CAST OFF THE BRITISH YOKE

The Old Dominion
and
American Independence

1763–1776

Michael Cecere

HERITAGE BOOKS
2014

HERITAGE BOOKS

AN IMPRINT OF HERITAGE BOOKS, INC.

Books, CDs, and more—Worldwide

For our listing of thousands of titles see our website
at
www.HeritageBooks.com

Published 2014 by
HERITAGE BOOKS, INC.
Publishing Division
5810 Ruatan Street
Berwyn Heights, Md. 20740

Copyright © 2014 Michael Cecere

Heritage Books by the author:

*An Officer of Very Extraordinary Merit: Charles Porterfield
and the American War for Independence, 1775–1780*

Captain Thomas Posey and the 7th Virginia Regiment

Cast Off the British Yoke: The Old Dominion and American Independence, 1763–1776

Great Things Are Expected from the Virginians: Virginia in the American Revolution

In This Time of Extreme Danger: Northern Virginia in the American Revolution

They Are Indeed a Very Useful Corps: American Riflemen in the Revolutionary War

*They Behaved Like Soldiers: Captain John Chilton and the
Third Virginia Regiment, 1775–1778*

To Hazard Our Own Security: Maine's Role in the American Revolution

Wedded to My Sword: The Revolutionary War Service of Light Horse Harry Lee

International Standard Book Numbers
Paperbound: 978-0-7884-5568-1
Clothbound: 978-0-7884-9047-7

Contents

Acknowledgements

My acknowledgements begin, as my research always does, with the Simpson Library at the University of Mary Washington in Fredericksburg. Their extensive collection of resources on the American Revolution is invaluable to anyone who studies this important time period. The resources of the Rockefeller Library in Williamsburg, particularly the digital collection of the Virginia Gazette, were also immensely useful to my research.

I owe much gratitude to my friends in the 7th Virginia Regiment, a Revolutionary War reenacting unit with many knowledgeable members. Norm Fuss, Drummond Ball, Buzz Deemer, Ron Phelps, and Rob Friar all took the time to assist me with my inquires and accompany me on my many visits to the sites discussed in the book. My interest and knowledge of the American Revolution has been greatly enriched by my long involvement with Revolutionary War reenacting, and the many friendships I have formed in this hobby are a reward onto itself.

Virginia in 1775

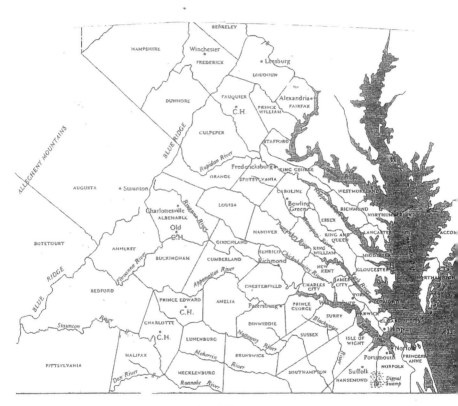

Counties of Virginia (1775)

Southeastern Virginia

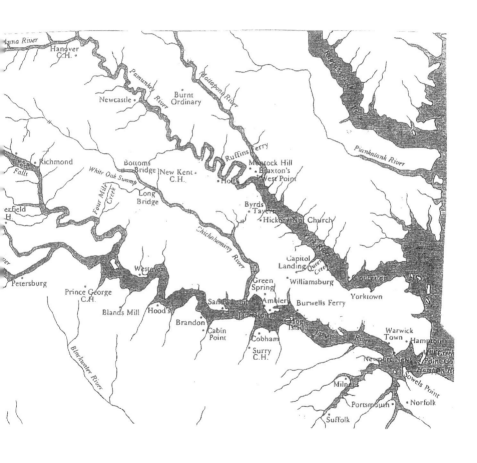

Introduction

The large crowd that waited outside Virginia's capitol in Williamsburg on May 15th, 1776 cheered wildly when the unanimous vote was announced. All 112 delegates to the 5th Virginia Convention had voted to instruct Virginia's delegation in Philadelphia at the Continental Congress to

> DECLARE THE UNITED COLONIES FREE AND INDEPENDENT STATES, absolved from all allegiance to, or dependence upon, the crown or parliament of Great Britain.[1]

Alexander Purdie's Virginia Gazette observed that a great celebration was held in Williamsburg the day after the historic vote with, "everyone seemingly pleased that the dominion of Great Britain was now at an end."[2] As far as the folks gathered in the capital were concerned, Virginia had declared its independence.

Six weeks later, on July 2, 1776, the Continental Congress in Philadelphia adopted Virginia's resolution for American independence. America's 170 year connection with Great Britain was formally and officially severed.

This unprecedented action, which was inconceivable just a few years earlier, was the result of a thirteen year dispute between Britain and her American colonies, a dispute that first emerged in 1763 on the heels of one of Great Britain's greatest foreign policy achievements.

---

[1] Alexander Purdie, Virginia Gazette, 17 May, 1776, 3
[2] Ibid.

It was the actions of the British Parliament in the wake of England's victory in the French and Indian War that planted the seeds of dissention between Britain and her American colonies. Thirteen years before the colonies declared their independence from Britain, Virginians had gathered in Williamsburg to cheer the end of a different conflict, the French and Indian War.[3] This long, costly war between Britain and France for dominance over North America ended victoriously for Great Britain (and her colonies) in 1763. The Treaty of Paris formally transferred possession of Canada to Britain and recognized England's claim to the territory west of the Appalachian Mountains. Virginia's colonial leaders in the House of Burgesses proudly acknowledged the colony's connection to Great Britain as well as the important role Virginia played in the war:

> *Our dependence upon Great Britain we acknowledge and glory in as our greatest happiness and only security; but this is not the dependence of a People subjugated by the arms of a Conqueror, but of Sons sent out to explore and settle a new World, for the mutual benefit of themselves and their common Parent.... By such a spirit and by such principles...hath our conduct ever been influenced and we hope we may, without arrogance, take* [some credit]...*for the part we took in the late war, when we did, as far as we were able, contribute to the success of the British arms.*[4]

---

[3] George Reese, ed., "Governor Fauquier to the Earl of Egremont, 7 September, 1763," *The Official Papers of Francis Fauquier,* Vol. 2, (Charlottesville: The University Press of Virginia, 1981), 1028

[4] Reese, ed., "Second Address of the House of Burgesses to Governor Fauquier, 27 May, 1763," *The Official Papers of Francis Fauquier,* Vol. 2, 964

The view that the colonists were not a conquered people but rather the sons of Englishmen sent to settle a new world appealed to the vast majority of Virginians. George Mason, one of the landed gentry of Fairfax County, presented perhaps the best explanation of the colonists' view of their position in the British Empire in a letter to London merchants in 1766:

> *Let our fellow-subjects in Great Britain reflect that we are descended from the same stock with themselves, nurtured in the same principles of freedom...that in crossing the Atlantic Ocean, we have only changed our climate, not our minds, our natures and dispositions remain unaltered; that we are still the same people with them in every respect....*[5]

Mason and his fellow Virginians believed that as Englishmen, they were entitled to the same rights and privileges as their brethren in Great Britain, rights long guaranteed under the British constitution. Up until 1763, Virginians were content that these rights were indeed respected by Britain. They lived under a system that historians describe as salutary or benign neglect in which the colonists were allowed to largely rule themselves.

Changes in British colonial policy and administration in 1763 (triggered primarily by the enormous financial debt Great Britain incurred during the French and Indian War) ended this period of salutary neglect. A struggle between the colonial legislatures in America and the British parliament over political supremacy arose in its place. This struggle

---

[5] Robert Rutland, ed., "To the Committee of Merchants in London, 6 June, 1766," *The Papers of George Mason,* Vol. 1, (University of North Carolina Press, 1970), 68

lasted twenty years and ultimately ended with Britain's recognition of American independence in 1783.

It was never pre-ordained that the struggle between Britain and her American colonies would end that way. In fact, during the decade leading up to the Revolutionary War, political reconciliation with Britain was the goal of the colonists. They sent numerous appeals and petitions to British authorities requesting a redress of their grievances. For a time it looked like these actions, combined with economic measures (boycotts) had convinced British leaders to repeal their burdensome new colonial policies.

Relations between British and colonial leaders turned increasingly confrontational, however, in 1774 and within two years, Virginians overwhelmingly supported independence from Great Britain.

The question this book seeks to answer is what specifically occurred in the years leading up to the spring of 1776 to convince Virginians, and ultimately the other 12 American colonies, to cast off their allegiance to Great Britain and embrace independence.

Chapter One

"The People...have become more attentive to their Liberties."

1763-1773

Great Britain faced an enormous fiscal crisis in 1763. Its national debt (which exploded during the French and Indian War to a level that was barely manageable) had nearly bankrupted the nation.[1] British taxpayers groaned under the increased tax burden and British leaders desperately sought ways to slash expenses and raise revenue. They looked to the American colonies as a possible solution to their troubles.

Proclamation of 1763 and the Sugar Act of 1764

One way to reduce military expenditures was to limit conflicts between the colonists and Indians in North America that might require British military intervention. British leaders decided that the best way to limit such conflicts was to restrict contact between the colonists and Indians, so in October 1763 a royal proclamation was issued by King George III that prohibited settlement of the newly secured land west of the Appalachian Mountains. This proclamation surprised and annoyed many colonists, particularly those who looked to

---

[1] Edmund S. Morgan, *Prologue to Revolution: Sources and Documents on the Stamp Act Crisis, 1764-1766*, (Chapel Hill, NC: University of North Carolina Press, 1959), 1

prosper through speculative western land sales. Prominent Virginians like George Washington, Thomas Jefferson, and George Mason, fell into this group and were highly displeased by the Proclamation. They viewed the measure as an arbitrary dictate from across the ocean, but also recognized that there was little they could do to stop it.

The colonists were even more troubled to learn in 1764 that they were to bear the brunt of the costs of maintaining a large British military presence in North America through new trade regulations (the Sugar Act) and stricter enforcement of existing trade laws. The colonists argued that if France was no longer a threat to the colonies and the proclamation line limited conflict with the Indians, why was there a need to garrison so many British troops in the colonies? They also reminded the British Ministry that the French and Indian War had left their own colonial governments deeply in debt.

Furthermore, they argued, the new trade regulations would reduce colonial commerce and hamper the colonists' ability to buy goods manufactured in Britain.[2] In other words, the Sugar Act would actually reduce colonial trade with Britain and harm British manufacturers. Bostonians expressed the view of many colonists when they declared at a town meeting in mid-1764 that

> *Our trade, as it is now, and always has been conducted, centers in Great Britain, and in return for manufactured* [goods] *affords* [Britain] *more ready cash, beyond any comparison, than can possibly be*

---

[2] "Instructions to Representatives in the General Assembly at a Town Meeting in Boston, 28 May, 1764," *The Massachusetts Gazette & Boston News-Letter*, 31 May, 1764, 2

expected by [the proposed Sugar Acts]. *We are ultimately yielding large supplies to the revenues of the mother country, while we are labouring for a very moderate subsistence for ourselves. But if our trade is to be curtail'd in its most profitable branches, and burthens...laid upon that which...remain, we shall be so far from being able to take off the manufactures of Great Britain, that it will be scarce possible for us to earn our bread.*[3]

Although many colonists were troubled by what they viewed as parliamentary meddling into colonial affairs through the Proclamation of 1763 and the Sugar Act of 1764, few argued that Parliament did not have the right to pass such misguided policies.

It was another matter entirely, however, when word reached the colonies in 1765 that Parliament had levied a stamp tax on the colonists.

The Stamp Act 1765

Colonial opposition to the new stamp tax was immediate and widespread and challenged the very authority of Parliament to impose such a tax (or by implication to rule the colonies.) Petitions and resolutions were adopted throughout the colonies, a Stamp Act Congress convened in New York to consider economic measures against Britain, and violence against British officials erupted in Massachusetts and was threatened in other colonies including Virginia.

---

[3] Ibid.

When he reflected on the events of 1765 in his journal, Massachusetts lawyer John Adams was astonished at what had occurred:

The Year 1765 has been the most remarkable Year of my Life. That enormous Engine, fabricated by the british Parliament, for battering down all the Rights and Liberties of America, I mean the Stamp Act, has raised and spread, thro the whole Continent, a Spirit that will be recorded to our Honour, with all future Generations. In every Colony, from Georgia to New Hampshire inclusively, the Stamp Distributors and Inspectors have been compelled, by the unconquerable Rage of the People, to renounce their offices. Such and so universal has been the Resentment of the People, that every Man who has dared to speak in favour of the Stamps, or to soften the detestation in which they are held...has been seen to sink into universal Contempt and Ignominy. The People, even to the lowest Ranks, have become more attentive to their Liberties, more inquisitive about them, and more determined to defend them, than they were ever before known or had occasion to be.... Our Presses have groaned, our Pulpits have thundered, our Legislatures have resolved, our Towns have voted, The Crown Officers have every where trembled, and all their little Tools and Creatures, been afraid to Speak and ashamed to be seen.[4]

---

[4] John Adams, Diary 11, entry for 18 December 1765, *Adams Family Papers*, Massachusetts Historical Society

The colonists' strong opposition to the Stamp Act surprised the British Ministry. Officials in London considered the act an appropriate measure to help offset the massive British debt generated from the French and Indian War. For the colonists, however, the question of whether they should contribute to the reduction of Britain's war debt was not the issue, it was the method of taxation adopted by Parliament that troubled the colonists, not the amount of the tax.

Virginia's Reaction to the Stamp Act

Virginians were long accustomed to paying taxes levied by their own representatives. In order to pay for the operation of the colonial government, the House of Burgesses adopted a variety of duties and fees on such items as hogsheads of tobacco (50,000 exported in 1762), wheeled carriages, and imported horses. Fees were also assessed on every ship passenger, (indentured servant, slave, or free person) who landed in Virginia.[5] Taxes on tithables (every male over 16 years old as well as female slaves over 16 years old) and real estate taxes on landowners were also levied to help pay for the large war debt Virginia generated in the 1750's and early 1760's.[6] All of these taxes, in addition to the levies passed by local church vestries to maintain and operate the parishes and assist the poor, amounted to a significant tax obligation for Virginians.

These internal taxes, levied by the Virginia House of Burgesses and the local church vestries, were not the only financial expenses Virginians incurred. The British

---

[5] Reese, ed., "Report on the Colony, 30 January, 1763," *The Official Papers of Francis Fauquier*, Vol. 2, 1009-1022
[6] Ibid.

Parliament exercised its own authority over the colonies to regulate colonial trade. This authority, long established by the Navigation Acts of the 1600's, involved a series of trade regulations and tariffs (duties on imported goods) that were designed to encourage the colonists to buy British goods instead of foreign produced goods. Most colonists viewed these tariffs (imposed by Parliament) as external taxes and accepted them because of their optional nature. One could avoid the tariffs by simply purchasing British or colonial made goods. Thus, raising revenue for the British treasury was not the primary purpose of such tariffs, but rather, they were designed to regulate colonial trade by promoting domestic commerce over foreign commerce.

Parliament's stamp tax, however, had a much different purpose; it taxed items (anything made of paper) that had no substitute. Legal documents such as licenses, commissions, and contracts as well as common writing paper and even newspapers and playing cards were subject to the tax. A tax on such documents and items was impossible for the colonists to avoid and had nothing to do with regulating trade. Instead, it was designed to raise revenue for the British treasury through an internal tax on the colonists.

This was completely unacceptable to most colonists. If the stamp tax was allowed to stand, it would establish a dangerous precedent, taxation of the colonists without their representation in Parliament. It would also signal a significant and dangerous expansion of parliamentary power over the colonies. The outcry from the colonists against the Stamp Act was thus loud and adamant.

Opposition to a stamp tax had actually developed in Virginia a year before Parliament adopted the measure when reports reached the colony in 1764 that the British Ministry was considering it.

Richard Henry Lee of Westmoreland County was one of the first in Virginia to sound the alarm. Lee hailed from one of the most politically powerful families in Virginia and had already developed a reputation as a political firebrand for his bold stance against the slave trade in 1758. Educated in England, Lee possessed a keen political mind and rousing literary and oratorical skills. He expressed his concern about the expansion of parliamentary rule over the colonists to a friend in London in May 1764:

> *The right to be governed by laws made by our representatives, and the illegality of taxation without consent are such essential principles of the British constitution, that it is a...wonder how men, who have almost imbibed* [these principles] *in their mother's milk...should be of opinion that the people of America were to be taxed without consulting their representatives!*[7]

Six month later, the House of Burgesses, troubled by reports that the British Ministry was seriously considering a direct tax on the colonies, appealed to Parliament and King George III to reject the idea. The burgesses asserted that

---

[7] James C. Ballagh, ed., "Richard Henry Lee to ------ , 31 May, 1764," *The Letters of Richard Henry Lee,* Vol. 1, (NY: Macmillan Co., 1911), 5-6

> *It* [is] *a fundamental Principle of the British Constitution, without which Freedom can no Where exist, that the People are not subject to any Taxes but such as are laid on them by their own Consent, or by those legally appointed to represent them....*[8]

The burgesses claimed that since there were no colonial representatives in Parliament, that body had no authority to levy an internal tax on the colonies.

The British Parliament disagreed and passed the Stamp Act in March 1765. As feared, the tax required colonists to use stamped paper for legal and business documents, writing paper and newspapers. Once the tax took effect on November 1st, heavy fines would be levied on anyone caught violating the act.

The House of Burgesses was in session when reports of the Stamp Act's passage reached Virginia. The initial response of Virginia's leaders was surprisingly subdued. Many burgesses, including the House Speaker, John Robinson, preferred to wait for Parliament's reply to their earlier petition before they took action.

Other burgesses were not so patient. Twenty nine year old Patrick Henry, of Hanover County, boldly proposed a set of resolutions that challenged Parliament's authority. Henry was a first term burgess who, despite humble origins and a limited education, was an exceptional orator. George Mason, one of Virginia's best political thinkers, described Henry as

---

[8] William J. Van Schreeven and Robert L. Scribner, ed., "Address, Memorial, and Remonstrance of the General Assembly to King, Lords, and Commons Respectively in Opposition to a Proposed Stamp Tax, 18 December, 1764," *Revolutionary Virginia: The Road to Independence,* Vol. 1, (Charlottesville: University Press of Virginia, 1973), 11

By far the most powerful speaker I ever heard. Every word he says not only engages but commands the attention; and your passions are no longer your own when he addresses them. [9]

Henry's first three resolutions asserted that the American colonists possessed the same rights and privileges as native-born Englishmen and that taxation without representation violated the British constitution. The fourth resolution noted the tradition of colonial self-rule in local matters, a tradition long upheld by past kings and parliaments.

Although these resolutions generated a good deal of discussion in the House of Burgesses, they were approved by narrow margins. Henry's last resolve, however, ignited impassioned arguments and a very close vote:

The General Assembly of this Colony have the only and exclusive Right and Power to lay Taxes...upon the inhabitants of this Colony and that every Attempt to vest such Power in any person or persons other than the General Assembly has a manifest Tendency to destroy British as well as American Freedom. [10]

This resolve openly challenged the authority of King George III and Parliament and troubled many conservative burgesses. They forcefully opposed the measure. Patrick Henry responded with a warning to King George III to heed

---

[9] Robert A. Rutland, ed., "George Mason to Martin Cockburn, 26 May, 1774," *The Papers of George Mason,* Vol. 1, (University of North Carolina Press, 1970), 190

[10] Van Schreeven and Scribner, ed., "Resolutions Offered by Patrick Henry in Condemnation of the Stamp Act, 29-30 May, 1765," *Revolutionary Virginia: The Road to Independence,* Vol. 1, 18

the fate of Julius Caesar and Charles I, both of whom were killed trying to usurp power. Although this threat prompted shouts of "treason" in the assembly, Henry's fifth resolution passed by one vote.[11] It was overturned the next day in another close vote, but not before copies of the resolves were sent to neighboring colonies and appeared in newspapers outside of Virginia. The one gazette or newspaper published in Virginia in 1765 was printed by Joseph Royal whose strong support for the King dissuaded him from printing the resolves in his gazette.[12]

Despite the reluctance of Mr. Royal to challenge the action of the King and Parliament, opposition to the Stamp Act spread throughout Virginia and the other colonies. The freeholders of Westmoreland County proclaimed that the stamp tax was an attempt to *"reduce the People of this Country to a State of abject and detestable slavery."* They pledged to *"exert every Faculty to prevent the Execution of the said Stamp Act."*[13] The county court in Northampton County declared the Stamp Act unconstitutional and in Norfolk, self-proclaimed Sons of Liberty adopted a series of resolves to oppose, *"the oppressive and unconstitutional...Stamp Act."*[14] The inhabitants of Norfolk proclaimed:

---

[11] Ibid., 16

[12] Ibid.

[13] Van Schreeven and Scribner, ed. "Resolutions of the Westmoreland Association in Defiance of the Stamp Act, 27 February, 1766," *Revolutionary Virginia: The Road to Independence,* Vol. 1, 24

[14] Purdie and Dixon, *Virginia Gazette,* 21 March and 4 April 1766, 3

If we quietly submit to the execution of the Stamp Act, all our claims to civil liberties will be lost, and we, and our posterity [will] *become absolute slaves.*[15]

They therefore pledged to

Sacrifice their lives and fortune in concurrence with the other Sons of Liberty in the American provinces, to defend and preserve those invaluable blessings transmitted to us by our ancestors.[16]

To most Virginians, the amount of the stamp tax was inconsequential compared to the precedent the tax would establish. Many feared that the Stamp Act marked the beginning of unchecked parliamentary rule over the colonists. Colonel George Washington of Fairfax County reported that Virginians

Look upon this unconstitutional method of Taxation as a direful attack upon their Liberties, and loudly exclaim against the Violation.[17]

Like their southern brethren, many northern colonists decried the stamp tax as an attack on their constitutional rights. In June, the Massachusetts House of Representatives sent a circular letter to all the colonial legislatures calling for a Stamp Act Congress to meet in New York in October. Nine

---

[15] Ibid.

[16] Ibid.

[17] W.W. Abbot and Dorothy Twohig, eds. "George Washington to Francis Dandridge, 20 September, 1765," *The Papers of George Washington: Colonial Series,* Vol. 7, (Charlottesville: University Press of Virginia, 1990), 395-396

colonies sent delegates to the meeting, but Virginia was not one of them. Governor Francis Fauquier refused to convene a special session of the House of Burgesses to select delegates, so Virginia had no representatives to send to New York.

The Stamp Act Congress met in New York for nearly three weeks and closed with a statement to Parliament proclaiming that the American colonists were English citizens, entitled to the same rights as native-born Englishmen. They also complained that the new duties under the Sugar Act placed a large burden on colonial trade and asserted that the stamp tax violated the principle of no taxation without representation.[18]

More forceful opposition to the Stamp Act was displayed in Boston two months prior to the Stamp Act Congress when a mob ransacked the office and home of Andrew Oliver, the appointed stamp tax distributor for Massachusetts. Oliver barely escaped with his life and resigned his commission the next day.[19] Two weeks later, a similar assault occurred on the residence of Lieutenant Governor Thomas Hutchinson.

The threat of violence was also used to intimidate British officials in Virginia. Although no property was destroyed, an angry crowd in Williamsburg "persuaded" George Mercer, the official stamp distributor for the colony, to resign his position in October. Such attacks, or in some cases the threat of attack, convinced most of the appointed stamp distributors in the colonies to resign their lucrative commissions over the fall. As a result, when the Stamp Act went into effect on November 1st, Georgia was the only colony prepared to enforce it.

---

[18] Edmund S. Morgan, *Prologue to Revolution: Sources and Documents on the Stamp Act Crisis, 1764-1766,* 62-63

[19] Edmund Morgan and Helen Morgan, *The Stamp Act Crisis: Prologue to Revolution,* (Chapel Hill, NC: University of North Carolina Press, 1953), 123-126

Business and legal affairs temporarily came to a halt in most of British America as the absence of stamp tax distributors made it impossible to legally transact business or hold court. A backlog of court cases soon created pressure on the courts to ignore the law and resume hearings without the stamps.

Merchants in Boston, New York, and Philadelphia employed a different approach to protest the stamp tax; they launched a boycott of British goods. By the close of 1765 hundreds of colonial merchants were withholding business orders with their counterparts in Britain. This action soon had the desired effect.

Repeal of the Stamp Act 1766

The sharp decline in mercantile orders from the American colonists over the winter of 1765-66 spurred many merchants in Britain to petition Parliament to repeal the Stamp Act. Their claims of dire economic consequences caused by the steep reduction in colonial trade resonated with Parliament.[20] A new group of ministers, headed by the Marquis of Rockingham, replaced the former administration that had introduced the Stamp Act, and they were open to the idea of repeal, moving to do so in March, 1766. Virginians learned of the happy news two months later through published letters in Alexander Purdie and John Dixon's new Virginia Gazette. Many of the letters published in the gazette urged the colonists not to gloat over their sudden success:

---

[20] Ibid., 271

Blessed to God the act is repealed, after a terrible struggle. O that Boston, that America may be truly thankful and humble, and frugal, and not insult the parliament in their rejoicings....[21]

Prevail upon [the colonists] *to mix discretion with this great joy, that you do not exult as conquerors, but receive the blessing (now confirmed to you) with thankfulness and gratitude.*[22]

George Mason, one of the landed gentry of Fairfax County, resented the idea that the colonists should be grateful to Parliament for reversing something that was wrong in the first place. In a public letter to a committee of London merchants, Mason asserted that as Englishmen, the colonists possessed the same rights and privileges as native Britons, rights that they expected to pass on to their children:

We claim nothing but the liberty and privileges of Englishmen, in the same degree, as if we still [lived] *among our brethren in Great Britain; these rights have not been forfeited by any act of ours; we cannot be deprived of them, without our consent, but by violence and injustice; we have received them from our ancestors, and, with God's leave, we will transmit them, unimpaired, to our posterity.*[23]

---

[21] "Extract of a letter from a Rev. Divine in London dated March 3, 1766," Purdie & Dixon, *Virginia Gazette*, 23 May, 1766, 2

[22] "Extract of a letter from a Gentleman in London to his friend in New York, February 27," Purdie & Dixon, *Virginia Gazette*, 23 May, 1766, 2

[23] Rutland, ed., "To the Committee of Merchants in London, 6 June, 1766," *The Papers of George Mason*, Vol. 1, 68

Disinterested in such colonial claims, Parliament was determined to assert its authority over the colonies and passed the Declaratory Act ahead of its repeal of the Stamp Act. The Declaratory Act proclaimed that

> *The said colonies...in America have been, are, and of right ought to be, subordinate unto, and dependent upon the imperial crown and Parliament of Great Britain; and that the king...with the advice and consent of...Parliament...hath...full power and authority to make laws...to bind the colonies and people of America, subjects of the crown of Great Britain, in all cases whatsoever.*[24]

The colonists had long recognized the authority of the King over them, but this new assertion that they were also subordinate to Parliament was troubling to many. A year passed before Parliament's authority was once again tested.

Townshend Duties : 1767

In the four years since the end of the French and Indian War little had been done to effectively address Britain's crushing debt crisis. The Stamp Act only increased the financial burden on Britain by disrupting trade and commerce with the colonies, and the Sugar Act earned little revenue. Desperate for a way to shift some of the financial cost of the empire to the colonies and determined to re-assert Parliament's authority over the colonists, Parliament adopted the

---

[24] Henry Steele Commager, "The Declaratory Act, 18 March, 1766," *Documents of American History*, (New York: Appleton-Century-Crofts, 1963), 60-61

Townshend Duties in 1767. This act placed tariffs on a list of goods shipped to the colonies from Britain. The newly taxed items included tea, glass, paint, and paper. The British Ministry argued that since the colonists had long accepted Parliament's right to tax imports, they could not legally oppose the new duties because the goods being taxed were imported from Britain to the colonies.

The colonists replied that past duties (tariffs) were designed to regulate trade by discouraging the purchase of foreign goods, but the Townshend Duties were placed on many goods that the colonists could only legally purchase from England. In other words, since there was no foreign competition for many of the newly taxed items, there was no need to levy a duty on them. The colonists argued that the duties on these imports were really just a veiled attempt by Parliament to raise revenue from the colonists. That made the Townshend Duties an internal tax, and the colonists believed that they were the only ones who could impose internal taxes on themselves.

The Virginia House of Burgesses objected to the Townshend Duties in a series of petitions to Parliament and the King in 1768. They conceded that

Parliament may make Laws for regulating Trade of the Colonies...But a tax imposed upon such of the British Exports, as are necessaries of Life, to be paid by the Colonists upon Importation...not with the most distant view to [regulate] Commerce, but merely to raise a Revenue [is] a Tax internal to all Intents and Purposes.[25]

---

[25] Van Schreeven and Scribner, ed.,"To the Right Honorable The Spiritual and Temporal In Parliament Assembled, 16 April, 1768," *Revolutionary Virginia: The Road to Independence,* Vol. 1, 58

Virginians simply could not accept the idea of British taxation that was designed to raise revenue for the British treasury. They contended that such taxes violated the British constitution because they were levied by a legislative body in which the colonists had no representation. The House of Burgesses complained that

> *To say that the Parliament of Great Britain has the constitutional Authority and Right to impose internal Taxes on the Inhabitants of this Continent, who are not and...cannot be Represented in the house of Commons, is...to command them to bid Adieu to their natural and civil Liberties and prepare for a state of Slavery.*[26]

This view was shared by colonists throughout America. In New York, hand-bills were circulated that claimed that "*duties laid for the sole purpose of raising money are* [internal] *taxes* [and] *attempts to* [levy] *such should be instantly and firmly opposed.*"[27]

Boston merchants led the opposition to the Townshend Duties with a pledge to boycott the list of taxed goods.[28] The Massachusetts legislature followed with a circular letter to the other colonies in February 1768 stating that

---

[26] Ibid.

[27] Ellen Chase, *The Beginnings of the American Revolution : Based on Contemporary Letters, Diaries, and other Documents,* Vol. 1, (Port Washington, NY: Kennikat Press, 1970), 85

[28] Boston Merchants Broadside, 31 October, 1767, Massachusetts Historical Society

*Duties on the People of this province with the sole &
express purpose of raising a Revenue, are
Infringements of* [the colonists'] *Natural &
Constitutional Rights because* [they] *are not
represented in the British Parliament....*[29]

The British Ministry objected to the circular letter and demanded that it be rescinded, but the Massachusetts legislature refused. When Massachusetts Governor Francis Bernard announced the postponement of the autumn 1768 meeting of the colonial legislature for fear that such a gathering might provoke increased unrest (which had become a common occurrence and an effective tool to intimidate British customs agents), Boston's leaders called for a special convention.

Frustrated by the constant harassment and intimidation of government officials and the extra-legal activities of Massachusetts's leaders, Governor Bernard asked the British government to send troops to Boston to re-establish order. Two regiments arrived on October 1st, 1768 and were greeted by the townsfolk with fierce resentment. Two more regiments squeezed into Boston in November. Despite frequent verbal altercations and fistfights between the soldiers and townsfolk, a tense calm descended over the town.

---

[29] Harry A. Cushing, ed., "The House of Representatives of Massachusetts to the Other House of Representatives, 11 February, 1768," *The Writings of Samuel Adams,* Vol. 1, (NY:G.P. Putnam's Sons, 1904), 185-186

Non-Importation Association : 1769

The military occupation of Boston spurred Virginians like Colonel George Washington to support stronger opposition to Parliament's policies. In the spring of 1769, Washington wrote to his friend and neighbor, Colonel George Mason, to urge strong action in defense of their rights:

> *At a time when our lordly Masters in Great Britain will be satisfied with nothing less than the deprivation of American freedom, it seems highly necessary that some thing shou'd be done to avert the stroke and maintain the liberty which we have derived from our Ancestors....*[30]

Washington added that while it was every man's duty to defend his freedom with force if necessary, violence should only be used as a last resort.[31] He suggested, instead, that a boycott of British goods was the next logical step for the colonies:

> *Addresses to the Throne, and remonstrances to Parliament, we have already...proved the inefficacy of; how far then [will] their attention to our rights & priviledges...be awakened or alarmed by starving their Trade & manufacture? The northern Colonies, it*

---

[30] Rutland, "George Washington to George Mason, 5 April, 1769," *The Papers of George Mason,* Vol. 1, 96-98

[31] Ibid.

appears, are endeavouring to adopt [a boycott]*... Upon the whole... I think... that it ought to be tried here....*[32]

Mason replied to Washington the same day. He supported a boycott and proclaimed that he was ready to sacrifice the "comforts of life" to preserve his liberty:

Our All is at Stake, & the little Conveniencys & Comforts of Life, when set in Competition with our Liberty, ought to be rejected not with Reluctance but with Pleasure....[33]

Mason was confident that a boycott would quickly get Britain's attention and cause English manufacturers to pressure Parliament to redress American grievances:

We may [reject all English] *Finery... & confine ourselves to* [home grown] *Linnens and Woolens... It is amazing how much this (if adopted in all the Colonys) wou'd lessen American Imports, and distress the various Traders & Manufacturers in Great Britain – This wou'd quickly awaken their Attention – they wou'd see, they wou'd feel the Oppressions we groan under, & exert themselves to procure us Redress.*[34]

Mason drafted a boycott plan and sent it with Washington to the House of Burgesses in Williamsburg. When Virginia's new governor, Lord Botetourt learned of the plan, he dissolved

---

[32] Ibid.

[33] Rutland, "George Mason to George Washington, 5 April, 1769," *The Papers of George Mason,* Vol. 1, 99

[34] Ibid.

the assembly to prevent its consideration. Undeterred, the dismissed burgesses met at a nearby tavern and approved most of Mason's proposals. They urged their fellow colonists to *"promote & encourage Industry & Frugality & discourage all manner of Luxury & Extravigance."*[35] Ninety-four burgesses joined a voluntary association to boycott the taxed items.[36] Most of the other colonies adopted similar measures, and by the fall of 1769, a continent wide boycott of select British goods was implemented.

The boycott was somewhat effective in the northern colonies, where imported goods from Britain were channeled through local merchants, but it was less effective in Virginia and the southern colonies because individual planters often traded directly with British merchants and felt less pressure to observe the boycott. Some Virginia gentlemen were reluctant to sacrifice their English comforts. To counter this, a second association was drafted in 1770 to strengthen the enforcement provisions of the boycott. County committees were authorized to search for contraband (boycotted goods). They were also instructed to publish the names of boycott violators in the Virginia gazettes.

Boston Massacre 1770

Back in Boston, tension between the townsfolk and British troops (which were reduced to two regiments in the summer of 1769 in a failed effort by their commander, General Thomas Gage, to placate Boston's inhabitants) was on the rise again.

---

[35] Van Schreeven and Scribner, ed., "Non-importation Resolutions of the Former Burgesses, 18 May, 1769," *Revolutionary Virginia: The Road to Independence,* Vol. 1, 75
[36] Ibid. 76-77

The problem was largely of General Gage's making; the rules under which the British army operated in Boston restricted their conduct and invited insult and injury from the public and civil authorities. A frustrated General Gage noted that

> *The People were as Lawless and Licentious after the Troops arrived, as they were before. The Troops could not act by Military Authority, and no Person in Civil Authority would ask their aid. They were there contrary to the wishes of the Council, Assembly, Magistrates and People, and seemed only offered to abuse and Ruin. And the Soldiers were either to suffer ill usage and even assaults upon their Persons till their Lives were in Danger, or by resisting and defending themselves, to run almost a Certainty of suffering by the Law.*[37]

The tension between the colonists and troops finally erupted into bloodshed on March 5, 1770 when a detachment of British troops fired into a large crowd that was taunting and pelting them with ice and snowballs. The incident, dubbed the Boston Massacre by the colonists, resulted in five dead colonists and an outraged public. The next day, thousands of Bostonians gathered to demand the removal of the British soldiers from Boston. Within days, the 14th and 29th British Regiments relocated to Castle Island in Boston Harbor. Months later, a Boston jury cleared all but two of the soldiers of any wrongdoing. The two convicted soldiers were found guilty of manslaughter and branded on their thumbs as a punishment.

---

[37] Hiller B. Zobel, *The Boston Massacre*, (New York: W.W. Norton, 1970), 180-81

Surprisingly, news of the bloodshed in Boston did not spur an enormous outcry in Virginia or the other colonies outside of New England. Much bigger news from England soon grabbed the attention of the colonists.

Repeal of the Townshend Duties 1770

By the spring of 1770 many members of Parliament, frustrated by the failure of yet another set of taxes to help relieve their enormous debt, were ready to make a change. The disruption of trade caused by the colonial boycott and the added expense of the troops in Boston cost Britain significantly more than the revenue collected from the Townshend Duties. The duties had become another drain on the treasury and just three years after their adoption (in March 1770) all but one of the duties were repealed by Parliament.

Parliament's decision was mainly an economic, not political one; the British Ministers and their supporters in Parliament continued to claim that it had the authority to tax the colonists. To emphasize this point the tax on tea was maintained. Although some of the colonists called for a continuation of the boycott until the duty on tea was also repealed, merchants in New York and Philadelphia ceased to participate and the boycott dissolved. British goods, including small quantities of taxed tea, once again flowed into the colonies.

Parliament's repeal of the Townshend Duties helped ease tensions between the colonies and Great Britain. The brief respite ended in 1772 when the colonists learned that the British Ministry had assumed responsibility for paying the salaries of the Massachusetts governor and other royal appointees. This gave these officials more independence from the Massachusetts legislature (which used to control their pay).

By itself, this change may not have troubled the legislators, but in the climate of 1772, where distrust between the colonists and Britain remained high, the change triggered alarms. Some feared that it was another step toward the British Ministry's goal of destroying popular government in the colonies by removing the ability of the people, through their elected representatives in the colonial legislature, to influence appointed officials. A town meeting in Boston in November 1772 asserted that

> *There is abundant Reasons to be alarmed that the plan of Despotism which the Enemies of our invaluable Rights have concerted, is rapidly hastening to a completion and* [we] *can no longer conceal our impatience under a constant, unremitted, uniform Aim to inslave us.... Making* [executive officials] *not only intirely independent of the People...but absolutely dependent on the crown (which may hereafter be worn by a Tyrant) both for their Appointment and Support, we cannot but be extremely alarm'd at the mischievous Tendency of this Innovation.*[38]

Boston's leaders responded to this policy change by forming a committee of correspondence, which was designed to keep fellow colonists informed of the latest news and

---

[38] Circular Letter from the Freeholders of Boston, 20 November, 1772, Massachusetts Historical Society

generate more support from them. The House of Burgesses in Virginia formed their own committee of correspondence in March 1773 and similar committees soon appeared throughout the colonies as well as in a number of Virginia counties.[39]

Boston Tea Party 1773

Parliament was bothered by the formation of these committees but did nothing to stop them. Their attention was focused on a plan to save the financially troubled East India Company, which was burdened with a huge surplus of tea due in large part to a significant decrease in British tea consumption among the American colonists. To help the East India Company unload its surplus tea and remain solvent, Parliament passed the Tea Act in early 1773. On the surface the Tea Act appeared to benefit the American colonists. East India Company agents in the colonies were given a monopoly to sell taxed tea directly to the colonists at a lower price than all their competitors, even those who sold smuggled Dutch tea.

The potential financial savings of this new arrangement for the colonists created a dilemma for colonial leaders. Although some colonists had resumed drinking taxed English tea when the boycott collapsed in 1770, many others, at the urging of local leaders, had continued to boycott tea. As a result, colonial leaders could argue in 1773 that most colonists, as evidenced by their refusal to purchase East India tea, still opposed the tea tax as unconstitutional.

---

[39] Van Schreeven and Scribner, ed., "Resolutions of the House of Burgesses Establishing a Committee of Inter-colonial Correspondence, 12 March, 1773," *Revolutionary Virginia: The Road to Independence,* Vol. 1, 91

This argument would unravel, however, if the colonists purchased large amounts of the surplus East India tea at its bargain prices. Colonial leaders feared that Parliament would interpret a surge in British tea sales as tacit acceptance of the tea tax. This would be the precedent Parliament needed to reaffirm the Declaratory Act.

Colonial leaders were determined to prevent this from happening and undertook efforts to block the delivery of the surplus tea in Charleston, Philadelphia, New York, and Boston. They succeeded without mishap in all the ports except Boston. On December 16th, 1773, scores of Bostonians took the extreme measure of dumping the controversial tea into Boston Harbor. This action outraged Parliament and the King; they interpreted the act as a blatant challenge to their authority and responded forcefully.

Chapter Two

"The Crisis is Arrived when we must Assert our Rights or Submit…"

1774

Virginians learned about the Boston Tea Party in mid-January 1774. Although most opposed the Tea Act and the tea shipments to America, few approved of the destruction of the tea in Boston. One writer to Purdie and Dixon's *Virginia Gazette* observed that

> *The Lives of the* [Tea] *commissioners* [have] *been notoriously threatened and their Properties notoriously invaded at Boston, by a Set of lawless Rioters…Is there no Danger to Liberty when every Merchant is liable to have his House, Property, and even Life, invaded or threatened by a Mob, who may be assembled at any Time….*[1]

Such scenes of "lawlessness" disturbed Virginians (who maintained a healthy respect for private property). As a result, few endorsed the actions of the Bostonians and everyone waited anxiously for Parliament's response. While they waited, the attention and concern of many Virginians turned to other matters, particularly to reports of Indian unrest in the west. Their attention shifted back to Boston in mid-May when

---

[1] Purdie & Dixon, *Virginia Gazette*, 20 January, 1774

news of Parliament's reaction to the "tea party' in Boston Harbor reached Virginia.

Outraged by the destruction of private property, the British Parliament moved to punish the entire city of Boston through the Boston Port Act. This act closed Boston harbor to all trade and commerce. British warships and soldiers were sent to Boston to enforce the port closure and help keep order in the "lawless" city. The port would only be reopened upon payment for the destroyed tea.

Many Virginians learned about these developments through the weekly newspapers. There were four gazettes printed in Virginia in 1774, three located in the capital and a fourth in Norfolk. Like all of their competitors, Purdie & Dixon's *Virginia Gazette* (printed in Williamsburg) reacted strongly to the Boston Port Act. On May 19th, they published an extract of a letter from London that characterized Parliament's actions as more sinister than just a simple demand for restitution for the tea:

> *Extract of a Letter from London, March 19, 1774*
>
> *A Bill is now in Parliament to stop up the Port of Boston, till the King pleases to restore it. This is, in Fact, to destroy the Town, because the Inhabitants have had Spirit enough to declare that they will be free, and the Ministers say it is intended as an Example to all the other Colonies, whenever they shall dare to assert their Rights.*[2]

Rind's Gazette reported that four regiments of troops and a very formidable British fleet would, "*soon make its*

---

[2] Purdie & Dixon, *Virginia Gazette*, 19 May, 1774, 4

appearance in the American ocean," presumably to enforce the coercive measures against Boston.[3]   Accounts of Parliament's heavy handedness towards Boston, coupled with concern that such policies might soon be directed at other colonies, heightened the fears of Virginians regarding the intentions of the British Ministry.

A moment of decision had arrived for all of the colonists. They could either stand and support Boston or shy away and abandon Massachusetts to its fate.

Virginia Rallies to Boston's Side

As word spread about Parliament's harsh response to the "tea party" in Boston, more and more Virginians concluded that the British measures were a dangerous abuse of parliamentary power.   Edmund Pendleton, a moderate burgess from Caroline County, expressed the view held by many of his fellow colonists:

> *Tho' it should be granted that the Bostonians did wrong in destroying the tea, yet the Parliament giving Judgement and sending ships and troops to* [punish the entire city] *in a case of Private property is* [an] *Attack upon constitutional Rights, of which we could not remain Idle Spectators.....*[4]

Landon Carter of Richmond County also viewed Parliament's actions as excessive, recording (inaccurately) in his diary that

---

[3] Rind, *Virginia Gazette*, 26 May, 1774, 2

[4] David John Mays, ed., "Edmund Pendleton to Joseph Chew, 20 June, 1774," *The Letters and Papers of Edmund Pendleton,* Vol. 1 (Charlottesville: University Press of Virginia, 1967), 93

Great alarms in the Country. The Parliament of England have declared war against the town of Boston and rather worse; for they have attacked and blocked up their harbour with 3 line of Battle Ships and 6 others, and landed 8 regiments there to subdue them to submit to their taxation; as this is but a Prelude to destroy the Liberties of America, The other Colonies cannot look on the affair but as a dangerous alarm.[5]

On May 24th, George Mason, Patrick Henry, and Thomas Jefferson joined a committee of burgesses in Williamsburg to draft a resolution in support of Massachusetts. The committee proposed that Virginians observe June 1st (the day the Boston Port bill took effect) as a day of fasting and prayer for the people of Boston. Their proposal easily passed the House of Burgesses but angered the quick tempered Royal Governor John Murray, the Earl of Dunmore. Lord Dunmore thought the resolution insulted Parliament and the King, so he dissolved the House of Burgesses on May 26th. With important work such as the renewal of the court fees and militia laws still to be completed, Dunmore's action had significant consequences for both legal and commercial transactions as well as the defense of the colony.

At the time of the assembly's dissolution, however, most of the burgesses were focused on producing a strong response to Parliament's crack down on Boston. Many of the dismissed burgesses gathered at a tavern near the capitol to discuss additional ways to support Massachusetts. On May 27th,

---

[5] Jack P. Greene, ed., *The Diary of Landon Carter of Sabine Hall, 1752-1778, Vol. 2,*(Charlottesville: Univ. Press of Virginia, 1965), 817-818

eighty-nine of them declared that Parliament's actions against Massachusetts were not only a grievous violation of the British constitution, but a systematic effort to reduce all of the American colonists to a state of slavery:

> *With much grief we find that our dutiful applications to Great Britain for security of our just, ancient, and constitutional rights, have been not only disregarded, but that a determined system is formed and pressed for reducing the inhabitants of British America to slavery, by subjecting them to the payment of taxes, imposed without consent of the people or their representatives; and that in pursuit of this system, we find an act of the British parliament, lately passed, for stopping the...commerce of the town of Boston...until the people there submit to the payment of such unconstitutional taxes...a most dangerous attempt to destroy the constitutional liberty and rights of all North America....*[6]

The burgesses accused the East India Company of colluding with Parliament to deprive the colonies of their rights. They pledged to boycott all of the company's goods, except spices and saltpeter, until the acts against Massachusetts were repealed.[7] They also called for a general meeting of the colonies to foster greater unity among them:

---

[6] Van Schreeven and Scribner, ed.,"An Association Signed by 89 Members of the late House of Burgesses, 27 May 1774," *Revolutionary Virginia: The Road to Independence,* Vol. 1, 97-98

[7] Ibid.

We are further clearly of opinion, that an attack, made on one of our sister colonies, to compel submission to arbitrary taxes, is an attack made on all British America, and threatens ruin to the rights of all, unless the united wisdom of the whole be applied. And for this purpose it is recommended... [that] *deputies from the several colonies of British America meet in general congress.*[8]

Satisfied with these measures, most of the dismissed burgesses left the capital the next day to return to their homes. A few were still in Williamsburg when Peyton Randolph, the chairman of Virginia's Committee of Correspondence, received news from the north. Colonial leaders from New England and the mid-Atlantic colonies proposed a boycott of all British goods and the assembly of a general congress in Philadelphia to discuss the crisis. Randolph summoned the representatives that were still in Williamsburg to discuss the news. They decided that a colony wide convention was necessary to select and instruct Virginia's delegation to the Philadelphia congress.[9] Counties were instructed to send two representatives to Williamsburg in early August to attend the convention.

Some counties in Virginia, eager to take decisive action, passed their own resolutions in support of Boston prior to the convention. The freeholders of Prince William County were the first to do so on June 6th. They passed a set of resolves that re-asserted the principle of no taxation without representation and endorsed a boycott of all British goods to

---

[8] Ibid.
[9] Ibid., 99-100

pressure Britain to change its policy towards Boston.[10] Loudoun County passed similar resolves a week later.

Additional Measures Against Massachusetts

Reports of additional punitive parliamentary acts against Massachusetts reached Virginia in mid-June and intensified support for the beleaguered colony to the north. Part of Massachusetts's ancient 1691 charter was revoked and royal appointees replaced elected officials on the executive council, (the upper chamber of the colonial legislature). Special town meetings (beyond the annually scheduled one for each town) were forbidden without the governor's consent. Perhaps most troubling to Virginians was passage of the Administration of Justice Act, which allowed the Massachusetts governor to transfer court cases of government officials to Britain (out of reach of hostile Massachusetts juries). Many colonists feared that this measure would allow royal officials to act with impunity from the law because the colonists would have no way to hold them accountable for their actions.

In addition to these measures (which together with the Port Bill became known as the Intolerable Acts) were reports of still more British troops heading to Boston to join General Thomas Gage, the newly appointed military governor of the colony. All of these measures and reports over the summer prompted a growing number of counties in Virginia to embrace a boycott of British goods as a demonstration of support for Massachusetts.

---

[10] Rutland, ed.,"Prince William County Resolves, 6 June, 1774," *The Papers of George Mason*, Vol. 1, 101

To Boycott or Petition

Not every Virginian approved of a boycott, however. Bryan Fairfax, a good friend and neighbor of George Washington's, wrote to Washington in early July and expressed his opposition to such a measure. Fairfax thought that a general boycott would be too provocative and difficult to implement and he argued that the colonists should send another petition to England, instead.[11]

George Washington was skeptical of Fairfax's position. He replied to his friend the next day and maintained that a boycott was overdue:

> *As to your political sentiments, I would heartily join you in them...provided there was the most distant hope of success. But have we not tried this already? Have we not addressed* [Parliament] *? And to what end? Did they deign to look at our petitions? Does it not appear, as clear as* [the sun]*...that there is a regular, systematic plan formed to fix the right and practice of taxation upon us? Does not the uniform conduct of Parliament for some years past confirm this...Is there anything to be expected from petitioning after this? Is not the attack upon the liberty and property of the people of Boston...plain and self-evident proof of what they are aiming at? Do not the subsequent bills...for depriving Massachusetts of its charter...convince us that the administration is determined to stick at nothing to carry its point? Ought we not, then, to put*

[11] Beverly H. Runge, ed., "Bryan Fairfax to George Washington, 3 July, 1774," *The Papers of George Washington: Colonial Series,* Vol. 10, (Charlottesville, VA: University Press of Virginia, 1995), 107-108

our virtue and fortitude to the severest test? With you I think it a folly to attempt more than we can execute...yet I think we may do more than is generally believed, in respect to the non-importation scheme.[12]

Bryan Fairfax remained troubled by what he viewed as a policy of confrontation among his fellow Virginians. He wrote another letter to Washington two weeks later in mid-July and urged restraint. He believed that patient petitions and appeals to Britain had the best chance of changing British policy. Fairfax wanted to wait for the outcome of yet another colonial petition to Parliament before stronger actions were taken. He told Washington that

Americans ought to consider the Majority of the english Parliament...as acting from honest tho' erroneous principles...Whatever Corruption there may be in the Parliament, whatever unjust designs some Men may have, we ought to gain the Affections of those who mean well; we should strive to conciliate the Affections of [England].... It is incredible how far a mild Behavior contributes to a Reconciliation in any dispute between Man & Man....[13]

Fairfax repeated his fear that an aggressive approach towards Parliament would only offend and anger that body and result in the rejection of colonial appeals.

---

[12] Runge, ed., "George Washington to Bryan Fairfax, 4 July, 1774," *The Papers of George Washington: Colonial Series,* Vol. 10, 109-110

[13] Runge, ed., "Bryan Fairfax to George Washington, 17 July, 1774," *The Papers of George Washington,* Vol. 10, 115-116

Colonel Washington, however, had already abandoned hope that petitions would sway Parliament. He responded to his friend on July 20th:

> *I see nothing to induce a belief that the Parliament would embrace a favorable opportunity of repealing acts, which they go on with great rapidity to pass, in order to enforce their tyrannical system;* [In fact], *I observe…that* [parliament] *is pursuing a regular plan at the expense of law and justice to overthrow our constitutional rights and liberties. How can I expect any redress from a measure which has been ineffectually tried already?*[14]

Washington then reminded Fairfax what was at stake in the dispute:

> *For Sir, what is it we are contending against? Is it against paying the duty of three pence per pound on tea because* [it is] *burthensome? No, it is the right only, we have all along disputed, and to this end we have already petitioned his Majesty in as humble and dutiful manner as subjects could do. Nay, more, we applied to* [Parliament] *setting forth, that, as Englishmen, we could not be deprived of* [our constitutional rights].[15]

Washington maintained that Parliament's harsh treatment of Massachusetts demonstrated its intention to enforce arbitrary

---

[14] Runge, ed.,"George Washington to Bryan Fairfax, 20 July, 1774," *The Papers of George Washington*, Vol. 10, 129
[15] Ibid.

rule over all the colonies. He ended with a simple explanation of his position:

> *I think the Parliament of Great Britain hath no more right to put their hands into my pocket, without my consent, than I have to put my hands into yours for money; and this being already urged to them in a firm, but decent manner, by all the colonies, what reason is there to expect anything from their justice?*[16]

The freeholders of Fairfax County apparently agreed with Colonel Washington and selected him as one of their convention delegates in mid-July.[17] They also proceeded to pass a set of resolves that reiterated the views of neighboring Prince William and Loudoun County and ended with the assertion that

> *It is our greatest Wish and Inclination, as well as interest, to continue our Connection with, and Dependence upon the British Government; but tho' we are its Subjects, we will use every Means which Heaven hath given us to prevent our becoming its Slaves.*[18]

---

[16] Ibid.

[17] Rutland, ed., "Fairfax County Resolves, 18 July, 1774," *The Papers of George Mason,* Vol. 1, 209

[18] Ibid.

The 1ˢᵗ Virginia Convention

In early August delegates from throughout Virginia gathered in Williamsburg to attend a special convention convened to select representatives for the upcoming continental congress in Philadelphia and to draft instructions for the representatives. Governor Dunmore was out of town, at the head of a military expedition against the Indians on the frontier. Many of the delegates arrived from their county and town committees with instructions for bold action. They met in the capitol and selected Peyton Randolph, George Washington, Patrick Henry, Richard Henry Lee, Edmund Pendleton, Benjamin Harrison, and Richard Bland as delegates to the general Congress in Philadelphia. The Convention then instructed the delegates to simultaneously reaffirm Virginia's desire for close ties with Britain and defend the colonists' constitutional rights:

> *We desire that* [the delegates to Congress] *will express...our Faith and true Allegiance to his Majesty King George the Third...and that we are determined...to support him in the legal Exercise of all his just Rights and Prerogatives...We sincerely...wish most ardently a Return of that... Affection and commercial Connexion that formerly united both Countries, which can only be effected by a Removal of those Causes of Discontent* [the Intolerable Acts] *which have of late unhappily divided us. It cannot admit of a Doubt but that British Subjects in America are entitled to the same Rights and Privileges as their Fellow Subjects possess in Britain; and therefore, that the Power*

assumed by the British Parliament to bind America by their [laws] *in all Cases whatsoever, is unconstitutional, and the Source of these unhappy Differences.*[19]

The Virginia Convention gave Parliament until November 1st, 1774, to repeal its acts against Massachusetts or face a general boycott. Other provisions called for a ban on the further importation of slaves and a ban on the consumption of tea. The Convention even went as far as to authorize a ban on colonial exports to Britain in September 1775 if Parliament remained intransigent with its policies.[20]

With Virginia's representatives to the Congress selected and their instructions drafted, the convention's work was complete and it adjourned on August 6th. The congress in Philadelphia was to convene in early September so the appointed delegates to the congress hurried to get their affairs in order and start their journey northward.

---

[19] Van Schreeven and Scribner, ed., "The Convention of 1774: Instructions To the Deputies Elected to Attend the General Congress, 6 August, 1774," *Revolutionary Virginia: The Road to Independence,* Vol. 1, 236-238

[20] Ibid.

Chapter Three

"These Gentlemen from Virginia appear to be the most spirited and consistent of any."

Fall: 1774

Peyton Randolph, Richard Henry Lee, Benjamin Harrison, and Richard Bland were the first Virginia delegates to arrive in Philadelphia in early September. They dined at the City Tavern with delegates from several other colonies, one of whom was John Adams, of Massachusetts. Mr. Adams was quite impressed by the Virginians and recorded in his diary that

> These Gentlemen from Virginia appear to be the most spirited and consistent of any. Harrison said he would have come on foot rather than not come. Bland said he would have gone, upon this Occasion, if it had been to Jericho.[1]

George Washington, Patrick Henry, and Edmund Pendleton arrived the following day and undoubtedly impressed Adams as well.

---

[1] Paul H. Smith, ed., "John Adams Diary, 2 September, 1774," *Letters of Delegates to Congress: 1774-1789*, Vol. 1, (Washington, D.C.: Library of Congress, 1976), 7

Congress formally met for the first time on September 5th, not in the Pennsylvania capitol building, (known today as Independence Hall) but in nearby Carpenter's Hall. This recently constructed building was much smaller than the capitol and the delegates found themselves in very close quarters with each other, but they were determined to deliberate privately and without any meddling from the conservative Pennsylvania Assembly, something that would be impossible to avoid if they met in the capitol building.

Although Massachusetts was at the center of the dispute with Britain, the delegates chose Peyton Randolph, Virginia's Speaker of the House of Burgesses, to preside over the Congress. Randolph was a political moderate from Williamsburg, universally esteemed by Virginians, and his selection garnered good will among the southern delegates.

The delegates followed Randolph's selection as President of the Congress with a debate over voting procedures. Patrick Henry proposed that colonies with larger populations be allotted more votes in Congress than the less populated colonies. A delegate from Rhode Island countered that since every colony was prepared to sacrifice and suffer equally in the dispute with Great Britain, the colonies should have an equal voice in Congress.[2] The issue was settled when the delegates realized that they had no reliable information to accurately determine the population size of the thirteen colonies. They decided that the only practical solution was to give each colony one vote in the Congress.

Once the procedural matters were settled, the delegates tackled the main issue, a unified response to the Intolerable

---

[2] Smith, "James Duane's Notes on the Debates, 6 September, 1774," *Letters of Delegates to Congress*, Vol. 1, 30-31

Acts. Patrick Henry set the benchmark for colonial unity when he boldly proclaimed:

> *The Distinctions between Virginians, Pennsylvanians, New Yorkers, and New Englanders, are no more. I am not a Virginian, but an American!*[3]

The Massachusetts delegates were undoubtedly pleased by Henry's display of unity. It remained to be seen whether the rest of the congress shared his view.

A week of deliberations provided John Adams with the answer. He informed his wife in mid-September that

> *Congress will, to all present Appearance, be well united...A Tory here is the most despicable Animal...The Spirit, the Firmness, the Prudence of* [Massachusetts] *are vastly applauded and We are universally acknowledged the Saviours and Defenders of American Liberty.*[4]

Congress Rejects Militant Measures

Such strong support for Massachusetts convinced John Adams to draft a resolution on September 30th that went beyond punitive economic measures against Britain. Adams believed it was time to better organize the colonial militias. His resolution

---

[3] Ibid., 28

[4] Smith, "John Adams to Abigail Adams, 14 September, 1774," *The Letters of Delegates to Congress*, Vol. 1, 69-70

Recommended to all the Colonies, to establish by Provincial Laws, where it can be done, a regular well furnished, and disciplined Militia, and where it cannot be done by Law, by voluntary Associations, and private Agreements.[5]

Richard Henry Lee proposed a similar measure on October 3rd and claimed that

Since it is quite unreasonable that the Mother Country should be at the expence of maintaining Standing Armies in North America for its defence and [so the Ministry] *may be convinced that it is unnecessary and improper as North America is able, willing, and under Providence determined to Protect Defend and Secure itself, The Congress do most earnestly recommend it to the several Colonies that a Militia be forthwith appointed and well disciplined and that they be well provided with Ammunition and Proper Arms.*[6]

Although all of the delegates in Philadelphia were united in their opposition to the Intolerable Acts, the debate that ensued in early October over the proposed militia resolutions of Adams and Lee revealed that Congress differed significantly on how to respond to Parliament's crack down on Boston.

Opponents of Adams's and Lee's resolutions (which included Virginians Benjamin Harrison and Richard Bland)

---

[5] Smith, "John Adams Proposed Resolutions, 1 October, 1774," *The Letters of Delegates to Congress*, Vol. 1, 132

[6] Smith, "Richard Henry Lee's Proposed Resolutions, 1 October, 1774," *The Letters of Delegates to Congress*, Vol. 1, 140

called the resolutions nothing short of a declaration of war that undermined the true purpose of the Continental Congress, which was to adopt the best means to affect a reconciliation with Britain.[7]   They preferred trade restrictions on both imports and exports that would impact British manufacturers and spur them to pressure Parliament to resolve the dispute peacefully.

Proponents of the militia resolutions, however, like Patrick Henry, argued that

> *A preparation for Warr is necessary to obtain peace -- America is not Now in a State of peace...all of the Bulwarks of Our Safety, of Our Constitution are thrown down,* [and] *We are Now in a State of Nature. We ought to ask Ourselves the Question should the plans of* [non-exportation and non-importation] *fail of success – in that Case Arms are Necessary, & if then, it is Necessary Now.*[8]

Henry went on to assert that

> *Arms are a Resource to which We shall be forced, a Resource afforded Us by God & Nature, & why in the Name of both are We to hesitate providing them Now whilst in Our power.*[9]

For a majority of the delegates who still preferred to think in terms of a peaceful reconciliation, Henry's assertions were disturbing and his recommended course of action dangerous.

---

[7] Smith, "Silas Deane's Diary,", 3 October, 1774," *The Letters of Delegates to Congress*, Vol. 1, 138

[8] Ibid., 139

[9] Ibid.

As a result, the proposals to encourage each colony to strengthen its militia were defeated and much to the chagrin of Adams, Lee, Henry, and a few other delegates, Congress shifted its attention solely to economic measures against Britain.

Disappointed by the refusal of Congress to support measures to strengthen the colonial militias, John Adams became decidedly less confident about the effectiveness of the assembly and complained to his wife in mid-October that

> *I am wearied to Death with the Life I lead. The Business of the Congress is tedious, beyond Expression. This Assembly is like no other that ever existed. Every Man in it is a great Man – an orator, a Critick, a statesman, and therefore every Man upon every Question must shew his oratory, his criticism and his Political Abilities. The Consequence of this is, that Business is drawn and spun out to an immeasurable Length. I believe if it was moved and seconded that We should come to a Resolution that Three and two make five, We should be entertained with Logick and Rhetorick, Law, History, Politicks and Mathematicks, concerning the Subject for two whole Days, and then We should pass a Resolution unanimously in the Affirmative.*[10]

Two more weeks passed before the delegates finally agreed on a course of action. The plan they adopted was similar to the proposals of the Virginia Convention earlier that summer. A boycott of British goods and the discontinuation of the slave

---

[10] Smith, "John Adams to Abigail Adams, 9 October, 1774," *Letters of Delegates to Congress*, Vol. 1 164

trade were approved for December 1st, 1774. If Parliament persisted with the Intolerable Acts, a ban on all colonial exports to Britain would follow on September 1st, 1775. Congress also called on the American colonists to be more frugal and industrious and to avoid extravagant activities like horse-racing, gambling, plays, and dances. Committees were authorized in every county, city, and town to enforce these provisions.[11]

Fairfax County Ponders a Stronger Response

Although the Continental Congress, the Virginia Convention, and nearly every county committee in Virginia favored economic measures to oppose the British ministry's actions against Boston, one county in northern Virginia, led by Colonel George Mason, boldly embraced more aggressive measures in mid-September (two weeks before similar measures were rejected by the Continental Congress). Like their brethren throughout Virginia, the freeholders of Fairfax County initially opted (at their July 17th meeting in Alexandria) for economic sanctions against Britain. However, in the weeks following the adoption of the Fairfax Resolves, distressing newspaper reports caused many to question whether economic sanctions went far enough to oppose Parliament.

Within days of the adoption of the Fairfax County Resolves on July 17th, reports that additional British regiments were en route to Boston to reinforce the four regiments already there appeared in the weekly Virginia gazettes. Alarmed at the

---

[11] Journal of Continental Congress, 20 October, 1774, 75-80
(Accessed via the Library of Congress website at www.loc.gov)

increasing size of the British military in Massachusetts, many Virginians questioned the real purpose of such a large force. Did the British Ministry's plans extend beyond the occupation of Boston? Might other colonies be occupied as well?

Equally worrisome was news in late July that Parliament was about to consider a bill calling for new regulations on all the American colonies, not just Massachusetts.[12] This fostered the concern of many colonists that the true intention of the British Ministry was to subjugate all of British North America.

Prompted by these alarming reports, writers to the Virginia gazettes boldly proclaimed in late July the willingness of Virginians to fight for their constitutional rights. *"Do they think we will submit to Tyranny in our own Land?"* asked one writer. *"The Country which our Fathers purchased with their Blood, we will defend with our Blood."*[13] This view was echoed a week later by a self described American Cato who reminded readers that, *"With the Sword our Forefathers obtained their constitutional Rights, and by the Sword it is our Duty to defend them."*[14]

Threat from Canada

The possibility of armed conflict seemed to increase on the eve of the Virginia Convention in August when it was reported in the newspapers that General Gage

> *Has received the strongest Assurances from the Governour of Canada that 10,000 of his Majesty's truly loyal Subjects of that Province are ready to*

[12] Purdie & Dixon, *Virginia Gazette,* 21 July, 1774 , 1
[13] Ibid.
[14] Purdie and Dixon, *Virginia Gazette*, 28 July, 1774, 1

march at the shortest Notice...against all factious and disaffected Persons whatsoever.[15]

This threat to employ thousands of Canadian militia against the colonists (soldiers who years earlier had been bitter opponents of the British) angered many American colonists. Yet, most of the delegates to the Virginia Convention restrained their anger and endorsed economic sanctions as the most appropriate way to oppose Parliament.

Virginians outside of the Convention, however, particularly in Fairfax County, took notice of these late summer reports and began to question whether economic sanctions were a strong enough response to Parliament.

King George III Backs Parliament

The concern of Virginians only intensified in September when they learned the disappointing news of King George III's unqualified support for Parliament's actions against Massachusetts. It was commonly believed among many colonists that although the British Ministry and Parliament were under the sway of corrupt ministers bent on oppressing (some went as far to say enslaving) the colonists, the English people and the King would surely rise to America's defense.

An account of the King's speech to Parliament in June appeared in Purdie and Dixon's *Virginia Gazette* in early September and dashed this hope. King George III declared that

---

[15] Ibid.

I have long seen, with Concern, a dangerous Spirit of Resistance to my Government, and to the Execution of the Laws, prevailing in the Province of Massachusetts Bay, in New England. It proceeded, at length, to such an Extremity as to render [Parliament's] *immediate interposition indispensably necessary.... Nothing that depends on me shall be wanting to render* [Parliament's interposition] *effectual. It is my most anxious Desire to see my deluded Subjects in that Part of the World returning to a Sense of their Duty, acquiescing in that just Subordination to the Authority* [of Parliament] *and maintaining that due Regard to the commercial Interests, of this Country....*[6]

Many of the King's "deluded subjects" believed that King George had the situation backwards. It was he who had been deluded and misinformed by corrupt ministers of his government. Although the colonists were discouraged by the King's speech, they remained hopeful that he would eventually come to see the crisis in its proper light and intervene to protect the rights of his loyal subjects in America.

The Quebec Act

The disappointment and anxiety caused by the King's endorsement of Parliament's actions was further exacerbated by news in September of Parliament's passage of the Quebec Act. This new law extended Quebec's boundary to the Ohio River and continued southwestward all the way to the

---

[6] "King's Speech to Parliament, June 13, 1774," Purdie and Dixon, *Virginia Gazette,* 8 September, 1774, 2

Mississippi River. In addition to effectively restricting future westward expansion of many of the American colonies, the Quebec Act also allowed the inhabitants of Quebec to govern themselves in civil matters under their old French laws and legal customs and perhaps worst of all to many American colonists, maintain their Catholic faith. The level of religious intolerance was high in a number of American colonies so Parliament's embrace of Quebec's French Catholic population generated a great deal of displeasure and much concern in the colonies. Some viewed it as a plot by Parliament to garner French-Canadian support so that they might be better able to militarily subdue and control the thirteen colonies.

Massachusetts Gunpowder Raid

One other incident grabbed the attention of many Virginians in mid-September and possibly caused Fairfax County's freeholders to adopt more forceful measures against the British than a boycott. A week before the Fairfax freeholders met in Alexandria, an account of a bloody British raid outside of Boston circulated in the Virginia newspapers. The wildly inaccurate account claimed that British troops had seized a large supply of gunpowder stored outside of Boston and fired upon colonists who opposed the raid.[17] The account further claimed that the British troops fled back to Boston where the navy bombarded a portion of the town.[18]

Much of New England was alarmed by this report and militia forces mustered and marched throughout the region before the account was discovered to be grossly inaccurate.

---

[17] Purdie and Dixon, *Virginia Gazette,* 15 September, 1774, 3
[18] Ibid.

No blood had been spilled during the raid and Boston had not been fired upon. General Gage's troops did seize 250 barrels of Massachusetts gunpowder, however, and much of New England did rally to resist the British when the alarm was sounded. Both the brazen act of General Gage and the firm response of the New England colonists were noticed throughout the continent and foreshadowed more serious confrontations ahead.

Fairfax County Independent Militia Company

It was with all of these reports and developments in mind that the leaders and freeholders of Fairfax County gathered (two months after the adoption of their July resolves) to debate a new measure penned by Colonel George Mason. His proposal to form an independent company of volunteer militia was bold and provocative and seemingly lacked any legal foundation. Yet, Mason, who was considered one of Virginia's top legal minds, insisted that such a militia company was necessary.

Laws for the regulation of the militia in Virginia dated back to the 1730's and were periodically renewed in the years leading up to 1774, (most recently in 1771) but when Governor Dunmore suddenly dissolved the House of Burgesses in May 1774 he denied the assembly the chance to renew the expired militia law. This meant that the authority to assemble, discipline and train the various county militias no longer existed.

When conflict with the Indians erupted on the frontier in the summer of 1774, self preservation motivated many frontiersmen to serve in Lord Dunmore's expedition. With their homes and families in danger, the western counties had little trouble raising volunteers to fight, thus, the expired militia law was not needed to compel the militia to turn out on the frontier.

However, the threat of Indian attack was small in the tidewater and northern neck counties of Virginia so the absence of the militia law actually undermined efforts to better train and organize the county militias. As a result, the military preparedness of much of Virginia's militia force had declined. With this in mind, the gentlemen and freeholders of Fairfax County acted, declaring on September 21st, 1774, that

> *In this Time of extreme Danger, with the Indian Enemy in our Country, and threat'ned with the Destruction of our Civil-rights, & Liberty, and all that is dear to British Subjects & Freemen; we the Subscribers, taking into our serious consideration the present alarming Situation of all the British Colonies upon this Continent as well as our own, being sensible of the Expediency of putting the Militia of this Colony upon a more respectable Footing, & hoping to excite others by our Example, have voluntarily freely & cordially entered into the following Association.... That we will form ourselves into a Company, not exceeding one hundred Men, by the Name of The Fairfax independent Company of Voluntiers....*[19]

Although the company was open to the first one hundred men who met the unit's requirements, those requirements were difficult for most freeholders to achieve. Clearly Mason's aim was to attract men of a certain social and financial stature into the company's ranks. Colonel Mason noted as much when he

---

[19] Rutland, ed., "Fairfax County Militia Association 21 September, 1774," *The Papers of George Mason*, Vol. 1, 210-211

observed months later that the company was comprised of, *"Gentlemen of the first fortune and character...*[who] *have submitted to stand in the ranks as common soldiers.*"[20]

Those who joined agreed to outfit themselves (at their own expense) in a, *"regular Uniform of Blue, turn'd up with Buff...Buff Waist Coat & Breeches, & white Stockings.*"[21] They also pledged to equip themselves with a good fire-lock (musket) and all of the necessary military accoutrements of a soldier. Company officers would be chosen annually from among the ranks, and the volunteers pledged to meet regularly, *"for the Purpose of learning & practicing the military Exercise & Discipline."*[22] The expectation was that the Fairfax Independent Militia Company would present a sharp example for their fellow Virginians to emulate.

Interestingly, the volunteers were instructed to obtain at least six pounds of gunpowder, twenty pounds of lead, and fifty gun flints.[23] This was far above the normal amount expected of an individual soldier for such items and suggests that each volunteer was also expected to equip additional soldiers if it became necessary to expand the militia forces of the county.

This highlights the fact that the Fairfax Independent Company of Volunteers was not formed as a typical county militia force, but rather, it was meant to serve as a training vehicle in which future militia officers learned the military arts. Colonel Mason explained this view months later when

---

[20] Rutland, ed., "Remarks on the Annual Elections of the Fairfax Independent Company, April 1775, *The Papers of George Mason*, Vol. 1, 229

[21] Ibid.

[22] Ibid.

[23] Ibid.

objections to the election of new company officers were raised. Mason noted that the independent company was originally formed

> *To rouse the attention of the public, to introduce the use of arms and discipline, to infuse a martial spirit of emulation, and to provide a fund of officers; that in case of absolute necessity, the people might be the better enabled to act in defence of their invaded liberty.* [24]

One way to, *"provide a fund of officers,"* was to annually rotate the company's officers through regular elections. The one exception to this policy was reserved for the gentleman who served as the company's overall commander, Colonel George Washington. His stature and military experience made him an invaluable member of the company and the thought of reducing him to the ranks via rotation was inconceivable. Colonel Mason defended this view, noting that

> *The exception made in favor of the gentleman who by the unanimous voice of the company now commands it, is a very proper one, justly due to his public merit and experience.* [25]

---

[24] Ibid.
[25] Ibid., 231

Prince William Independent Company of Cadets

Fairfax County was not the only county in the fall of 1774 to turn to Colonel George Washington for leadership. Neighboring Prince William County also formed an independent militia company and named it the Independent Company of Cadets.

Thomas Montgomery, a merchant from Prince William County, reported to a committee of the House of Burgesses in 1775 that the Prince William independent company was formed in September 1774.[26] Six weeks later, on November 11th, 1774, the leaders of the company appealed to Colonel Washington to, *take command of this company as their Field Officer, and* [requested] *that he will be pleas'd to direct the fashion of their uniform.*[27] The men who delivered this request (Thomas Blackburn, Richard Graham, and Philip Richard Francis Lee) were also instructed to, *acquaint* [Colonel Washington] *with the Motto of the Company* [Aut Liber, aut nullus: Either Liberty or Death]"[28]

---

[26] "Testimony of Thomas Montgomery of PWC 14 June, 1775," *Journal of the House of Burgesses*: 1773-1776, 236

[27] Stanislaus M. Hamilton, ed. "Extract from the Minutes of the Independent Company of Cadets of the 11th, November, 1774," *Letters to Washington & Accompanying Papers*, Vol. 5 (Boston & New York: Houghton Mifflin, Co., 1902, 68-69

[28] Ibid.

Military Preparations Spread.....Slowly

Support for the formation of independent militia companies in Virginia, while far from universal in the fall of 1774, gained currency among some Virginians as speculation about Parliament's intentions increased. A letter in Pinkney's gazette in late October highlighted the fears of a growing number of colonists about Parliament's intentions:

As it is confidently asserted that the Canadians are to be poured in on the back parts of our provinces, the English troops in our front, and our governors forbid giving assent to militia laws, [it is] *high time that we should look around us and enter into associations for learning the use of arms, and to chuse officers; so that if ever we should be attacked, we may be able to defend ourselves, and not be drove like sheep to the slaughter.*[29]

The prospect of being driven like sheep to slaughter apparently did not concern Henry Lee II of Prince William County. He confidently informed his cousin William in England in early October that the colonists were ready to fight if necessary:

If Genl Gage Dares to pull a trigger the English troops will rue the Day, the Colonys are determined as One Man if things should be reduced to Extremitys, to repell force by force....[30]

---

[29] Pinkney, *Virginia Gazette*, 27 October, 1774, 2
[30] "Henry Lee II to William Lee, 1 October, 1774," *Lee-Ludwell Papers*, Virginia Historical Society

Three weeks later, while the Continental Congress in Philadelphia adopted economic measures against Britain, Nicholas Cresswell, a British visitor recently arrived in Virginia, observed that the inhabitants of Fairfax County behaved as if they were on the brink of war:

> *Everything here is in the utmost confusion. Committees are appointed to inspect into the Characters and Conduct of every tradesman, to prevent them selling Tea or buying British Manufactures. Some of them have been tarred and feathered, others had their property burnt and destroyed by the populace. Independent Companies are raising in every County on the Continent...and train their Men as if they were on the Eve of War...*[Contributions are raised] *in every Colony on the Continent for the relief of the people of Boston. The King is openly cursed, and his authority set at defiance. In short, everything is ripe for rebellion. The New Englanders by their canting, whining, insinuating tricks have persuaded the rest of the Colonies that the Government is going to make absolute slaves of them.*[31]

Although Cresswell's claim that independent companies were forming all over the continent was greatly exaggerated, his observations of Alexandria, Virginia in late October 1774 certainly attested to the lengths many Virginians were willing to go to resist Parliament.

Perhaps influenced by the same rhetoric and actions witnessed by Nicholas Cresswell, two additional northern Virginia counties (Loudoun and Spotsylvania) formed their own independent militia companies in the early winter of

---

[31] Nicholas Cresswell, "24 October, 1774," *The Journal of Nicholas Cresswell*, (The Dial Press: NY, 1974), 43-44

1774. Cresswell actually observed Loudoun County's "ragged" independent company exercise on a visit to Leesburg on December 13th.[32] Two days later, the Spotsylvania County Committee recommended to the inhabitants of their county the formation of independent companies of public spirited gentlemen.[33]

Additionally, the independent militia companies of Williamsburg -- which welcomed Lord Dunmore back with great fanfare from his successful expedition against the Indians in the west in December -- and Norfolk, which was formed long before 1774 for reasons unrelated to the dispute with Britain, brought to six the total number of independent companies of militia that existed in Virginia in 1774.[34] This small number, out of 60 plus counties and towns, demonstrated the continued preference of most Virginia jurisdictions for economic measures such as those adopted by the Continental Congress in October against the British. Events would soon cause many Virginians to reconsider this stance.

---

[32] Cresswell Journal, 13 December, 1774, 51

[33] Robert L. Scribner, ed., *Revolutionary Virginia: The Road to Independence,* Vol. 2, (Charlottesville: University Press of Virginia, 1975), 196-97

[34] John Pendleton Kennedy, ed., *Journal of the House of Burgesses*: 1773-1776, (Richmond: VA, 1905), 232-33

Chapter Four

"If we wish to be free...
We must fight!"

Winter and Spring: 1775

Gunpowder and Arms Ban

While county committees throughout Virginia met in early December to discuss implementation of Congress's non-importation agreement, more disturbing reports from England appeared in the newspapers. Dixon and Hunter's gazette printed a letter from England that revealed a shocking new British policy aimed at the colonies. *"This Day's Gazette,"* wrote a correspondent from London, *"contains a Proclamation prohibiting the Exportation of Gunpowder, Arms, Ammunition, and Saltpeter, during the Space of six Months."*[1]

Concerned about reports of the, *"amazing Quantities of fire-arms &ct.,"* that were about to be shipped to America, British authorities sprang into action and suspended all such shipments.[2] A correspondent to Dixon and Hunter's gazette noted that, *"Two Vessels laden with Gunpowder, and other military Utensils, bound for the other side of the Atlantick, were stopped...in Consequence of the King's Proclamation."*[3]

---

[1] Dixon and Hunter, *Virginia Gazette, Supplement*, 8 December, 1774, 2
[2] Ibid.
[3] Ibid.

British officials were clearly worried that colonial opposition to their policies could turn violent and their solution was to deny the colonists the means to resist.

Along with the troubling news about the gunpowder and arms restrictions, the gazettes were also filled with reports of ever more British reinforcements sailing to the colonies, specifically two regiments for New York and hundreds of Marines with a second naval fleet to Boston.[4] These reports suggested to a growing number of Virginians (and their fellow American colonists) that the British Ministry was preparing to use armed force to exert its will.

Colonists in New Hampshire and Rhode Island reacted strongly to the news of the gunpowder prohibition by storming lightly guarded British forts to seize the arms and gunpowder stored inside. Amazingly, no blood was shed in these incidents, but property was damaged and stolen and British authorities were furious.

No such incident occurred in Maryland, but the colony did attract the attention of many Virginians in December when it established a colony-wide subscription (voluntary tax) of three shillings per tithable to raise funds for gunpowder and arms. Maryland's leaders also called for all freemen in the colony between the ages of 16 to 50 to serve in their respective county militia companies.

Although most Virginians continued to place their reliance on economic sanctions to change Parliament's policies, colonial leaders like George Washington acted to prepare for conflict if it erupted. Responding to requests from the independent militia companies of both Fairfax and Prince William counties, Colonel Washington made arrangements in

---

[4] Ibid.

Philadelphia to obtain military drill manuals, muskets, officers' sashes, and accoutrements for each company.

Colonel Washington was not alone in his efforts to procure military supplies for his fellow Virginians. The committees of Dunmore and Northampton County both took steps to procure gunpowder in early January. Dunmore County (in the northwest region of Virginia) made arrangements to purchase and store all of the gunpowder in the possession of local merchants while Northampton County (on the eastern shore) offered a reward to the first person in the county who could manufacture 500 pounds of gunpowder.[5] When confirmation of the King's ban on powder and arms exports to America appeared in the Virginia Gazettes in January, (in the form of a circular letter from the Secretary of State for North America, Lord Dartmouth, to the various colonial governors), more county committees in Virginia acted.[6]

Young James Madison of Orange County observed on January 20th that some counties, including his own, had moved beyond securing gunpowder and arms and were forming independent militia companies like those formed in 1774:

We are very busy at present in raising men and procuring the necessaries for defending ourselves and our friends in case of a sudden invasion. The extensiveness of the demands of the Congress, and the pride of the British nation, together with the wickedness of the present ministry, seem, in the judgment of our politicians, to require a preparation

---

[5] Scribner, ed., *Revolutionary Virginia: The Road to Independence,* Vol. 2, 229, 231

[6] Dixon & Hunter, *Virginia Gazette,* 14 January, 1775, 1

for extreme events. There will, by the Spring I expect, be some thousands of well-trained, high spirited men ready to meet danger whenever it appears, who are influenced by no mercenary principles, but bearing their own expenses, and having the prospect of no recompense but the honor and safety of their country.[7]

While Orange County and a few other counties moved to establish independent militia companies, Fairfax County once again went significantly further and acted to expand and organize its entire county militia force:

Fairfax County Committee of Safety
January 17, 1775

Resolved, That this Committee do concur in opinion with the Provincial Committee of the Province of Maryland, that a well regulated Militia, composed of gentlemen freeholders, and other freemen, is the natural strength and only stable security of a free Government, and that such Militia will relieve our mother country from any expense in our protection and defence, will obviate the pretence of a necessity for taxing us on that account, and render it unnecessary to keep Standing Armies among us – ever dangerous to liberty; and therefore it is recommended to such of the inhabitants of this County as are from sixteen to fifty of age to choose a

---

[7] Gaillard Hunt, ed., "James Madison to William Bradford Jr., 20 January, 1775," *The Writings of James Madison*, Vol. 1, (New York: J.P. Putnam's Sons, 1900), 28

Captain, two Lts. an Ensign, four sgts. four cpls. and one Drummer for each Company; that they provide themselves with good Firelocks, and use their utmost endeavors to make themselves masters of the Military Exercise [of 1764].[8]

This resolution signaled a significant expansion of military preparation in Fairfax County and demonstrated the county's willingness to lead Virginia's opposition against Parliament's policies and actions. The legality of the committee's actions (to act on its own without legislation from the House of Burgesses) was open to debate, but the fact that it recommended (instead of required) the county's inhabitants to organize themselves into militia companies and pay three shillings per tithable person to raise funds for the purchase of gunpowder and other supplies, avoided the legal issue of whether the committee had the authority to compel such measures.

Three weeks after adoption of this resolution, Colonel George Mason sent a draft of a more detailed militia plan to Colonel Washington and invited him to, *"make such Alterations as you think necessary."*[9] The plan opened with a justification of the committee's actions in February 1775:

Threatened with the Destruction of our antient Laws & Liberty, and the Loss of all that is dear to British Subjects & Freemen, justly alarmed with the Prospect of impending Ruin,-- firmly determined at the hazard

---

[8] Rutland, ed., "Fairfax County Committee of Safety Proceedings, 17 January 1775," *The Papers of George Mason,* Vol. 1, 212

[9] Rutland, ed., "George Mason to George Washington, 6 February, 1774," *The Papers of George Mason,* Vol. 1, 214

of our Lives, to transmit to our Children & Posterity those sacred Rights to which ourselves were born; and thoroughly convinced that a well regulated Militia, composed of the Gentlemen, Freeholders, and other Freemen, is the natural Strength and only safe & stable security of a free Government...WE the Subscribers, Inhabitants of Fairfax County, have freely & voluntarily agreed...to enroll & embody ourselves into a Militia for this County....[10]

Mason's plan raised the minimum age of militia service in Fairfax County by two years and specified that all able bodied freemen in the county between 18 and 50 years old should join militia companies under officers of their own choosing and serve until, *"a regular and proper Militia Law for the Defence of the Country shall be enacted by the Legislature of this Colony."*[11] The men who joined these companies pledged to outfit and equip themselves in a uniform manner and, *"perfect ourselves in the Military Exercise & Discipline...."*[12]

George Mason and George Washington assumed much of the responsibility for purchasing gunpowder and raising funds for the Fairfax militia, splitting the cost of a large shipment of gunpowder from Philadelphia (worth over 350 pounds in Pennsylvania currency) in mid-February and collecting the three shilling fee per tithable from those willing and able to pay.[13]

---

[10] Rutland, ed., "Fairfax County Militia Plan for Embodying the People, 6 February, 1775," *The Papers of George Mason*, Vol. 1, 215-216
[11] Ibid.
[12] Ibid.
[13] Rutland, ed., "George Mason to George Washington, 17-18 Feb. 1775," *The Papers of George Mason*, Vol. 1, 220-225

Military Preparations Spread in Virginia

Possibly inspired by the example of Fairfax County and undoubtedly influenced by Britain's steady military build-up in Massachusetts and Parliament's new efforts to halt gunpowder and arms shipments to the colonies, more Virginia counties acted to improve their military preparedness in February 1775. Caroline and Cumberland counties took measures to secure gunpowder, Isle of Wight and Fauquier counties moved to form militia companies, (Fauquier offered command of its company to George Washington), and Spotsylvania county (which had already formed a militia company) exercised their troops, making a, *"poor appearance,"* according to Nicholas Cresswell, who witnessed them drill in Fredericksburg.[14]

More Disappointing News from England

For every county that took these aggressive measures, however, another clung to the hope that the economic sanctions adopted by the Continental Congress would succeed and make military preparations unnecessary. Such hope dimmed when news of the King's continued strong support for Parliament, and the results of England's parliamentary elections the previous fall, reached Virginia in February. King George III declared in a speech to both houses of Parliament in late November, 1774, that

---

[14] Scribner, ed., *Revolutionary Virginia: The Road to Independence,* Vol. 2, 284, 287, 317, and Vol. 3 41, 43, 56, 75 ; also Runge, ed., "16 February, 1775," *The Papers of George Washington,* Vol. 10, 263-64

It gives me much concern that I am obliged, at the opening of this Parliament, that a most daring spirit of resistance and disobedience to the law prevails in the province of Massachusetts Bay, and has, in [many] parts of it, broke forth in fresh violence of a very criminal nature. These proceedings have been countenanced and encouraged in other of my colonies, and unwarrantable attempts have been made to obstruct the commerce of this kingdom, by unlawful combinations. I have taken such measures, and given such orders, as I have judged most proper and effectual in carrying into execution the laws that were passed in the last session of the late Parliament, for the protection and security of the commerce of my subjects and for the restoring and preserving peace, order, and good government in the province of Massachusetts Bay; and you may depend upon my firm and steadfast resolution to withstand every attempt to weaken or impair the supreme authority of this legislature over all the dominions of my Crown; the maintenance of which I consider as essential to the dignity, the safety, and the welfare of the British empire.[15]

George Mason, in a letter to his friend George Washington, lamented the tone of the King's speech and wondered if perhaps the King had not yet seen the petition from the Philadelphia Congress:

---

[15] Dixon & Hunter, *Virginia Gazette*, 4 February, 1775, 2

I suppose You have seen the King's Speech, & the Addresses of both Houses in the Last Maryland Paper; from the Style in which they speak of the Americans I think We have little Hopes of a speedy Redress of Grievances; but on the Contrary we may expect to see coercive & vindictive Measures still pursued. It seems as if the King either had not received, or was determined to take no Notice of the Proceedings of the Congress.[16]

Richard Henry Lee was also troubled by the latest reports from England, noting that, *"All America has received with astonishment and concern the* [King's] *Speech to Parliament.*[17] Lee's concern increased when reports about the autumn parliamentary elections in Britain reached the colonies. Lee and many other colonists had long given up hope that the current British administration would see the error of their ways and reverse their ill-advised and unconstitutional policies, but they had continued to hope that the King and English people would come to their defense and force Parliament to halt its oppressive actions.

The King's firm demonstration of support for Parliament left only the English people as an effective ally to the American colonists. Lee had acknowledged their importance in a letter to his brother, Arthur, in England:

---

[16] Rutland, ed., "George Mason to George Washington, 6 February, 1775," *The Papers of George Mason*, Vol. 1, 214

[17] Ballagh, ed.,"Richard Henry Lee to Arthur Lee, 24 Feb. 1775," *The Letters of Richard Henry Lee,* Vol. 1, 130

The wicked violence of the Ministry is so clearly expressed, as to leave no doubt of their fatal determination to ruin both Countries, unless a powerful and timely check is interposed by the Body of the people…. [Perhaps] the proceedings of the last Continental Congress when communicated to the people of England will rouse a spirit that proving fatal to an abandoned Ministry may save the whole Empire from impending destruction.[18]

Surely, hoped Lee and many other colonists, the British people would recognize the wrongs done to their brethren in America and vote out the corrupt leaders and their supporters in Parliament and elevate prominent Whigs like, Edmund Burke, John Wilkes, and William Pitt, all of whom had championed the American cause in Parliament for years.

The desired election results, however, never materialized. In fact, the fall parliamentary elections brought very little change in the membership of Parliament and the issue of the American colonies barely registered for most of the English electorate.[19]

Discouraged by the election results, colonists like Samuel Chase, a delegate to the Continental Congress from Maryland, concluded in early 1775 that the colonists could only look to themselves and God for the defense of their constitutional rights. Chase expressed his disillusionment with both the English political system and English people in a fiery letter to

---

[18] Ibid.

[19] Lewis Namier and John Brooks, *The History of Parliament : The House of Commons, 1754-1790*, (Oxford University Press, 1964)

James Duane, a fellow congressional delegate from New York:

> *If justice were to decide the dispute I would be confident, but when I reflect on the enormous Influence of the Crown, the System of Corruption introduced at the Art of Government...the open & repeated Violations, by Parliament, of the Constitution, at Home, the regular, arbitrary System of Colony administration, the several acts related to Massachusetts, the Quebec bill, and the Re-election of the Members of the last Parliament, I have not the least Dawn of Hope in the Justice, Humanity, Wisdom, or Virtue of the British Nation. I consider them as one of the most abandon'd & wicked People under the Sun. They openly sell themselves & their Posterity to their Representatives, who as openly traffic their Integrity & Honor to the Minister. The Roman Senate in the Reigns of Claudius, Caesar, or Nero, were not more servilely wicked, than the present House of Commons...Our Dependence must be on God & ourselves.*[20]

A Posture of Defense

If the colonists did have only God and themselves to depend on, Richard Henry Lee was confident that they could still prevail. In the same letter in which Lee had expressed hope that the English people would rise up to support the

---

[20] Smith, "Samuel Chase to James Duane 5 Feb, 1775," *Letters of Delegates to Congress,* Vol. 1, 304

colonists, he also bragged about the deadly aim of Virginia's frontier riflemen:

> *This one County of Fincastle can furnish 1000 Rifle Men that for their number make the most formidable light Infantry in the World. The six frontier Counties can produce 6000 of these Men who from their amazing hardihood, their method of living so long in the woods without carrying provisions with them, the exceeding quickness with which they can march to distant parts, and above all, the dexterity to which they have arrived in the use of the Rifle Gun. There is not one of these Men who wish a distance less than 200 yards or a larger object than an Orange. – Every shot is fatal.*[21]

For the many colonists who still thought in February 1775 that talk of armed resistance to Britain was foolishly premature and even criminal, writers to the weekly gazettes like, "A Watchman," convincingly warned of the dangers of complacency and appeasement.   Drawing upon the ancient lessons of Carthage (whose people surrendered their weapons to Rome in return for the promise of peace but were instead enslaved) "A Watchman" warned the colonists of a potentially similar fate:

---

[21] Ballagh, ed., "Richard Henry Lee to Arthur Lee, 24 February, 1775," *Letters of Richard Henry Lee*, Vol. 1, 130-131

To the INHABITANTS of BRITISH AMERICA
Friends and Countrymen,
At a time when ministerial tyrants threaten a people with the total loss of their liberties, supineness and inattention on their part will render...their ruin....
Equally inexcuseable with the Carthegenians will the AMERICANS be if they suffer the tyrants, who are endeavouring to enslave them, to possess themselves of all their forts, castles, arms, ammunition, and warlike stores. What reason can be given by them for such cowardly and pusillanimous conduct? Perhaps it may be said that there yet remains some gleam of hope that the British ministry may do us justice, restore us to our liberties, and repeal those oppressive acts which now hang over America; and was this even probable, it would hardly justify such a conduct. But what foundation have we for such hope? If this be the intention of the ministry, is a formidable fleet and numerous army, necessary to bring it about? Could they not have given up their plan for enslaving America without seizing all the strong holds on the continent; upon all the arms and ammunition? And without soliciting and finally obtaining an order to prohibit the importation of war like stores in the colonies? Does this speak the language of peace and reconciliation, or does it not rather speak that of war, tumult and desolation? And shall we, like the Carthegenians, peacefully surrender our arms to our enemies, in hopes of obtaining, in return, the liberties we have so long been contending for? Be not deceived, my

countrymen, should the ministry ever prevail upon you to make that base and infamous surrender, they will then tell you...what those liberties are, which they will in future suffer you to enjoy....[22]

Reminding readers that, "*whenever a power exists in a state over which the people have no control, the people are completely enslaved,*" "A Watchman" rejected Parliament's claim of authority over the colonies and called on colonists throughout America to better prepare themselves for armed conflict:[23]

I am far from wishing hostilities to commence on the part of America; but still hope that no person will, at this important crisis, be unprepared to act in his own defence, should he by necessity be driven thereto. And I must here beg leave to recommend to the consideration of the people of this continent, whether, when we are by an arbitrary decree prohibited the having of arms and ammunition by importation, we have not, by the law of self preservation, a right to seize upon all those within our power, in order to defend the LIBERTIES which GOD and nature have given to us.[24]

A little over a month later, Patrick Henry would make a similar argument.

---

[22] "A Watchman, 16 February, 1775," Pinkney *Virginia Gazette*, 2
[23] Ibid.
[24] Ibid.

Tensions Mount in Massachusetts

In the weeks leading up to Patrick Henry's fiery "Liberty or Death" speech at the 2nd Virginia Convention in Richmond, tension throughout the colonies steadily increased. The occupation of Boston, with reportedly fourteen regiments, an enormous naval fleet, and even more reinforcements on the way, strongly suggested that the British Ministry intended to use force against the colonists.[25] In fact, months of tense encounters between Boston's inhabitants and the occupying British troops left the Redcoats eager for a confrontation. British Major John Pitcairn of the British Marines expressed the view of many British soldiers in Boston in a letter to Lord Sandwich in early March:

Orders are anxiously expected from England to chastise those very bad people. The General had some of the Great Wigs, as they are called here, with him two days ago, when he took that opportunity of telling them, and swore to it by the living God, that if there was a single man of the King's troops killed in any of their towns he would burn it to the ground. What fools you are, said he, to pretend to resist the power of Great Britain; she maintained last war three hundred thousand men, and will do the same now rather than suffer the ungrateful people of this country to continue in their rebellion. This behavior of the General's gives great satisfaction to the friends of Government [Tories]. I am satisfied that one active campaign, a smart action, and burning of two

---

[25] Dixon and Hunter, *Virginia Gazette*, 11 February, 1775, 2

or three of their towns, will set everything to rights.
Nothing now, I am afraid, but this will ever convince
those foolish bad people that England is in earnest.
What a sad misfortune it was to this country, the
repealing of the Stamp Act; every friend to
Government here asserts in the strongest terms that
this has been the cause of all their misfortunes.[26]

Although the colonists were unaware of Major Pitcairn's sentiments, it had become increasingly evident to the Provisional Congress of Massachusetts over the winter that armed conflict with General Gage's force was likely and they instructed their constituents in Massachusetts to plan accordingly. Virginians read about these developments in early March in the various Virginia gazettes:

IN PROVINCIAL CONGRESS,
CAMBRIDGE, February 9, 1775.
To the inhabitants of MASSACHUSETTS BAY.

Friends and fellow sufferers,
Fleets, troops, and every implement of war, are sent
into the province, with apparent design to wrest from
you that freedom which it is your duty, even at the
risk of your lives, to hand inviolate to
posterity....Though we deprecate a rupture with the
mother state, yet we must still urge you to every
preparation for your necessary defence; for unless
you exhibit to your enemies such a firmness as shall
convince them that you are worthy of that freedom

---

[26] William Clark, ed., "Major John Pitcairn to Lord Sandwich, 4 March, 1775," *Naval Documents of the American Revolution*, Vol. 1, (Washington, 1964), 125

your ancestors fled here to enjoy you have nothing to expect but the vilest and most abject slavery.[27]

CAMBRIDGE, February 15.
WHEREAS it appears to this congress, from the present disposition of the British ministry and parliament, that there is real cause of fear that the reasonable and just applications of this continent to Great Britain, for "peace, liberty, and safety," will not meet with a favourable reception, but, on the contrary, from the large reinforcement of troops expected in this colony, the tenor of intelligence from Great Britain, and general appearances, we have reason to apprehend that the sudden destruction of this colony in particular is intended, for refusing, with the other colonies, tamely to submit to the most ignominious slavery:
Therefore resolved, that the great law of self preservation calls upon the inhabitants of this colony immediately to prepare against every attempt that may be made to attack them by surprize; and it is upon serious deliberation, most earnestly recommended to the militia in general, as well as the detached part of it in minute men, that they spare neither time, pains, nor expence, at so critical a juncture, in perfecting themselves forthwith in military discipline, and that skilful instructors be provided for those companies which are not already provided therewith.... And it is recommended to the towns and districts in this colony, that they encourage such persons as are skilled in the manufactory of fire arms and bayonets, diligently to

---

[27] Pinkney, *Virginia Gazette*, 9 March, 1775, 2

apply themselves thereto, for supplying such of the inhabitants as shall be deficient.[28]

These accounts in the Virginia gazettes must have weighed heavy on the minds of Patrick Henry and his fellow convention delegates as they gathered at what is now St. John's Church in Richmond in late March to select representatives to the next Continental Congress (scheduled to meet in Philadelphia in May) and provide them with instructions.

Rumors of Reconciliation Persist

Not all of the news in the Virginia gazettes, however, was contentious and discouraging. A number of letters from England appeared in the Virginia newspapers in March suggesting that the colonial boycott was having a positive effect on British opinion and that English merchants had appealed to Parliament to end the dispute with the colonies. Other reports claimed (inaccurately it turned out) that the Continental Congress's petition had been graciously received by the King who laid it before Parliament for its consideration.[29]

The unanimity, firmness and moderation, of the resolutions of the general congress [and] the universal approbation these [resolutions] meet with here, have roused the merchants and disconcerted the ministers. As yet, however, they appear

---

[28] Pinkney, *Virginia Gazette,* 9 March, 1775, 3
[29] Pinkney, *Virginia Gazette,* 16 March, 1775, 2-3

unresolved unwilling to retract, and unable to proceed.[30]

Incredibly, one letter from London even suggested that Parliament was ready to repeal the Intolerable Acts and grant representation of the colonies in Parliament.

LONDON, January 10.
IT is said that a plan is now agitating in the cabinet to conciliate matters between the mother country and America, by repealing the disagreeable acts, and admitting them to be represented by eighty members in the house of commons.[31]

Such reports gave hope to those colonists, including many at the 2nd Virginia Convention, who believed that peaceful reconciliation with Britain was still possible.

2nd Virginia Convention

One Virginian who was not at all swayed by such reports, however, was Patrick Henry. On the fourth day of the 2nd Virginia Convention in Richmond, the delegate from Hanover County rose to propose that Virginia *"Be immediately put into a posture of defense."*[32] Henry believed more than ever that armed conflict with Britain was inevitable and he urged Virginia to assume a war footing.

---

[30] Ibid.

[31] Pinkney, *Virginia Gazette,* 23 March, 1775, 2

[32] Scribner, ed., *Revolutionary Virginia: The Road to Independence,* Vol. 2 366-367

Henry's proposal to expand the colony's military preparedness was opposed by moderates like Edmund Pendleton and Robert Carter Nicholas. They argued that such a move was too confrontational and would provoke Parliament. They urged patience and scoffed at the idea of fighting Britain: *"Where* [are] *our* [military] *stores...our arms...our soldiers...the sinews of war,"* they asked? Henry's proposal might be brave, they said, *"but it was the bravery of madmen."*[33]

Patrick Henry replied to his critics and in doing so delivered one of the greatest speeches in American history. He acknowledged the patriotism of the opposition but suggested that they had, *"shut* [their] *eyes against a painful truth."*[34] Henry was alarmed by Britain's military buildup in Massachusetts and asked the delegates a pointed question:

> *Are fleets and armies necessary...* [for] *reconciliation? Have we shown ourselves so unwilling to be reconciled, that force must be called in to win back our love? Let us not deceive ourselves, sir. These are the implements of war and subjugation—the last arguments to which kings resort...I ask gentlemen, sir, what means this martial array, if its purpose be not to force us to submission...Has Great Britain any enemy in this quarter of the world, to call for all this accumulation of navies and armies? No, sir, she has none. They are meant for us, they can be meant for no other.*

[33] William Wirt, *Sketches in the Life and Character of Patrick Henry,* (Philadelphia, 1817), 136
[34] Ibid. 138

They are sent over to bind and rivet upon us those chains which the British ministry have been so long forging....[35]

Henry then recounted the failure of the numerous pleas and petitions sent to Britain over the past decade:

In vain, after these [appeals and petitions] *may we indulge the fond hope of peace and reconciliation. There is no longer any room for hope. If we wish to be free...we must fight! I repeat it, sir, we must fight!*[36]

Henry confidently exclaimed that, "*Three million people, armed in the holy cause of liberty...are invincible by any force which our enemy can send against us.*"[37] He then asserted that conflict was inevitable and urged the delegates to prepare the colony for it:

There is no retreat, but into submission and slavery! Our chains are forged. Their clanking may be heard on the plains of Boston! The war is inevitable – and let it come!! I repeat it sir, let it come!! It is vain, sir, to extenuate the matter. Gentlemen may cry, peace, peace – but there is no peace. The war is actually begun! The next gale that sweeps from the north will bring to our ears the clash of resounding arms! Our brethren are already in the field! Why stand we here idle? What is it that gentlemen wish?

---

[35] Ibid. 139
[36] Ibid. 140
[37] Ibid. 141

What would they have? Is life so dear, or peace so sweet, as to be purchased at the price of chains and slavery? Forbid it, Almighty God! I know not what course others may take; but as for me, give me liberty, or give me death![38]

Henry's stirring appeal worked, and his resolution passed by a narrow margin. A committee was formed to, "*prepare a Plan for embodying, arming and disciplining such a Number of Men,*" as was sufficient to put the colony into a posture of defense.[39] The committee, made up of leaders like Patrick Henry, George Washington, Richard Henry Lee, Thomas Jefferson, and Edmund Pendleton, drafted a plan by the next day and it was adopted by the Convention a day after that. It began by recommending that the colony diligently put into execution the Militia Law of 1738, which the committee claimed, "*has become in force by the expiration of all subsequent militia laws.*"[40]

The militia law of 1738 instructed each county to place all free males over 21 into militia companies. Free blacks and Indians were denied weapons and were assigned servile tasks as pioneers, laborers, or in some cases, musicians. Free whites were given eighteen months to obtain the necessary weapons and accoutrements required for their company (either infantry or horse). Regular musters were to be held for training purposes and punishments and fines inflicted on those who disobeyed commands or acted mutinously.[41]

---

[38] Ibid.
[39] Scribner, ed., *Revolutionary Virginia: The Road to Independence,* Vol. 23, 66-6
[40] Ibid., 374
[41] William W. Henings, *The Statutes at Large Being a Collection of all the Laws of Virginia,* Vol. 5, (Richmond: J. & G. Cochran, 1821), 16-23

To address the immediate weakness of the colony's militia forces and bridge the gap until the 1738 militia law could be fully implemented, the Convention,

> *Recommended to the Inhabitants of the several Counties of this Colony that they form one or more volunteer Companies of Infantry and Troops of Horse in each County and be in constant training and Readiness to act on any Emergency.*[42]

The plan identified counties that should raise troops of horse and those better served to raise companies of infantry. Hunting shirts were the recommended uniform for all of the troops and the plan specified the number of officers and rank and file for each company along with their arms, gear, and even the military drill they were to use, his Majesty's 1764 Drill.[43] The plan also recommended that all of the county committees collect funds from their constituents to supply their militia companies with an adequate supply of ammunition and arms.[44]

The fact that the Convention recommended all of these measures to the counties suggests that the delegates recognized their own legal limitations as an extra-legal assembly. No provision was made for any county that refused to adopt these recommendations; such an unpleasant possibility was essentially ignored because the Convention recognized there was little it could legally do to enforce them.

---

[42] Scribner, ed., *Revolutionary Virginia: The Road to Independence,* Vol. 2, 375
[43] Ibid.
[44] Ibid.

This might account for the slow response of many counties in implementing the Convention's recommendations. The vote on Patrick Henry's resolution to adopt a posture of defense was very close and revealed a reluctance from nearly half of the representatives in the Convention to escalate the dispute with Britain. In the two weeks following the Convention only a handful of counties publically acknowledged the militia resolutions. Gloucester, Sussex, and Southampton County thanked the Convention for its efforts and expressed support for the resolutions and Albemarle County took measures to organize its militia companies.[45]

Mixed Messages from England

In the immediate aftermath of the 2nd Convention, the Virginia gazettes were full of a new wave of optimistic reports from Britain (written in late December and early January) on the growing support among the English people and merchants for the American cause. Writers claimed that Congress's petitions were well received by all who read them and that pressure on the Ministry to reconcile with the colonies was growing every day:

> *Extract from a letter from a Gentleman in London…*
> *December 24, 1774*
>
> *The proceedings of the General Congress, and of your colony, have had every effect you could wish, upon the people, the Parliament, the Ministry, and the Merchants…The Ministry begin to disavow*

---

[45] Robert Scribner, ed., *Revolutionary Virginia: The Road to Independence*, Vol. 3, (Charlottesville, VA: University Press of Virginia, 1977), 30, 33, 37, 39

individually the late measures.... You have everything to expect from that firmness and unanimity which have thus shaken their councils, confounded their plans, and set them mutually at variance....

Another letter, dated Jan. 4ᵗʰ, says:
The number of your friends among the people at large increase every day.... [The Ministry] are alarmed at the unanimity of the Congress.... For Heaven's sake, for your own sake, and that of posterity, do not relax your vigilance.[46]

Yet another letter from England dated January 4ᵗʰ from "*a merchant of great veracity*," reported that

We have this day had as numerous and respectable a meeting of the merchants and traders to America as I ever saw. We have agreed to petition Parliament on your behalf, unanimously.[47]

Dixon and Hunter's gazette included a very optimistic letter from London expressing confidence that the long running dispute between Great Britain and the colonies might soon be settled:

London, Jan. 4, 1775
The reasons why I hope the unhappy differences between Great Britain and the colonies will soon subside, are...that the deliberations of the celebrated Congress, are held in the highest esteem, by every

---

[46] Purdie, *Virginia Gazette*, 7 April, 1775, 2
[47] Ibid.

sensible man in this metropolis; our great patriot, Lord Chatham (William Pitt) *has declared, that he* [lacks] *words to express the great satisfaction he received in reading them....*[48]

Such accounts undoubtedly bolstered the hope of Virginians that the long dispute with Parliament might still be peacefully resolved. They may have also dampened the enthusiasm of some Virginians to implement the 2nd Convention's militia recommendations.

Much of this new found optimism and hope was shaken just a week later, however, by a string of reports in the newspapers outlining the increased military measures that the British Ministry had adopted. These new accounts from England, dated late January and early February, painted a foreboding scene of armed coercion and conflict:

Extract of a letter from a Gentleman in Glasgow...Jan.31,1775

Great preparations are making by the Ministry, to reduce the Americans to obedience. All meetings are to be deemed high treason; and it is said, some of the people of Boston are to be brought home in irons. Thirty ships of war are ordered out to guard your coast, and block up your ports, which are to admit of no export or import, but to and from Great Britain and her islands. God knows how this will end....[49]

Another letter from Glasgow declared

---

[48] Dixon and Hunter, *Virginia Gazette*, 8 April, 1775
[49] Purdie, *Virginia Gazette*, 14 April, 1775, 2

> *The American affairs now seem to wear a very gloomy aspect. Government seems resolved to enforce the late acts, which I fear will create disturbances, and may perhaps involve you in the calamities of a civil war.*[50]

On the morning of April 19th, just days after the publication of these letters, the long feared conflict between the colonists and British troops erupted on a village green in Massachusetts.

The colonists' dispute with England had entered a new phase in Massachusetts -- armed conflict -- and it remained to be seen if that conflict would extend all the way to Virginia.

---

[50] Ibid.

Chapter Five

"The whole country [is] in an actual state of rebellion."

April to June: 1775

When the British army marched into the Massachusetts countryside on the evening of April 18th, 1775 it was not their first such endeavor. Nearly two months earlier a large detachment of British troops landed near the Massachusetts village of Marblehead, up the coast from Boston, in an effort to seize military supplies stored in neighboring Salem. The raid failed to capture any military stores, but it did include some creative diplomacy that defused a tense and nearly combative encounter. An account of the incident appeared within days in the Essex gazette:

Last Sabbath the Peace of the Town was disturbed by the coming of a Regiment of the King's Troops...A Transport arrived at Marblehead...covered with Soldiers, who having loaded and fixed their Bayonets, landed with great Dispatch; and instantly marched off. Some of the Inhabitants suspecting they were bound to Salem, to seize some Materials there preparing for an Artillery, dispatched several Messengers to inform us of it. These Materials were

*on the North Side of the North River, and to come at
them it was necessary to cross a Bridge, one Part of
which was made to draw up...the Regiment marched
off with a quick Pace, in a direct Course for the
North Bridge; just before their Entrance upon which,
the Draw-Bridge was pulled up...The Colonel who
led them expressed some Surprize; and then turning
about, ordered an Officer to face his Company to a
Body of Men standing on a Wharf on the other Side
of the Draw-Bridge, and fire. One of our Townsmen
(who had kept along Side the Colonel)...instantly told
him he had better not fire, that he had no Right to fire
without further Orders, "and if you do fire (said he)
you will be all dead Men." The company neither
fired or faced....* [1]

Colonel Alexander Leslie consulted with his officers and
declared to the colonists that *"he would maintain his Ground,
and go over the Bridge before he returned, if it was a Month
first."* [2] The townspeople replied that he could stay as long as
he liked, but the bridge would not be lowered. They then
asked Colonel Leslie what his purpose was for crossing the
bridge. Leslie replied that he had orders to cross it and that he
must comply with those orders. After a ninety minute
standoff, a compromise was reached:

---

[1] Clark, ed., "Essex Gazette, Tuesday, February 21 to 28, 1775," *Naval
Documents of the American Revolution*, Vol. 1, 114-16
[2] Ibid.

Finally the Colonel said he must go over; and if the Draw-Bridge were let down so that he might pass, he pledged his Honour he would march not above thirty Rods beyond it, and then immediately return. The Regiment had now been on the Bridge about an Hour and an Half; and every Thing being secured, the Inhabitants directed the Draw-Bridge to be let down. The Regiment immediately passed over, marched a few Rods, returned, and with great Expedition went back to Marblehead, where they embarked on board the Transport without Delay.[3]

Lexington and Concord

Two months after this tense but comical incident, General Gage ordered a much larger detachment of troops to seize a large cache of military stores reportedly hidden in the town of Concord, eighteen miles northwest of Boston. On the evening of April 18th, about 800 troops crossed the Charles River and marched rapidly towards Concord, hoping to catch the townsfolk by surprise. Ahead of them rode a handful of colonists determined to alarm the countryside of their approach and thwart the raid.

Thanks to the efforts of Paul Revere and William Dawes the alarm reached Lexington (a small village just six miles from Concord directly on the British army's route of march) around midnight. Captain John Parker mustered the village militia on the green while Samuel Adams and John Hancock, who were in Lexington on their way to the Continental Congress in Philadelphia, prepared to flee.

---

[3] Ibid.

Approximately 75 men were gathered on Lexington Green when the British column arrived at dawn. The militia were under orders to hold their fire. Similar orders were issued to the British troops, some of who formed on the green facing the militia. While two companies of British light infantry faced the militia on the green with bayonets fixed, Major John Pitcairn of the Royal Marines rode ahead and ordered the militia to lay down their arms and disperse. Captain Parker wisely ordered his men to comply and most were in the process of doing so when a shot rang out. Although the origin of the shot will never be known, each side believed the other fired it. The British troops on the green responded with a scattering of musket fire followed by a disorderly bayonet charge toward the militia. Months of pent up anger at the colonists was unleashed on the green, and for a few moments the British officers lost control of their men. Seventeen colonists were killed or wounded in the incident before the officers restored order and continued their march to Concord.[4]

When the British arrived at Concord, they found little of military value there. The military supplies and militia were gone. While part of the British force searched the town, detachments were sent beyond Concord to search a few sites. One of these detachments secured a bridge about half a mile outside of town. The detachment soon faced hundreds of militia who were determined to cross the bridge. Musket fire erupted from both sides and each suffered casualties.[5] The outnumbered British regulars fled back to Concord where they found their commander, Colonel Francis Smith, preparing to

---

[4] David Hackett Fischer, *Paul Revere's Ride*, (New York: Oxford University Press, 1994), 188-200
[5] Ibid., 212-214

return to Boston. The British retraced their route, but this time they encountered hundreds of militiamen from the surrounding area who fired at them from behind stone walls, trees, and buildings. Casualties among the British officers were extreme, and by the time Colonel Smith's men reached Lexington, nearly all order had broken down.

The expedition was saved by the timely arrival of British reinforcements under Lord Hugh Percy. The ever cautious General Gage had ordered Percy's 1,000 man force to follow Smith's expedition just in case trouble erupted.[6] They left Boston later than planned and arrived in Lexington just in time to save Smith's detachment.

Percy's men joined the fight, and the combined British force continued on towards Boston. The militia persisted in their attacks on the British and caused Lord Percy to redirect his march to Charlestown Neck, a peninsula located across the Charles River from Boston. British cannon from nearby ships covered the narrow crossing point of Charlestown Neck and prevented the militia from continuing their pursuit.

Hundreds of minute-men gathered at Cambridge and other areas outside of Boston ready to resume the fight if the British ventured out of Boston again. There was little chance of that happening. Many of Smith's and Percy's exhausted troops collapsed where they halted, desperate to rest after their long ordeal. Nearly 275 of their number were casualties of the day's fight. Less than half that number fell among the militia.[7]

---

[6] Ibid., note 36, 412-13
[7] Ibid., 321

The Williamsburg Gunpowder Incident

While much of New England was in an uproar over the engagement at Lexington and Concord, Virginians went about their business on April 19th unaware of the crisis to the north. Just forty-eight hours after the bloodshed at Lexington, however, a confrontation erupted in Williamsburg over the seizure of 15 half barrels of gunpowder stored in the colony's powder magazine in the center of town.

In the early morning hours of April 21st, twenty armed men from the *HMS Magdalen* landed at Burwell's Ferry on the James River and rapidly marched to Williamsburg, four miles away.[8] Their orders, at the behest of Governor Dunmore, were to seize a supply of gunpowder stored in the powder magazine in the center of Williamsburg and transport it back to their ship. Lord Dunmore explained the rationale behind this provocative act in a letter to his superiors in England:

The series of dangerous measures pursued by the people of this colony against government, which they have now entirely overturned and particularly their having come to a resolution of raising a body of armed men in all of the counties, made me think it prudent to remove some gunpowder which was in a magazine in this place where it lay exposed to any attempt that might be made to seize it, and I had reason to believe the people intended to take that step.[9]

---

[8] Clark, "Journal of His Majesty's Schooner Magdalen, 20 April, 1775," *Naval Documents of the American Revolution*, Vol. 1, 204

[9] K. G. Davies, ed., "Governor Earl of Dunmore to Earl of Dartmouth, 1 May, 1775," *Documents of the American Revolution,* Vol. 9, (Irish University Press), 107-108

Hoping to remove the gunpowder in secret and avoid a confrontation, the small British naval detachment entered the capital in the pre-dawn hours unnoticed. Armed with a key to the magazine provided by the governor, they quickly loaded 15 half barrels of gunpowder onto a wagon and started back to their ship.

At some point in the operation the British sailors and marines were discovered and the alarm spread throughout town, but not before the detachment escaped back to their ship with the powder. Lord Dunmore recalled that, "*Drums were then sent through the city,* [and] *the independent company got under arms.*"[10] Anxious city residents gathered at the courthouse, directly across from the magazine, in the dim light of dawn and learned what had happened. Benjamin Waller recalled that, "*the People...were much alarmed and assembled some with and others without Arms.*"[11] Attorney General John Randolph who lived close to the courthouse confirmed that, "*many of the people were under arms at the courthouse,*" and Purdie's Virginia Gazette described the whole city as, "*alarmed and much exasperated....*"[12]

A few hundred yards from the courthouse, just around the corner at the Governor's Palace, Lord Dunmore heard the commotion created by the agitated crowd. He reported to the British Ministry after the incident that

---

[10] Ibid.

[11] Kennedy, ed., "Benjamin Waller Testimony," *Journal of the House of Burgesses*: 1773-1776, 231-32

[12] Kennedy, ed., "John Randolph Testimony," *Journal of the House of Burgesses*: 1773-1776, 233 and Purdie, *Virginia Gazette Supplement*, 21 April, 1775, 3

All the people assembled and during their consultation continued threats were brought to my house that it was their resolution to seize upon or massacre me and every person found giving me assistance if I refused to deliver the powder immediately into their custody. [13]

Dunmore's concern for his safety may have been valid as Purdie's gazette reported that, *"numbers got themselves in readiness to repair to the palace."* [14]   Luckily for Dunmore, Peyton Randolph and other respected leaders of the city were able to calm the irate crowd and prevent them from marching on the Governor's Palace. Instead, a meeting of the Common Hall (governing body of the city) was held and after much deliberation, a formal address to the governor was drafted. It expressed the city's alarm at the removal of the gunpowder from the public magazine, *"while they were sleeping in their beds,"* and asserted that the magazine remained the best place to store the powder, especially given recent talk of possible slave insurrections. The address concluded with a polite request that Governor Dunmore explain his motives for removing the powder and that it be immediately returned to the magazine. [15] A delegation of city leaders, accompanied by Speaker Randolph, went to Dunmore's residence to deliver the address and retrieve the governor's reply.

Realizing the precarious situation he was in, Governor Dunmore admitted to Lord Dartmouth after the incident that

---

[13] Davies, ed., "Dunmore to Dartmouth, 1 May, 1775," *Documents of the American Revolution*, Vol. 9, 108

[14] Purdie, *Virginia Gazette Supplement*, 21 April, 1775, 3

[15] Scribner, ed., *Revolutionary Virginia: The Road to Independence* Vol. 3, 55

With their armed force at a little distance…I thought proper, in the defenceless state in which I [found] myself, to endeavour to soothe them and answered verbally to the effect that I had removed the powder (lest the Negroes might have seized upon it) to a place of security from whence when I saw occasion I would at any time deliver it to the people.[16]

Dunmore further explained to the delegation that he had the powder removed before dawn, "*to prevent any alarm,*" and that, "*he was surprised to hear the people were under arms on this occasion, and that he should not think it prudent to put the powder into their hands in such a situation.*"[17]

Barely able to contain his anger at what he viewed as, "*one of the highest insults that could be offered to the authority of His Majesty's government,*" Dunmore ignored the delegation's warning that his reply would be unsatisfactory to the crowd outside.[18] As the delegation left to deliver his reply, Dunmore prepared for the worst, arming himself and his aides and servants.

To the governor's great surprise and relief, Williamsburg's leaders convinced the assembled crowd and independent militia company that Dunmore's response was satisfactory and they dispersed and returned to their homes.[19] The situation

---

[16] Davies, "Dunmore to Dartmouth, 1 May, 1775," *Documents of the American Revolution,* Vol. 9, 108

[17] Scribner, ed., *Revolutionary Virginia: The Road to Independence* Vol. 3, 55

[18] Davies, ed., "Dunmore to Dartmouth, 1 May, 1775," *Documents of the American Revolution,* Vol. 9, 108

[19] Kennedy, ed., "Testimony of Mayor John Dixon," *Journal of the House of Burgesses*: 1773-1776, 233

remained calm until evening when, according to Benjamin Waller

> *A Report prevailed that the Marines were landed, and intended to Town;* [the residents] *expressed great uneasiness and went with their Arms to the Magazine to guard it, but soon dispersed except a few who acted as patrole that Night....*[20]

Although the reported landing of British marines proved to be false, the armed Virginians who gathered at the magazine to challenge the marines demonstrated a degree of resistance to British authority that had rarely been seen in Virginia.

Anger at Dunmore Grows

The following day, Lord Dunmore sparked another uproar when he lost his temper in public and unleashed a verbal tirade against the colonists. Mayor John Dixon, like most of Williamsburg, learned of Dunmore's outburst secondhand and noted the impact it had on the capital's inhabitants:

> *The Inhabitants appeared to be in perfect tranquility til a Report was spread by his Excellency's throwing out some threats respecting the Slaves, when there seemed to be great uneasiness but nothing more was done but doubling the usual Patrole...*[21]

Dixon's recollection of Dunmore, "*throwing out some threats,*" was a reference to the governor's chance encounter

---

[20] Kenney, ed., "Testimony of Benjamin Waller," *Journal of the House of Burgesses*: 1773-1776, 231-232

[21] Kennedy, "Testimony of Mayor John Dixon," *Journal of the House of Burgesses*: 1773-1776, 233

with Dr. William Pasteur outside the governor's palace. Dr. Pasteur reported that he met the highly agitated governor on the street the morning after the powder was seized and that Dunmore, "*seemed greatly exasperated at the Peoples having been under Arms.*"[22] Doctor Pasteur assured the governor that many of the people realized the rashness of their actions and regretted it, but Dunmore would not be placated and unleashed a tirade in response. Pasteur recalled that

> *His Lordship then proceeded to make use of several rash expressions and said that tho' he did not think himself in Danger yet he understood some injury or insult was intended to be offered to the Captains Foy and Collins,* [Dunmore's aide and the captain of the *H.M.S. Magellen*] *which he should consider as done to himself as those Gentlemen acted intirely by his particular Directions.*
>
> *That his Lordship then swore by the living God that if a Grain of Powder was burnt at Captain Foy or Captain Collins, or if any Injury or insult was offered to himself, or either of them, that he would declare Freedom to the Slaves, and reduce the City of Williamsburg to Ashes. His Lordship then mentioned setting up the Royal Standard, but did not say that he would actually do it, but said he believed, if he did he should have a Majority of white People and all the Slaves on the side of Government, that he had once fought for the Virginians, and that, by GOD, he would let them see that he could fight against them,*

---

[22] Kennedy, ed., "Testimony of Dr. William Pasteur," *Journal of the House of Burgesses*:1773-1776, 231

and declared that in a short Time, he could depopulate the whole Country.[23]

Reports of Dunmore's volatile outburst and rash threats spread quickly through Williamsburg, surprising no one and reinforcing a growing belief among many Virginians that Dunmore cared little for their safety or their interests.

This view was further supported by a letter from London (printed in the local gazettes on the day of the powder incident) that claimed that Lord Dunmore had willfully exaggerated the unrest in Virginia in a letter to his superiors in London in late December in order to alarm the Ministry into action. The London correspondent, (who was likely a member of Parliament who supported the colonists) noted that

> *A scene of greater confusion, misrule, and injustice, cannot be conceived, than is described in a letter of Lord Dunmore's dated Dec. 24th, as is now prevailing in the province of Virginia.* [According to Dunmore] *Committees are appointed in every county, to enforce what they call the laws of the Congress...* [and] *Armed companies are raised in every county, to enforce the orders of these committees....*[24]

The negative characterization of Virginia that Dunmore's December letter to the Ministry presented was followed a week later by the publication of a large passage of his actual letter. Dunmore's prediction that, *"The lower class of people... will discover that they have been duped by the richer sort..."* and his claim that, *"The arbitrary proceedings of these*

---

[23] Ibid., 231

[24] Purdie *Virginia Gazette, Supplement*, 21 April, 1775, 2

committees…cannot fail producing quarrels and dissention…" outraged many colonists.[25] Clearly Governor Dunmore viewed the colonists, and their opposition to Parliament's policies, with contempt and disdain, and the feeling of the colonists towards Dunmore was becoming mutual.

Had Virginians been aware of the contents of a letter Lord Dunmore wrote to Lord Dartmouth on May 1st, 1775, they would have been even angrier. Declaring the unrest in Virginia over the seized gunpowder an *"insurrection"* caused by the *"rebellious spirit"* of the people, Dunmore reported that *"parties of armed men were continually coming into town from the adjacent counties…offering fresh insults,"* and that, *"2,000 armed men"* in Fredericksburg were preparing to march on the capital to force him to return the powder.[26] Dunmore noted that since he could not, *"make any effectual resistance,"* against such an overwhelming force, he had sent his wife and children to a British warship in the York River out of fear for their safety. Dunmore was determined, however, to remain in the capital to assert royal authority and he expected city officials to once again intervene to stop the marchers from Fredericksburg from entering Williamsburg. Dunmore informed Lord Dartmouth that

> *I have already signified to the magistrates of Williamsburg that I expect them on their allegiance to fall upon means of putting a stop to the march of the people now on their way before they enter the city, that otherwise I shall be forced and it is my fixed*

---

[25] Purdie, *Virginia Gazette, Supplement,* 28 April, 1775, 3

[26] Davies, ed., "Dunmore to Dartmouth, 1 May, 1775," *Documents of the American Revolution,* Vol. 9, 109

purpose to arm all my own Negroes and receive all others that will come to me whom I shall declare free...[27]

The Governor added that if the magistrates and loyal Virginians did not, "*repair to my assistance,*" he would consider

The whole country in an actual state of rebellion and myself at liberty to annoy it by every possible means, and that I shall not hesitate at reducing their houses to ashes and spreading devastation wherever I can reach.[28]

Dunmore confidently concluded his letter to Lord Dartmouth by asserting that

I am persuaded that if His Majesty should think proper to add to a small body of troops to be sent here a quantity of arms, ammunition and other requisites for the service, I could raise such a force from among Indians, Negroes and other persons as would soon reduce the refractory people of this colony to obedience.[29]

Luckily for Lord Dunmore, his views and proposals in his May 1st letter to Lord Dartmouth remained undisclosed to the public.

---

[27] Ibid.
[28] Ibid.
[29] Ibid., 110

Militia on the March

That was not the case concerning the news of the seized powder in Williamsburg, which spread quickly throughout Virginia and reached Fredericksburg on April 24th, the same day that the Spotsylvania Independent Militia Company mustered for drill. The officers of the militia company (Hugh Mercer, Alexander Spotswood, and George Weedon) dispatched messengers to neighboring counties and called for a general muster of neighboring militia companies in Fredericksburg on Saturday April 29th. Their intention was to form a mounted corps of light horse militia and ride to Williamsburg to recover the stolen gunpowder:

> *A number of Public spirited Gentn should embrace this opporty to show their Zeal in the grand Cause by marching to – Wmsbg to enquire into this Affair and there to take such steps as may best answer the purpose of recovering the powder & securing the Arms now in the Magazine. To this End they have determined to hold themselves in readiness to march from this place as light horse on Saturday Morning....*[30]

The Spotsylvania company also sent riders to Williamsburg to learn the latest news. Mann Page Jr. and two other riders reached Williamsburg on Wednesday April 27th and were informed that Peyton Randolph and the city leaders of Williamsburg had the situation well under control. In fact, Speaker Randolph, aware of the volatile temper of the

---

[30] Clark, ed., *Naval Documents of the American Revolution*, Vol. 1, 214-15

governor, was alarmed to learn of the militia's planned march to Williamsburg and urged the riders to return to Fredericksburg as quickly as possible to halt the march. Randolph explained his decision in a letter to the militia leaders in Fredericksburg.:

> *His Excellency has repeatedly assured several Respectable Gentlemen, that the Powder shall be Return'd to the Magazine...*[and] *thinks that he acted for the best and will not be compell'd to* [do] *what we have abundant Reason to believe he would cheerfully do, were he left to himself.*[31]

Randolph expressed gratitude for the many offers of assistance that were sent to Williamsburg, including the latest from Fredericksburg, but asserted that the situation had stabilized and was under control:

> *It is our opinion and most earnest request that Matters may be quieted for the present; we are firmly persuaded that perfect Tranquility will be speedily Returned; By pursuing this Course we foresee no Hazard or even inconvenience that can ensue; whereas we are apprehensive...that violent measures may produce effects, which God only knows the consequences of.*[32]

Page returned to Fredericksburg at almost the same time that an express rider from the north with news of the bloodshed in Massachusetts (Lexington and Concord) passed

---

[31] Scribner, ed., *Revolutionary Virginia: The Road to Independence* Vol. 3, 63-64

[32] Ibid.

through town and alarmed everyone. British regulars had reportedly fired without provocation upon the Massachusetts militia, killing six and wounding four others.[33]   A second account claimed that 4,000 colonial militia had surrounded a brigade of British troops (1,000 strong) in Lexington and had killed 150 regulars at a loss of 50 of their own men.[34] Clearly, something significant had occurred in Massachusetts and the troops assembled in Fredericksburg must have wondered if the events to the north were in anyway related to their own crisis in Virginia.

Undoubtedly anxious about the news from Massachusetts, a large officer's council from 14 militia companies (representing 600 mounted militia) listened intently as Speaker Randolph's letter was read aloud. A heated debate on whether to proceed to Williamsburg followed. As Peyton Randolph was probably the most respected man in Virginia, his views held tremendous weight with those assembled and after much discussion it was agreed to heed Randolph's plea and cancel the march to the capital. Instead, the council publically condemned Lord Dunmore for his actions and pledged to re-assemble at a moment's notice to defend their rights or those of any sister colony that was unjustly invaded.[35]

Word of the cancellation of the march from Fredericksburg was welcomed by many in Virginia, but it was soon overshadowed by new reports in the gazettes. Accounts from England informed Virginians that Parliament had extended its strict trade restrictions (that had been imposed on the New

---

[33] Pinkney, *Virginia Gazette, Supplement*, 28 April, 1775, 2

[34] Ibid.

[35] Scribner, ed., "Spotsylvania Council, 29 April, 1775," *Revolutionary Virginia: The Road to Independence*, Vol. 3, 71

England colonies) to all of the colonies. This was Parliament's retaliation for the non-importation and non-exportation associations approved by the Continental Congress in the fall of 1774. Equally disturbing were reports that a royal proclamation issued in March declared the inhabitants of Massachusetts and certain individuals in other colonies, (including Peyton Randolph) actual rebels. Ironically, Randolph was doing everything in his power to calm Virginians and prevent an actual rebellion from erupting in Virginia.[36]

There were also the sketchy reports in the papers from Massachusetts of the confrontation between British troops and Massachusetts militia at Lexington that resulted in bloodshed.[37] It would be another week before further details from the north appeared in the gazette, but for Virginians like Patrick Henry, the bloodshed in Massachusetts, combined with Dunmore's seizure of the gunpowder in Williamsburg, was proof enough of a ministerial plot to subjugate all of the colonies, and he responded with action.

Henry's March on the Capital

Patrick Henry was surprised and disappointed when he learned that the militia gathered in Fredericksburg had cancelled their march on the capital. A week earlier, Henry had confided to two friends, Richard Morris and George Dabney, that Dunmore's seizure of the powder was a fortunate circumstance that would awaken and animate the public:

---

[36] Pinkney, *Virginia Gazette, Supplement,* 28 April, 1775, 2
[37] Ibid.

> *You may in vain talk to* [the people] *about the duties
> on tea, etc. These things will not affect them. They
> depend on principles, too abstracted for their
> apprehension and feeling. But tell them of the
> robbery of the magazine, and that the next step will
> be to disarm them, you bring the subject home to
> their bosoms, and they will be ready to fly to arms to
> defend themselves.* [38]

The news from Fredericksburg suggested that the animated
spirit Henry expected in the people had already waned.

Disappointed but determined, Henry delayed his journey to
Philadelphia to attend the 2nd Continental Congress and
instead, rode to Newcastle (a small town twenty miles
northeast of Richmond along the Pamunkey River) to meet
with the Hanover county committee and the independent
militia company.[39] Charles Dabney attended the meeting and
recalled years later that the militia waited most of the day for
the committee to decide what to do, "*there being some
disagreement among them....*"[40] In the late afternoon of May
2nd, Patrick Henry delivered a powerful address to the militia.
According to Henry biographer William Wirt, (who
reconstructed the essence of the speech from eyewitness
recollections) Henry

---

[38] Wirt, 137

[39] Note: Newcastle was a bustling colonial community and a crossing
point over the Pamunkey River in Hanover County that has since
completely disappeared).

[40] "Charles Dabney to William Wirt, Dec. 21, 1805," *Papers of Patrick
Henry* Rockefeller Library CWF, Microfilm

laid open the plan on which the British ministry had fallen to reduce the colonies to subjection, by robbing them of all the means of defending their rights: spread before their eyes in colours of vivid description, the fields of Lexington and Concord, still floating with the blood of their countrymen, gloriously shed in the general cause; showed them that the recent plunder of the magazine in Williamsburg, was nothing more than a part of the general system of subjugation;[41]

Henry presented those assembled with a stark choice exclaiming that

The moment was now come in which they were called upon to decide, whether they chose to live free, and hand down the noble inheritance to their children, or to become hewers of wood, and drawers of water to those lordlings, who were themselves the tools of a corrupt and tyrannical ministry -- he painted the country in a state of subjugation, and drew such pictures of wretched debasement and abject vassalage, as filled their souls with horror and indignation.[42]

Henry saw God's hand in the crisis and declared that

It was for them now to determine, whether they were worthy of this divine interference; whether they would accept the high boon now held out to them by

---

[41] Wirt, 138
[42] Ibid.

heaven--that if they would, though it might lead them through a sea of blood, they were to remember that the same God whose power divided the Red Sea for the deliverance of Israel, still reigned in all his glory, unchanged and unchangeable-- was still the enemy of the oppressor, and the friend of the oppressed.[43]

Henry ended his speech with a pragmatic observation, reminding those assembled that

no time was to be lost--that their enemies in this colony were now few and weak; that it would be easy for [the militia], *by a rapid and vigorous movement, to compel the restoration of the powder which had been carried off, or to make a reprisal on the king's revenues in the hands of the receiver general, which would fairly balance the account. That the Hanover volunteers would thus have an opportunity of striking the first blow in this colony, in the great cause of American liberty, and would cover themselves with never-fading laurels.*[44]

Swept up by Henry's speech, those assembled voted to march on Williamsburg under Patrick Henry's command. A party of sixteen men was detached to the residence of Richard Corbin in King and Queen County to demand compensation for the powder from the King's receiver-general (tax collector).[45] Ensign Parke Goodall commanded the

---

[43] Ibid., 138-39

[44] Ibid., 139

[45] "Nathaniel Pope to William Wirt, June 23, 1806," *Papers of Patrick Henry* Rockefeller Library CWF, Microfilm

detachment and was instructed to take Corbin prisoner if he refused to pay the 330 pounds demanded for the seized powder.[46] Goodall and his men reached Corbin's residence late in the evening of May 2nd and, adhering to instructions to treat the receiver-general with the utmost respect and tenderness, surrounded the house and waited until morning to announce their presence.[47]

Discovered in the morning by Mrs. Corbin, Ensign Goodall was informed that the receiver-general and the funds in his care were in Williamsburg. Eager to rejoin Henry and the rest of the militia at Doncastle's Ordinary in James City County and desirous to avoid offence to Mrs. Corbin, Ensign Goodall declined her invitation to search the house and marched off empty handed.[48]

Patrick Henry and the rest of the Hanover militia, reinforced by volunteers from New Kent and King William counties, were encamped at Doncastle's Ordinary, sixteen miles north of Williamsburg and waited for Ensign Goodall. Over 150 strong, they were described by one writer to Purdie's Virginia Gazette as, *"all men of property...well accoutered* [with] *a very martial appearance."*[49]

A day earlier Governor Dunmore, not yet aware of Henry's march but very aware of great "commotions and insurrections" in the colony, sought the advice of his council concerning a proclamation he wished to deliver. Released on May 3rd and printed in the gazettes soon after, Dunmore sought three objectives through his proclamation: justify the

---

[46] Ibid.
[47] Wirt, 140
[48] Ibid., 140-41
[49] Purdie, *Virginia Gazette, Supplement,* 5 May, 1775, 2

removal of the gunpowder, assert his desire *"to restore peace and harmony to this distracted country,"* and call on Virginians *to exert themselves in removing the discontents and suppressing the spirit of faction, which prevail among the people....*"[50] Overshadowed by newly arrived reports of Henry's march on Williamsburg, (which was clear evidence of the very spirit of faction Dunmore wished to suppress) the governor's proclamation had virtually no effect whatsoever except to demonstrate Dunmore's political impotency.

Fearful that Henry and his men would suddenly appear in the capital, Dunmore hastily prepared for battle. Captain Montague of the recently arrived warship *H.M.S. Fowey* rushed 43 men armed with swords, cutlasses, and bayonets (but no muskets) to the palace and threatened to bombard Yorktown if they were confronted or harassed on their march to Williamsburg.[51] They joined Dunmore's tiny force of armed servants at the palace. The governor also placed cannon before the palace and swore to fire on the town should Henry's troops dare enter.[52]

Henry, still at Doncastle's Ordinary, dismissed several appeals from Williamsburg's leaders to disband and turn back, but when Carter Braxton arrived in camp and proposed to ride to Williamsburg to convince his father-in-law, Richard Corbin, to issue payment for the powder, Henry agreed to remain at Doncastle's and await the outcome of Braxton's efforts. With the help of Thomas Nelson Sr. the respected president of the governor's council, Braxton returned on May

---

[50] Scribner, ed., "Dunmore's Proclamation, 3 May, 1775," *Revolutionary Virginia: Road to Independence,* Vol. 3, 80-81

[51] Pinkney, *Virginia Gazette,* 4 May, 1775

[52] Scribner, ed., *Revolutionary Virginia: The Road to Independence* Vol. 3, 9

4th with a bill of exchange for 330 pounds to pay for the gunpowder. Henry pledged to convey the money to the Virginia delegation in Congress who would use it to purchase gunpowder in Philadelphia for the colony.[53]

Satisfied with the gunpowder resolution but concerned that the public treasury in Williamsburg remained under threat from Dunmore, Henry wrote to the colonial treasurer, Robert Carter Nicholas and offered to provide a guard to transport the funds to a more secure location. Nicholas, who disapproved of Patrick Henry and his actions, curtly rejected the offer as unnecessary. Unfazed by Nicholas's response, Henry declared success and dismissed the troops under his command to their homes. He then struck out for Scotchtown (his home) to prepare for his journey to Philadelphia.

Just two days later, a relieved but angry Governor Dunmore issued a proclamation that essentially declared Patrick Henry and his followers outlaws:

> *Whereas...a certain Patrick Henry...and a Number of deluded Followers, have taken up Arms, chosen their officers, and styling themselves an Independent Company, have marched out of their County, encamped, and put themselves in a Posture of War, and have written and dispatched Letters to* [many] *Parts of the Country, exciting the People to join in these outrageous and rebellious Practices, to the great Terror of all his Majesty's faithful Subjects, and in open Defiance of Law and Government...*[I charge] *all Persons, upon their Allegiance, not to aid, abet, or give Countenance to, the said Patrick*

---

[53] Wirt, 142

> *Henry, or* [his followers] *but, on the Contrary, to oppose them and their Designs by every Means....*[54]

Once again, Dunmore's proclamation had little effect. In fact, it sparked a wave of support for Henry, who was praised by numerous county committees and was safely escorted northward to Maryland by parties of enthusiastic militia.

Although Henry's march on Williamsburg dominated the attention of many Virginians in early May, disturbing details of the bloodshed at Lexington and Concord soon regained the attention of Virginians. The Virginia gazettes printed a number of accounts in May of the fighting in Massachusetts as well as the militia's "siege" of Boston. The reports varied greatly and painted a confused situation that prompted one writer to Purdie's gazette to complain that it was difficult to determine the veracity of some of the reports:

> *We still seem to be in great suspense about our accounts from Boston, the authenticity of part of them being doubtful; however, we make not the least doubt there has been a smart engagement between the King's troops and the provincials, in which we hear the former have lost 302 men killed, wounded, and taken prisoner, and the latter 37.*[55]

This same letter cited claims from Massachusetts that 60,000 militia had turned out from New England and that 15,000 remained encamped outside of Boston constructing earthworks. Although the details remained uncertain,

---

[54] Scribner, ed., *Revolutionary Virginia: The Road to Independence* Vol. 3, 100-101

[55] Purdie, *Virginia Gazette, Supplement*, 12 May, 1775

Virginians realized that whatever was happening in Massachusetts was clearly significant.

Lord North's Olive Branch

Overlooked due to all of the attention over the gunpowder incident in Williamsburg and the bloodshed in Massachusetts was a controversial new reconciliation plan proposed by Lord North that surprisingly passed Parliament in late February.[56] The essence of Lord North's Olive Branch reconciliation proposal was a suspension of all of the taxes, duties, and restrictions (except those designed to regulate trade) for any colony that agreed to annually contribute to the common defense of the empire and the administration of colonial government. The amount to be contributed was left to each colony to decide (subject to approval by the King and Parliament), but it was expected to be based on the colony's ability to pay. A proponent of Lord North's plan summarized the view of most in Parliament regarding the colonists' obligations to the empire:

> *Seventy millions of debt, in the last war, was incurred solely on their account; and, in equity, the Americans ought to bear at least their fair proportion of it. The army and navy of England are employed for their protection, in common with the rest of the empire; they ought, therefore, to contribute both to the army and navy.*[57]

---

[56] Purdie, *Virginia Gazette, Supplement,* 21 April and 28 April and Pinkney, *Virginia Gazette Supplement,* 28 April
[57] Purdie, *Virginia Gazette,* 28 April, 1775, 2

Lord North himself doubted that many of the colonies would accept his proposal, but he argued that if only one or two did it would destroy the unity of the defiant colonies and make it easier to subdue them. North also argued that his proposal would have a good effect in England by demonstrating to British manufacturers (who largely sided with the colonists due to their boycott) the, "*moderation of Parliament, and the obstinancy and disaffection of the Americans*"[58]   Although much angst was expressed in Parliament about the sudden reversal of policy towards the Americans, North's reconciliation proposal easily passed the House of Commons, 274 to 88 in late February.

Debate over the proposal appeared in the Virginia gazettes in early May.   One English supporter of the colonists described North's plan as

> *A subterfuge too low and too thinly disguised to deceive the Americans.... It is evident to the world that this is only a villainous plan to divide them.... The Americans, my Lord, are too sensible and too brave to be drawn into any trap....*[59]

An American writer concurred, warning his fellow colonists to keep

> *The true character of the Ministry constantly in view; and disregard all plausible appearances of moderation and reconcilement (which are only hoisted out to deceive, and put us off guard) never remit our vigilance, faithful adherence to the association, and*

---

[58] Ibid.

[59] Purdie, *Virginia Gazette, Supplement*, 5 May, 1775

determination to be prepared for resisting force by force, until we know the repealing statutes are passed.... How, with any consistency, [continued the writer], *can we credit designs to redress us, when a ministerial majority in Parliament have declared the colony of Massachusetts Bay in rebellion, and the other colonies abetting them? When we find our publick magazines of ammunition privately removed in the night, and seven* [more] *regiments actually ordered to embark for North America?*[60]

Such accounts in the newspapers discouraged those who still held hope for reconciliation and caused Lord Dunmore, who had been instructed by Lord Dartmouth to convene the House of Burgesses so it could consider North's plan, to predict its rejection. He warned Dartmouth in a letter in mid-May that

The newspapers have already begun to prejudice the people against [Dartmouth's reconciliation plan] *and to call it only a ministerial device to divide the colonies....*[61]

But Dunmore did not place all the blame on the newspapers. Asserting that Virginians had abandoned reason and, *"thrown off every inclination to an accommodation of differences,"* Dunmore made a startling claim:[62]

---

[60] Ibid.

[61] Davies, ed., Dunmore to Dartmouth, 15 May, 1775, *Documents of the American Revolution,* Vol. 9, 134

[62] Ibid.

It is no longer to be doubted that independence is the object in view and I am of opinion that no warning will deter nor offers divert them from making every attempt their leaders advise to establish it.[63]

Most Virginians would have adamantly disagreed with Lord Dunmore about their desire for independence in May 1775. As alarmed as they were by the torrent of troubling events that swept Virginia and the colonies, Virginians would have argued that what was really needed was a change in policy and leaders in Parliament (and in the governor's palace in Williamsburg), not independence for the colonies.

In the weeks following Patrick Henry's march, Dunmore was strongly criticized by county committees throughout Virginia for the seizure of the gunpowder, his proclamations in early May, and even his letter to Lord Dartmouth written in late December of the preceding year. Committees declared that Dunmore had forfeited his right to govern and that he misrepresented Virginia's grievances and actions to Parliament. The distrust of the governor was so high that some suggested that his summons of the General Assembly to Williamsburg on June 1st, (specifically to consider Lord North's Olive Branch reconciliation plan), was actually a ploy to arrest colonial leaders.[64]

Such concerns prompted the Williamsburg Independent Militia company to meet Peyton Randolph (who returned from Philadelphia in late May to resume his seat as Speaker of the House of Burgesses) outside of town and escort him into the

---

[63] Ibid.

[64] John Selby, *The Revolution in Virginia: 1775-1783*, (Colonial Williamsburg Foundation, 1988), 41

capital with great fanfare. Guards were also posted at the Speaker's home in the center of Williamsburg to insure his safety.[65]

Collapse of Royal Government

After weeks of tension and crisis in the capital, Lord Dunmore had no desire to provoke another incident by threatening Speaker Randolph or any of the members of the House of Burgesses. The same consideration was apparently not shown by some of the burgesses who attended the assembly clad in the same course linen hunting shirts (tomahawks at their sides) that were worn by the independent militia companies.[66] Despite the defiance conveyed by such attire, the opening session of the House of Burgesses went smoothly, highlighted by Dunmore's address to the assembly in which he endorsed Lord North's Olive Branch reconciliation plan and laid the responsibility for calming the long running dispute on the burgesses. Dunmore defended Parliament's past actions and explained that all that was desired by the King and the, *"supreme legislature of the Empire"* was for the colonies to pay their fair share of the burden of operating the empire:

> *It must now be manifest, to all dispassionate People, that the Parliament, the high and supreme Legislature of the Empire, far from having entertained Thoughts...of oppressing the People of the Colonies, or of promoting the Interest of one, at the Expense of another...have only*

---

[65] Pinkney, *Virginia Gazette,* 1 June, 1775, 3

[66] Davies, ed., Dunmore to Dartmouth, June 25, 1775, *Documents of the American Revolution,* Vol. 9, 200-01

[asserted] *that the Whole, in Consideration of the Enjoyment of equal Rights, Privileges, and Advantages should be obliged, according to their Abilities and Situation, to contribute...towards the Burdens necessary for the Support of their Civil Government, and for the common Defence.*[67]

Dunmore noted that under Lord North's plan the colonists were left to decide for themselves a fair amount to contribute to the operation of the empire and if they accepted North's plan, it would be, *"Considered by his Majesty not only a Testimony of your Reverence for Parliament, but also as a Mark of your Duty and Attachment to our Sovereign...."*[68]

The governor concluded with an appeal to the burgesses:

I cannot conclude without exhorting you in the most earnest manner, to enter upon the Subject Matter, now recommended to you, with that Patience, Calmness, and Impartiality, which its great Importance requires, and to reflect upon the Benefits this Country hath received from the Support given to it by the Parent State, which I hope will animate your Zeal, now [that] you have it in your Power, to restore that Harmony and mutual confidence which rendered both Countries flourishing, and, in short, to pursue your true Interest, which will convert our present gloomy Apprehensions into Prospects of Peace, Happiness, and lasting Security.[69]

---

[67] Kennedy, ed., "1 June, 1775," *Journal of the House of Burgesses*: 1773-1776, 174-75

[68] Ibid.

[69] Ibid.

Although it took the House of Burgesses nearly two weeks to adopt an official reply to Lord North's reconciliation plan, the assembly responded to Dunmore's address within days and asserted that the crisis between England and the colonies was the result of the, "*Departure of his Majesty's Ministers from that wise System of Administration*," of past years.[70] In other words, the crisis of the last decade was all the fault of the British Ministry and their unconstitutional policies, begun in 1765 and carried to the present. The burgesses also took a swipe at Dunmore for consistently misleading the Ministry about the situation in Virginia:

> *However strangely this Country may have been misrepresented, we do solemnly avow the firmest and most unshaken Attachment to our most gracious Sovereign and his Government, as founded on the Laws and Principles of our excellent Constitution.*[71]

The House assured Dunmore that they would fully consider Lord North's plan and respond as soon as possible, but the Assembly's resolutions of approval for the proceedings of both the 1st Continental Congress and the 2nd Virginia Convention, bode ill for North's Olive Branch plan.[72] Many Virginians viewed North's plan for what is was, an effort to split the colonies, and Speaker Randolph wanted to delay consideration of North's proposal out of fear of undermining the Continental Congress, who were themselves considering

---

[70] Kennedy, ed., "5 June, 1775," *Journal of the House of Burgesses*: 1773-1776, 187-88

[71] Ibid.

[72] Ibid., 190

Lord North's plan.[73] Unity among the colonies was crucial and Peyton Randolph, along with most of his fellow burgesses, was determined to maintain it. He was assisted in these efforts by a new crisis at the powder magazine that seized everyone's attention in the capital.

On the night of June 3rd, (two days before the House of Burgesses responded to Dunmore's opening address) a party of young men broke into the powder magazine to retrieve weapons. A blast from a spring loaded musket showered them with shot. Pellets struck one youth in the arm and shoulder, seriously wounding him and another lost two fingers on his right hand.[74] The city was once again alarmed and many were outraged when they learned that spring guns (set to fire by a trip wire) had been secretly placed in the magazine. Purdie's gazette declared that, *"had any person lost his life, the perpetrator or perpetrators, of this diabolical invention, might have been justly branded with the…title of MURDERERS!"*[75] Pinkney's gazette pointed a finger straight at Dunmore, noting that, *"His lordship has displayed the most profound skill as an engineer…and it is imagined the adventure at the magazine on Saturday night, will be transmitted to the ministry as…proof of the expedience and efficacy of spring guns.*[76]

The spring guns proved to be of limited deterrence, however, as a large crowd gathered at the magazine two days later and in the presence of a few burgesses, carted away muskets and other military stores. A committee from the House of Burgesses approached Dunmore and requested that

---

[73] Selby, 42

[74] Dixon and Hunter, *Virginia Gazette,* 10 June, 1775, 2

[75] Purdie, *Virginia Gazette Supplement* , 9 June, 1775, 2

[76] Pinkney, *Virginia Gazette,* 8 June, 1775, 3

he instruct the Keeper of the Magazine to give them access so that they might examine the state of the magazine, but the governor, angered by what he saw as collusion between the burgesses and those who broke into the magazine, rejected the request, claiming that it had been improperly submitted.

A report spread through the city the next day (Tuesday June 6th) that a party of marines and sailors from the *H.M.S. Fowey* were marching to the governor's palace.[77] When members of the governor's council approached Dunmore to request that he order the landing party to return to their ship, he professed surprise that they were coming and agreed that if they were, he would send them back.[78] While this occurred, the Williamsburg independent militia company mustered at the magazine under Captain James Innes, "*determined to attack the said Marines and Sailors, if they should come.*"[79] Alas, they did not arrive, and it is unclear whether they were ever sent. What is clear is that Lord Dunmore had had enough of the disorder.

Dunmore Flees

A degree of calm settled upon the capital on Wednesday, June 7th, prompted in part by Governor Dunmore's new found cooperative attitude (he granted the House committee access to the magazine) and a resolution passed by the House of Burgesses that thanked the governor for his service against the Indians on the frontier in 1774.[80] In the evening, Lord

---

[77] Kennedy, ed., "6 June, 1775," *Journal of the House of Burgesses*: 1773-1776, 198

[78] Ibid.

[79] Ibid.

[80] Kennedy, ed., "7 June, 1775," *Journal of the House of Burgesses*:

Dunmore walked across town unmolested to visit one of his strongest supporters, John Randolph, Virginia's attorney general and brother of Speaker Peyton Randolph. There is no record of what they discussed, but it is likely that Dunmore either learned of or informed Randolph that the Virginia gazettes were going to print more damning excerpts of Dunmore's December 24th letter to Lord Dartmouth. The new excerpts, which were included in a letter from a correspondent in London that reached Virginia in early June, painted Lord Dunmore in the worst possible light:

Extract from a Letter from London

I...sent you a copy of such part of the earl of Dunmore's [December 24th] *letter to lord Dartmouth as had been laid before both houses of parliament; since which time I have had an opportunity of knowing the SECRET part of his lordship's letter, which was not laid before parliament, and as it particularly marks his character as governor of Virginia, in reference to the good people of that BRAVE colony, and will, I trust, be so instructive to the members of their house of burgesses as never hereafter to confide in him, but to consider and treat him as their confirmed enemy....*

After lord Dunmore had given his uncandid representation of Virginia, as transmitted to you [earlier], *he proceeded warmly to recommend to lord Dartmouth that some men of war* [ships] *should be stationed in Chesapeake Bay, to prevent the*

Virginians from carrying on any external trade, except with this country, and that all communication might be cut off between them and the northern colonies.... [Dunmore]...*observed that the COUNCIL, as well as the HOUSE OF BURGESSES, and almost EVERY PERSON OF FORTUNE AND CONSIDERATION IN THE COLONY except the ATTORNEY GENERAL* [John Randolph], *were* [as] *deeply engaged as the inferior planters in factious associations and plans of resistance, great outrages and disorders would soon take place among them, from the want of regular distribution of law; and therefore he strongly urged the king's ministers, as a sure method to increase their disorders, and which...could not fail to produce petitions from the RICH, praying for protections of* [Parliament], *that his majesty would, without delay, order HIMSELF, and all the other EXECUTIVE OFFICERS of Virginia, to withdraw from thence....* [81]

The London correspondent concluded with the suggestion that Lord Dunmore was a chief cause of the ongoing political crisis. *"Can you therefore, my dear sir, wonder that* [the Ministry] *perseveres in their ruinous and despotic system of American politics?"*[82]

Given all of the unrest that had occurred to date and that was sure to follow after the publication of this letter, Dunmore decided that it was time to withdraw to the safety of the *H.M.S. Fowey*. Early in the morning of June 8th, the governor

---

[81] Pinkney, *Virginia Gazette*, 8 June, 1775, 3

[82] Ibid.

and his family, (who had temporarily returned to the palace) accompanied by Captain Foy and his wife and a few of Dunmore's household servants, left the palace and made their way to the British schooner *Magdalen*, anchored in Queen's Creek. From there they sailed to the York River where Dunmore and his party transferred to the larger *H.M.S. Fowey*, anchored off of Yorktown. Dunmore justified his decision to leave in a letter to Lord Dartmouth a few weeks later:

> *My house was kept in continual alarm and threatened every night with an assault. Surrounded therefore as I was by armed men in the very place of my residence and in the neighborhood, who were raised in defiance of my authority and pay no obedience to it but assemble and act as their will directs, nor are they to be controlled even by the power which they are intended to support; and situated so far from any place where men-of-war can approach, the nearest being five miles, I could not think it safe to continue any longer in that city but judged it would be best in all respects for carrying on His Majesty's service to remove to the ship of war which is stationed here, where I have for the present fixed my residence and where most probably I shall be obliged to remain until I receive His Majesty's instructions.*[83]

To his credit, Dunmore delivered a similar, albeit more dramatic, explanation for his departure to the House of Burgesses:

---

[83] Davis, ed., Dunmore to Dartmouth, June 25, 1775, *Documents of the American Revolution,* Vol. 9, 201-02

Being now fully persuaded that my Person, and those of my Family likewise, are in constant danger of falling sacrifices to the blind and unmeasurable fury which has so unaccountably seized upon the minds and understanding of great numbers of People, and apprehending that at length some of them may work themselves up to that pitch of daringness and atrociousness as to fall upon me, in the defenceless state in which they know I am in the City of Williamsburg, and perpetrate Acts that would plunge this country into the most horrid calamities, and render the breach with the mother Country irreparable, I have thought it prudent...that I remove to a place of safety;[84]

For their part, the House of Burgesses expressed shock and dismay at Dunmore's actions, displaying a fair degree of amnesia regarding the unrest that had gripped the capital over the preceding month:

We...assure your Excellency, that it is with the greatest concern we find...that your Lordship entertains any suspicions of the personal security of yourself or family, as we can by no means suppose any of his Majesty's subjects in this Colony would meditate a crime so horrid and atrocious as you seem to apprehend.[85]

The House then criticized the governor, assured him that they desired order as much as he did, and pledged to do whatever was necessary to insure his safety and that of his family:

---

[84] Kennedy, ed., "8 June, 1775," *Journal of the House of Burgesses*: 1773-1776, 206
[85] Ibid., 207

We are fearful the step your Lordship hath taken, in removing from the seat of government, may [cause] a continuance of that great uneasiness which hath of late so unhappily prevailed in this Country. We cannot but express our concern that your Lordship did not think proper to communicate the ground of your uneasiness to us, as, from our zeal and attachment to the preservation of order and good government, we should have judged it our indispensable duty to have endeavoured to remove every cause of disquietude.... We assure your Lordship that we will cheerfully concur in any measure that may be proposed proper to the security of yourself and your family…[and] earnestly entreat your Lordship…to return, with your Lady and family, to the Palace; which we are persuaded will give the greatest satisfaction, and be the most likely means of quieting the minds of the People.[86]

Dunmore's reply was read to the House of Burgesses two days later. He reiterated that the, *"commotions among the People and their menaces and threats,"* and the unsupportive conduct of the burgesses which often countenanced, *"the violent and disorderly proceedings of the People,* were the chief cause of his flight."[87] The governor was also upset with the threats directed at the King's forces on June 6th, and the apparent usurpation of his executive authority by the House of Burgesses when they instructed the independent militia company to guard the magazine.[88]

---

[86] Ibid.

[87] Kennedy, ed., "10 June, 1775," *Journal of the House of Burgesses*: 1773-1776, 214-15

[88] Ibid.

When a body of Men assembled in the City of Williamsburg…with the approbation of everybody for the avowed purpose of attacking a party of the Kings forces, which, without the least foundation, it was reported were marching to my protection, and which, if true, ought to have been approved and aided, not opposed and insulted, by all good and loyal Subjects; when especially the House of Burgesses…has ventured upon a step fraught with the most alarming consequences, in ordering and appointing guards, without even consulting me, to mount in the city of Williamsburg, as is pretended, to protect the Magazine [which] *shews a design to usurp the executive power…*
I submit it to your own judgement whether I could reasonably expect any good effect from communicating the ground of my uneasiness to you. [89]

Dunmore accepted the burgesses offer to, "*cheerfully concur to any measure,*" that would insure his security and proposed five measures he wished to see the House implement:

1. Reopen the civil courts.
2. Disarm and dismiss the independent militia companies.
3. Demand the return of the stolen arms and equipment from the public magazine.
4. Stop harassing supporters of the government.
5. Accept Lord North's Olive Branch reconciliation plan. [90]

---

[89] Ibid.
[90] Ibid., 215

The House of Burgesses, of course, had no intention of implementing any of Dunmore's proposed measures. Instead, the burgesses adopted an address to Lord Dunmore on June 12th that rejected Lord North's reconciliation plan:

> *With pain and disappointment we must ultimately declare* [Lord North's plan] *only changes the form of oppression, without lightening its burden, we cannot, my Lord, close with the terms of that Resolution for these Reasons.*[91]

First, the burgesses declared, "*the British Parliament has no right to intermeddle with the support of civil Government in the Colonies. For us, not for them, has government been instituted.*"[92] Next, the burgesses noted that to obtain Parliament's exemption from unjust taxes, "*we must saddle ourselves with a perpetual tax adequate to the expectations...of Parliament alone.*"[93] In other words, Lord North's proposal would not give the colonists a real choice of whether to contribute an annual payment, such payments were a foregone conclusion.

The burgesses also objected to the fact that Lord North's plan did not repeal all of the offensive acts passed by Parliament in 1774 or address the enormous military build-up in Massachusetts, which they asserted could only be meant to coerce the colonists into submission.[94] Another objection was the continuation of Britain's trade monopoly over the colonies,

---

[91] Kennedy, ed., "12 June, 1775," *Journal of the House of Burgesses*: 1773-1776, 219

[92] Ibid.

[93] Ibid.

[94] Ibid.

something the colonists had previously accepted as their contribution to the British empire. The burgesses claimed that if they were to now make annual contributions to the common defense and civil governance of the colonies, they should be free of the restrictive Navigation Acts and be allowed to trade freely just as their brethren in England were free to do.[95]

Lastly, the burgesses reminded Lord Dunmore that they

> *Consider ourselves as bound in honor as well as interest to share one general fate with our Sister Colonies, and should hold ourselves base deserters of that union...were we to agree on any measures distinct and apart from them.*[96]

In other words, the House of Burgesses placed a high premium on continental unity and deferred to the will of the Continental Congress, which was still wrestling with Lord North's Olive Branch plan.

The burgesses' rejection of Lord North's plan marked the end of reconciliation efforts in Virginia for the time being. The House of Burgesses conducted two more weeks of business, but Dunmore's refusal to approve or even respond to any of the legislation meant that its passage was an exercise in futility.

The House concluded its session on June 24th and adjourned. By then few Virginians seemed to notice; their attention, like that of most of the colonists in America, had shifted northward to Philadelphia and Boston.

---

[95] Ibid., 220
[96] Ibid.

Chapter Six

"A Universal Appearance of War is put on."

Summer: 1775

While Virginians grappled with the departure of their governor, the stand-off between the British army in Boston and the New England militia outside the city approached its third month. In the weeks following Lexington and Concord, several skirmishes between the rebel militia and British regulars occurred in the vicinity of Boston, but nothing to the degree of April 19th. This changed in mid-June when General Gage sent 2,000 British troops across the Charles River to drive the rebels from their newly fortified position on Breed's Hill. The misnamed Battle of Bunker Hill ended in a British victory, but it came at an enormous cost. Over a thousand British regulars fell in the three assaults on the hill, more than three hundred fatally. American losses were less than half of the British. The carnage shocked both sides and significantly diminished chances for a peaceful resolution.

Reconciliation between England and her colonies remained the desire of the vast majority of Virginians in June of 1775; but even before news of the enormous bloodshed at Bunker Hill reached Virginia (in mid-July) Virginians worried that a peaceful settlement to the dispute was slipping away. The weekly gazettes were full of accounts in June of skirmishes outside of Boston. One newspaper reported in late June that

By every post from the northward, we receive advices
of smart skirmishes happening between ministerial
troops and provincials of New England.[1]

Letters from England also appeared in the gazettes that described additional British military preparations as well as bold boasts from British officials promising to rout the rebellious colonists. Dixon and Hunter's Virginia Gazette scoffed at a claim attributed to Sir Jeffery Amherst, a hero to the colonists for his service in the French and Indian War, "*that with 5,000 regular troops he would undertake the subjugation of the whole American continent.*"[2] The newspaper noted that General Gage had more than 5,000 British regulars in Boston, yet had failed to restore order in Massachusetts, much less the rest of the colonies. Parliament hoped to soon alter this by sending reinforcements to General Gage.

Congress Adopts the Army

The British Parliament was not alone in its preparations for war. After a month of hand wringing -- during which Congress applauded the seizure of Fort Ticonderoga in upstate New York but ordered an exact inventory of the garrison's military stores so that the supplies, "*may be safely returned when the restoration of the former harmony between great Britain and these colonies*...[is restored]" -- the Continental Congress finally acted decisively.[3] At the request of the

---

[1] Dixon and Hunter, *Virginia Gazette,* 24 June, 1775, 3
[2] Dixon and Hunter, *Virginia Gazette,* 24 June, 1775, 1
[3] Journal of the Continental Congress, Vol. 2, "18 May, 1775," 56
   (Access via the Library of Congress website)

Massachusetts Provincial Congress, the Continental Congress assumed responsibility for the army outside of Boston and authorized reinforcements in the form of ten rifle companies from Pennsylvania, Virginia and Maryland to join the army as soon as possible. The following day Congress appointed George Washington as commander-in-chief of the newly adopted continental army. Virginians learned of Washington's appointment from a letter in Purdie's gazette on June 23rd:

> *Col. WASHINGTON has been pressed to take the supreme command of the American troops encamped at Roxbury and I believe will accept the appointment, though with much reluctance, he being deeply impressed with the importance of that honourable trust, and dissident of his own (superior) abilities.*[4]

Washington revealed his anxiety at the appointment and concern for his abilities in letters to his family and friends:

> *I am now Imbarked on a tempestuous Ocean from whence, perhaps, no friendly harbor is to be found. I have been called upon by the unanimous Voice of the Colonies to the Command of the Continental Army – It is an honour I by no means aspired to – It is an honour I wished to avoid, as well from an unwillingness to quit the peaceful enjoyment of my Family as from a thorough conviction of my own Incapacity & want of experience in the conduct of so momentous a concern...*[5]

---

[4] Purdie, *Virginia Gazette Supplement*, 23 June, 1775,
[5] Philander D. Chase, ed., "George Washington to Burwell Bassett, 19 June, 1775," *The Papers of George Washington, Revolutionary War Series,* Vol. 1, (Charlottesville, VA: University Press of Virginia, 1985), 12-13

To his wife Martha, General Washington expressed similar concerns as well as genuine regret at his appointment. Yet, his sense of duty compelled him to accept:

It has been determined in Congress, that the whole Army raised for the defence of the American Cause shall be put under my care, and that it is necessary for me to proceed immediately to Boston to take upon me the Command of it. You may believe me my dear Patcy, when I assure you, in the most solemn manner, that, so far from seeking this appointment I have used every endeavour in my power to avoid it, not only from my unwillingness to part with you and the Family, but from a consciousness of its being a trust too great for my Capacity and that I should enjoy more real happiness and felicity in one month with you, at home, than I have the most distant prospect of reaping abroad, if my stay was to be Seven times Seven years. But, as it has been a kind of destiny that has thrown me upon this Service, I shall hope that my understanding of it, is designed to answer some good purpose.[6]

Washington's fellow delegates in Congress apparently did not share his lack of confidence in his abilities. In a letter to his wife, Silas Deane of Connecticut lavished praise on Washington and instructed his wife to welcome the general when he called upon her on his way to Boston:

---

[6] Chase, ed., "George Washington to Martha Washington, 18 June, 1775, *The Papers of George Washington,* Vol. 1, 3-4

Genl. Washington, will be with you soon, elected to that high Office by the Unanimous Voice of all America. I have been with him for a great part of the last Forty eight Hours, in Congress & Committee and the more I am acquainted with, the more I esteem him. He promises Me to call...[on] You. I wish to cultivate this Gentleman's acquaintance & regard, not from any sinister Views, but from the great Esteem I have of his Virtues, which do not shine in the View of the World by reason of his great Modesty, but when discovered by the discerning Eye, shine proportionately brighter. I know you will receive him as my Friend – what is more, infinitely more, his Country's Friend – who sacrificing private Fortune independent Ease, and every domestic pleasure, sets off at his Country's call to exert himself in her defence without so much as returning to bid adieu to a Fond partner & Family. Let Our youth look up to This Man as a pattern to form themselves by....[7]

Another Connecticut delegate, Eliphalet Dyer, revealed some of the other factors behind Washington's appointment:

You will hear that Coll. Washington is Appointed Genll or Commander in Chief over the Continental Army.... I believe he will be Very Agreeable to our officers & Soldiery. He is a Gent. Highly Esteemed by those acquainted with him, tho I don't believe [in military affairs] *he knows more than some of ours, but* [his appointment] *removes all jealousies, more*

---

[7] Smith, ed., "Silas Deane to Elizabeth Deane, 16 June, 1775, *Letters of Delegates to Congress*, Vol. 1, 493-94

firmly Cements the Southern to the Northern, and takes away the fear of the former lest an Enterprising eastern New England Genll proving Successful, might with his Victorious Army give law to the Southern & Western Gentry.[8]

As General Washington made his way north to assume command of the continental army at Cambridge, hundreds of volunteers assembled in frontier communities in Pennsylvania, Maryland, and Virginia to offer their services to the independent rifle companies authorized by Congress.

Rifle Companies

The two continental rifle companies from Virginia recruited men from the northwest region of the colony. Frederick County appointed Captain Daniel Morgan to lead one of the companies while Berkley County (now in West Virginia) appointed Hugh Stephenson to command the other company. Each commander hurried to form their company, Morgan mustered in Winchester while Stephenson mustered 25 miles to the northeast in Shepherdstown (West Virginia). Henry Bedinger, a member of Stephenson's company, recalled that

Volunteers presented themselves from every direction, in the vicinity of these Towns; [Winchester and Shepherdstown] *none were received but young men of Character, and of sufficient property to Clothe themselves completely, find their own arms,*

[8] Smith, ed., Eliphalet Dyer to Joseph Trumbull, 17 June, 1775, *Letters of the Delegates of Congress*, Vol. 1, 499-500

and accoutrements, that is, an approved Rifle, handsome shot pouch, and powder-horn, blanket, knapsack, with such decent clothing as should be prescribed, but which was at first ordered to be only a Hunting shirt and pantaloons, fringed on every edge, and in Various ways. Our Company was raised in less than a week. [Captain] Morgan had equal success.[9]

Peter Bruin, a member of Captain Morgan's company, noted that

So great was the enthusiasm of the moment that the difficulty did not depend on raising the number of men required but in selecting from those who crowded to the standard for admission, so that but a short time was employed in mustering and equiping the company.[10]

By mid July the rifle companies were on the march to Boston and were warmly received along the way. People marveled at their appearance and marksmanship. A resident of Frederick, Maryland noted that

Capt. Morgan, from Virginia, with his company of riflemen (all chosen), marched through this place on their way to Boston. Their appearance was truly martial; their spirits amazingly elated; breathing

[9] Danske Dandridge, "Henry Bedinger to --- Findley," *Historic Shepherdstown*, (Charlottesville, VA: Michie Co., 1910), 79

[10] John Dorman, ed., "Peter Bruin Pension Application," *Virginia Revolutionary Pension Applications*, Vol. 12 (Washington, D.C.: 1965), 3

nothing but a desire to join the American army and to engage the enemies of American liberties. [11]

Henry Bedinger, of Captain Stephenson's company, recalled that the riflemen were frequently greeted with cheers and kindness:

We were Met by a Number of Men and Women out of the Country who Brought us churns of Beer, Cyder, and Buttermilk, apples, cheries, etc, etc. We honoured them by firing at our parting. [12]

Such receptions continued all the way to Cambridge, where the companies joined the American army outside of Boston.

Williamsburg Becomes an Armed Camp

While the riflemen made the 600 mile march north to Boston, Virginia's capital was turning into an armed camp of its own. Speculation in late June about the possible arrival of 2,000 British troops in Virginia had prompted the residents of Williamsburg to appeal for assistance. [13]   On June 27th, the capital's inhabitants decided, "*to invite down, from a number of counties...250 men,*" to help protect the city. [14]

As far as Lord Dunmore was concerned, Williamsburg was already a fortified city. He wrote as much in a letter to Lord Dartmouth on the same day the residents of Williamsburg decided to seek more help:

---

[11] Dandridge, 95

[12] Ibid. 100

[13] Dixon and Hunter, *Virginia Gazette*, 24 June, 1775

[14] Scribner, ed., *Revolutionary Virginia: The Road to Independence*, Vol. 3, 218

A constant guard is kept in Williamsburg relieved every day from the adjacent Counties, and that place is become a Garrison, the pretence of which is the Security of the Person of their Speaker, who because he has been Chairman of the Congress, it is reported, (in order to inflame), that Government is anxious to Seize him.[15]

The "constant guard" that Dunmore described in Williamsburg included the capital's independent militia troops as well as volunteer detachments from nearby James City and New Kent counties. Dunmore also noted (no doubt with a great deal of frustration) that

Guards likewise Continually mount at the Town of York opposite to which the Men of War [on which Dunmore was staying] *lie, and thro' out the whole Country the greatest attention is paid to these Military preparations and a universal appearance of War is put on.*[16]

Dunmore's expectation of hostilities with the "rebels" prompted him to send his wife and children back to England in late June aboard the *H.M.S. Magdalen*. Despite protests from Virginians that Dunmore's decision was an over-reaction, the arrival in Williamsburg of militia troops from Goochland, Louisa, Spotsylvania, King George, Stafford and Albemarle counties in July added to the warlike atmosphere in the capital and suggested that Dunmore's concerns might be valid.

---

[15] Clark, ed., "Dunmore to Dartmouth, 27 June, 1775," *Naval Documents of the American Revolution*, Vol. 1, 764

[16] Ibid.

Purdie's gazette announced that all of the volunteers were, *"ready to take a crack with any ministerial troops that may be sent to molest us."*[17]

Lord Dunmore was also ready and eager to take a crack at the "rebels", but he lacked sufficient force to act. Instead, he remained aboard the *H.M.S. Fowey*, anchored off of Yorktown, where he dutifully reported to Lord Dartmouth in England on the deteriorating (and increasingly militant) situation in the colony:

> *A great number of people, horse and Foot, from various parts of the country have flocked to Williamsburg, armed and accoutered, and wearing uniforms.... They have made a Barrack of the Capital...and they have taken possession of the Park* [adjoining the Governor's Palace].[18]

Dunmore reported that in his absence his residence in Williamsburg (the Governor's palace) had been broken into a second time and that the intruders, *"broke open every lock...and carried off a considerable number of arms."*[19] The governor himself was nearly carried off in early July in a close encounter with a party of militia at his farmhouse (Porto Bello) on Queen's Creek, just a few miles outside of Williamsburg. Dunmore described the incident to Lord Dartmouth:

---

[17] Purdie, *Virginia Gazette,* 14 July, 1775

[18] Clark, ed., "Dunmore to Dartmouth, 12 July, 1775," *Naval Documents of the American Revolution,* Vol. 1, 873

[19] Ibid.

I happened...to go in the [Fowey's] *barge, to a Farm (my own property) about Seven miles from Williamsburg.... And Just after Captain Montague and I had done dinner... we were informed by my Servants that a body of men in Arms were Seen advancing directly to the House.... We had but just time to get into our boat and escape.*[20]

Two carpenters who accompanied Dunmore's small party in search of a new ship mast were seized by the militia and the "rebels" fired upon one of the governor's servants as he fled in a canoe, but the governor and the rest of his party escaped unharmed.[21] Aggrieved by this incident, Dunmore expanded his complaints to Lord Dartmouth to include the increasingly provocative actions of the militia posted in Yorktown:

We have now a Camp of these People behind the Town of York, not half a Cannon-Shot from the Ships; and the men are Continually parading in arms along the Shore Close to us, and at night we hear them challenge every boat or person that approached them.[22]

One of the things that had the militia on alert were reports of British landing parties robbing local inhabitants of livestock and other provisions. An account of one such incident appeared in a Pennsylvania gazette in late July:

---

[20] Ibid.
[21] Ibid.
[22] Ibid.

Gloucestertown, VA, July 13, 1775

It is certain that a boat from the Fowey or Otter landed several armed men on an island in the lower end of this country, who stole fourteen sheep and a cow. The owner of them alarmed his neighbours; but before they could arm themselves the robbers had made off.[23]

The militia was determined to halt these raids, and to demonstrate their resolve a large detachment of troops at Yorktown forcibly detained a landing party from the *H.M.S. Otter.* The detention of the landing party prompted a midshipman from the *Otter* to go ashore to investigate. He reported that

I walked up to their camp, which consisted of a few pales [fences] *covered with leaves, and found two hundred rebels round our men, whom they had been informed belonged to the Otter; and at my arrival vowed, that if they caught any belonging to the Fowey man of war, they would never let them go. I enquired into the reason why they detained the men, and was asked to whom they belonged; I answered to the King. The Captain of the Guard then asked me if I belonged to the Otter and* [whether] *any of the men or officers would venture on shore again. I told him, that both officers and men would, if they were ordered, come on shore to* [do their] *duty. They said they hoped they would behave themselves well, or they would get something they did not like. I replied that if saying*

---

[23] Clark, ed., "July 13, 1775" (Reported July 25th in PA Evening Post) *Naval Documents of the American Revolution,* Vol. 1, 881

they belonged to the King was impertinent, it was the answer they must always expect. Thus you see, [concluded the midshipman] *that the people of York, in Virginia, are worse than at Boston.*[24]

Lord Dunmore had reached a similar conclusion about the colonists, noting in a letter to Lord Dartmouth that they were "lawless ruffians" who displayed open rebellion:

The People of Virginia manifest open Rebellion by every means in their power, and they declare at the Same time that they are his Majesty's Most dutyfull Subjects...and that as designs have never been formed against my person, but that I may, whenever I please return to my usual Residence without the least danger; notwithstanding that my own Servants are prevented from passing with provisions which is thus cut off from me & denied to me, my people have been Carried off by the guard,; while my house has been a third time rifled, and is now entirely in the possession of these lawless Ruffians.[25]

Captain Charles Scott of Cumberland County, a veteran of the French and Indian War, may have actually agreed with Dunmore's characterization of the militia in Williamsburg as *"lawless ruffians"*. Selected by the officers in the capital to command this mixed force of volunteer militia, Scott faced the enormous challenge of instilling a degree of discipline in the

---

[24] Clark, ed. "A Midshipman on Board the Otter to a Friend in London, 11 July, 1775," *Naval Documents of the American Revolution,* Vol. 1, 866

[25] Clark, ed., "Dunmore to Dartmouth, 12 July, 1775, *Naval Documents of the American Revolution,* Vol. 1, 873

largely untrained and untried troops -- now 250 strong and encamped near the capital at Waller's Grove.[26]

The surprising departure of Dunmore and the British warships from the York River (they sailed to Norfolk on July 15th) actually made Captain Scott's task more difficult. With the threat to Williamsburg reduced, drill and guard duty in the capital grew mundane. Men who knew little of military discipline chafed at the inactivity of camp life and some fell into mischief. A council of officers adopted a set of regulations to instill greater discipline, but it had little effect:

> *Resolutions Adopted by the Officers at Williamsburg, July 18, 1775*
>
> *Resolved, That any private who may refuse when commanded on duty, or...deserts his post, goes to sleep or absents himself without leave of his officer, shall be punished as follows:*
>
> *For the first offence, he shall receive a reprimand from his own officer; for the second, that of the Commander-in-Chief before the whole battalion; and for the third, expulsion.*
>
> *Resolved, That any person who shall fire a gun without leave from the Commanding Officer, shall be taken into custody by the Officer of the Guard and there kept two hours without victuals or drink.*[27]

---

[26] R.A. Brock, ed., "George Gilmer to Thomas Jefferson in Papers, Military and Political, 1775-1778 of George Gilmer, M.D. of Pen Park, Albemarle Co., VA," *Miscellaneous Papers 1672-1865 Now First Printed from the Manuscripts in the Virginia Historical Society,* (Richmond, VA, 1937), 101 Henceforth known as the *Gilmer Papers.*

[27] Brock, ed., "Resolutions Adopted by the Officers at Williamsburg, 18 July, 1775," *Gilmer Papers,* 92-93

Not surprisingly, such light punishments had little effect on the troops, and the misconduct continued. Lieutenant George Gilmer of Albemarle County reluctantly placed much of the blame for the disorderly nature of the troops in Williamsburg upon Captain Scott:

> *Capt. Scott, our Commander-in-chief, who's goodness and merit is great, fears to offend, and by that every member is rather disorderly. We appear rather invited to feast than fight.*[28]

In fairness, the officers themselves demonstrated poor discipline (and judgment) and were gently reprimanded by the 3rd Virginia Convention in late July for seizing funds on their own initiative that were still held by some of the crown's revenue collectors. When the 3rd Virginia Convention in Richmond learned of the militia's unilateral action to seize the funds it immediately conveyed its disapproval and ordered the troops to desist in their actions. The chastised officers humbly responded with an appeal to the Convention to, *"lay down some certain line for our conduct, lest in our excessive zeal we should precipitate our Countrymen into unnecessary Calamities."*[29]

---

[28] Brock, ed., "George Gilmer to Thomas Jefferson," *Gilmer Papers*, 101

[29] Brock, ed., "To the President and Gentlemen of the Convention" *Gilmer Papers*, 109

Third Virginia Convention

The 3rd Virginia Convention had already been in session in Richmond for three weeks when the militia officers in Williamsburg appealed to the delegates for more guidance and instruction. A committee (formed on the third day of the convention) worked diligently to provide a plan to raise, "*a sufficient armed Force...under proper Officers for the Defence and protection of this Colony.*"[30] George Mason, a key member of the committee, described the enormous challenge that confronted the delegates:

> *I have not...had an hour which I could call my own. The committee... meets every morning at seven o' clock, sits till the Convention meets, which seldom* [ends] *before five in the afternoon, and immediately after dinner and a little refreshment sits again till nine or ten at night. This is hard duty, and yet, we have hitherto made but little progress....This will not be wondered at when the extent and importance of the business before us is reflected on – to raise forces for immediate service – to new model the whole militia – to render about one-fifth of it fit for the field at the shortest warning – to melt down all the volunteer and independent companies into this great establishment – to provide arms, ammunition, &c., -- and to point out ways and means of raising money, these are difficulties indeed!* [31]

[30] Scribner, ed., "Proceedings of Third Day of VA Convention," *Revolutionary Virginia: The Road to Independence,* Vol. 3, 319
[31] Rutland, ed., "George Mason to Martin Cockburn, 24 July, 1775," *The Papers of George Mason, Vol. 1,* 241

Nearly a month passed before the Convention adopted a detailed plan devised by the committee to better organize Virginia's military forces. The plan called for two regiments of regular (full time) soldiers raised for one year's service. Patrick Henry was selected to command the first regiment, which consisted of eight 68 man companies and totaled 544 men. [32] Colonel William Woodford, of Caroline County, was given command of the second regiment, which comprised 476 men in seven companies. [33] To raise this force, the Convention divided Virginia into sixteen districts and ordered each district (comprised of several counties) to recruit and send their company of regulars to Williamsburg as soon as possible.[34] The company of regulars from the eastern shore of Virginia remained there as a detached unit to help protect this isolated and vulnerable region of the colony.

The regular troops were not the only soldiers ordered to Williamsburg; hundreds of minutemen were ordered to march to the capital as well. They comprised a second tier of Virginia's new military establishment. The Convention authorized sixteen battalions of minutemen. These men were drawn from the ranks of the militia and were *"more strictly trained to proper discipline"* than the ordinary militia.[35] Each district was ordered to raise a 500 man battalion of minutemen *"from the age of sixteen to fifty, to be divided into ten companies of fifty men each."*[36] Like the regular troops, the

---

[32] William W. Henings, *The Statutes at Large Being a Collection of all the Laws of Virginia,* Vol. 9, (Richmond: J. & G. Cochran, 1821), 9

[33] Ibid., 10

[34] Ibid., 10, 16

[35] Ibid., 16

[36] Ibid., 16-17

minutemen were provided with proper arms as well as a hunting shirt and leggings.[37]

The last tier of Virginia's new military establishment was the traditional county militia. The Convention decreed that

> *All male persons, hired servants, and apprentices, above the age of sixteen, and under fifty years...shall be enlisted into the militia...and formed into companies....*[38]

Each member of the county militia had six months to furnish himself with

> *A good rifle...with a tomahawk,* [or a] *common firelock, bayonet, pouch, or cartouch box, three charges of powder and ball....* [Members of the militia] *shall constantly keep by him one pound of powder and four pounds of ball....*[39]

The militia companies were ordered to hold private musters every two weeks, except in the winter.

While the convention spent much of July and most of August organizing the colony's military force and establishing a set of regulations for the new troops (Articles of War), Lord Dunmore intensified his own efforts to strengthen his force.

---

[37] Ibid., 20
[38] Ibid., 27-28
[39] Ibid.

Dunmore Prepares for a Confrontation

Early in the morning of July 15th, two days before the 3rd Virginia Convention convened in Richmond, the *H.M.S. Otter*, with Lord Dunmore aboard, weighed anchor off of Yorktown and sailed for Norfolk. The *Otter* was joined by the 20 gun H.M.S. *Mercury*, which had arrived from New York to replace the Boston bound *H.M.S. Fowey*.[40] Onboard the *Fowey* was Captain Edward Foy, one of Lord Dunmore's closest advisors. He apparently parted with the governor on bad terms, writing to a Virginia loyalist at the time of his departure that, "*I am no longer interested in the fate of Lord Dunmore.*"[41] A few weeks later another strong supporter of the governor, John Randolph, the attorney general and brother of Peyton Randolph, also left Virginia.[42]

More frustrating for Dunmore than the departure of such key supporters, however, was the arrival of the *H.M.S. Mercury*, which replaced the *H.M.S. Fowey* in Virginia. Unlike Captain George Montagu of the *H.M.S. Fowey*, who had closely cooperated with Dunmore and earned the enmity of the colonists, Captain Montagu's replacement, Captain John Macartney of the *H.M.S. Mercury*, was far less cooperative with the governor and quickly incurred Dunmore's displeasure. Captain Macartney's first offense was to accept a dinner invitation on the eve of Dunmore's departure from Yorktown from Thomas Nelson Sr. of Yorktown, the president of the Governor's Council, who, along with most of

---

[40] Clark, ed. "Journal of His Majesty's Sloop Otter," *Naval Documents of the American Revolution*, Vol. 1, 893

[41] Selby, 47

[42] Ibid.

the Council, was viewed as a rebel by the governor.[43] Another point of contention with Dunmore was Macartney's initial refusal (along with Captain Matthew Squire of the *H.M.S. Otter*) to harbor runaway slaves aboard their ships, a policy that earned the two officers a public expression of gratitude from the residents of Norfolk in late July.[44]

Less than a week after Macartney's arrival, Dunmore wrote a scathing letter to Admiral Samuel Graves in Boston asking for the captain's removal:

> *As I have received every Assistance from Captain Montagu which it was possible to expect from Zeal and Assiduity, it is particularly unfortunate to his Majesty's Service that that Gentleman should be succeeded in the Command of his Majesty's Ships here by Captain Macartney who seems to be actuated altogether by Principles totally different, and to have principally at heart the making Friends among his Majesty's greatest Enemies in this Country. Hitherto instead of aiding me, he has very much prejudiced all the Measures which I have thought requisite to adopt for restoring his Majesty's lost Authority in this Government.*[45]

The hot tempered Dunmore went on to declare that

---

[43] Selby, 56

[44] Selby, 56 and Clark, ed., "Holt's Virginia Gazette, August 2, 1775," *Naval Documents of the American Revolution*, Vol. 1, 1048

[45] Clark, ed., "Lord Dunmore to Vice Admiral Samuel Graves, 17 July, 1775, *Naval Documents of the American Revolution*, Vol. 1, 903-04

> *It will be impossible for me ever…to apply to him for*
> *any Assistance…And as I think him utterly unfit for*
> *such a Command, I hope therefore You will by the*
> *most speedy means relieve him and send a different*
> *Person for the Command."* [46]

While Lord Dunmore -- and the crews aboard the handful of warships and tenders that protected him -- adjusted to their new anchorage in the Elizabeth River (between Norfolk and Portsmouth), some good news finally arrived for Dunmore on July 31st. A 60 man detachment of British regulars from the 14th Regiment at St. Augustine arrived aboard the sloop *Betsy*, and another 40 redcoats were expected momentarily. Purdie's gazette informed its readers of their arrival and speculated about their intentions:

> *Lord Dunmore reviewed his 60 body-guardsmen,*
> *lately arrived from St. Augustine…at Gosport and we*
> *hear, that he daily expects an additional*
> *reinforcement, of 40 more soldiers, from the same*
> *place. His Lordship it is said, as soon as they arrive,*
> *and when joined by the marines from the Mercury*
> *and Otter men of war, and a number of other select*
> *friends in different places, intends coming round to*
> *York town; from whence, if not prevented, it is likely*
> *he will pay us a visit in this city, although he cannot*
> *expect the same cordial reception as on former*
> *occasions, but will probably be received with such*

---

[46] Ibid.

illuminations &ct. as may make him forget his way to the palace.[47]

Mr. Purdie then made a stern declaration:

The good people of Virginia now consider Lord Dunmore as their mortal enemy, and will no longer brook the many insults they have received from him, which are daily repeated; and the "damn'd shirtmen," as they are emphatically called by some of his minions...will make [them regret] *before long, their ill-timed, base, and ungenerous conduct.*[48]

Although Dunmore acknowledged in a letter to Lord Dartmouth on August 2nd, that the newly arrived British troops were too few to restore order in this "distracted colony", he confidently declared that

[Were] *I speedily supplied with a few hundred more* [troops] *with Arms, Ammunition and the other requisites of War, and with full powers to act... I could in a few months reduce this Colony to perfect Submission.*[49]

---

[47] Purdie, *Virginia Gazette,* 4 August, 1775
[48] Ibid.
[49] Clark, ed., "Lord Dunmore to Lord Dartmouth, 2 Aug., 1775, *Naval Documents of the American Revolution,* Vol. 1, 1045

Norfolk

The inhabitants of Norfolk and the surrounding countryside were in a precarious situation. Threatened by warships offshore with scores of British regulars aboard and cut off from immediate support from Williamsburg by the broad James River, the residents of southern Virginia had to tread lightly so as to not provoke Lord Dunmore. One young lad, Alexander Main, a fifer in one of the city's volunteer militia companies, learned that the defiant act of wearing a hunting shirt in the presence of the governor was enough to warrant his seizure and detention aboard the *Otter*.[50] Although Main was soon released, anger over the incident caused the Norfolk Borough Committee to condemn John Schaw, a suspected supporter of Dunmore, for aiding the governor in the incident. The committee declared that

> *The said Schaw has herein shown himself a busy tool and enemy to American liberty, and as such, we advise every friend to his Country to have no further dealings or connections with him.*[51]

Although Schaw publically repented for his actions before the committee two days later, news of his "sincere repentance" did not appear in the local gazette in time to stop a large crowd from seizing and parading him about town to the tune of Yankee Doolittle (played by the aggrieved fifer, Alexander Main).[52] Terrified that he was about to be tarred and

---

[50] Clark, ed., "Minutes of the Norfolk Borough Committee, 8 Aug., 1775, *Navel Documents of the American Revolution*, Vol. 1, 1100

[51] Ibid.

[52] Scribner, ed., "Norfolk Borough Committee," *Revolutionary Virginia: The Road to Independence,* Vol. 3, 420

feathered, Schaw managed to escape to an alderman's house who persuaded the crowd to disperse on the promise that Schaw would report again to the committee the following day.[53] By then Schaw's repentance was reported and no further action was taken against him.

The Norfolk committee was not finished challenging supporters of Lord Dunmore, however. Andrew Sprowle, a prominent merchant from Portsmouth with warehouses in the adjacent village of Gosport, was summoned before the Norfolk committee to address accusations that he had offered his buildings in Gosport as housing for the troops of the 14th Regiment. Captain Macartney -- who on the same day that Sprowle was summoned had been praised for his "exemplary" conduct in the colony by John Holt's gazette -- interceded on Sprowle's behalf and expressed his astonishment that providing shelter to the King's troops was somehow improper:[54]

> *I am just informed by his Excellency Lord Dunmore, that Mr. Andrew Sprowle has received a summons to attend a Committee in Norfolk.... The accusations alleged against him are of a most extraordinary nature. In the summons he is charged with having harboured His Majesty's troops in the stores at Gosport. I am not surprised that a summons grounded upon such accusations should be alarming to Mr. Sprowle; particularly after the cruel and*

---

[53] Ibid.

[54] Clark, ed., "Holt, 9 Aug., 1775," *Naval Documents of the American Revolution*, Vol. 1, 1106

oppressive treatment Mr. Schaw lately received from a mob in Norfolk.[55]

Captain Macartney assured the mayor that he earnestly wished to promote the public peace and meant to do so, declaring

> *I am sent hither to be the guardian of a British colony; to protect His Majesty's Governor, and all the loyal subjects in the Province of Virginia. This is my duty, and should wish it to be known that my duty and inclination go hand in hand. The same principles that have induced me not to harbor the slaves of any individual in this province will operate with me to protect the property of all loyal subjects. As I have before observed, that I shall endeavour to promote the public peace of this province, it is hardly necessary to mention that I shall not remain an idle spectator, should any violence be offered to the persons or property of any of His Majesty's subjects.*[56]

Macartney observed that Virginians (like Mr. Sprowle) who remained loyal to and supported the constitutional government of the colony were, "*unjustly censored for their loyal conduct,*" and he asserted that, "*Men under these circumstances are more particularly entitled to my protection.*"[57] Thus, declared Captain Macartney, to best,

---

[55] Clark, ed., "Captain John Macartney to Paul Layall, Mayor of Norfolk, 12 August, 1775," *Naval Documents of the American Revolution,* Vol. 1, 1130

[56] Ibid.

[57] Ibid.

"preserve harmony" in Norfolk and suppress all *"party jealousies and animosities"*:

> *I shall, the first opportunity, place his Majesty's ship under my command abreast of the town; and I must assure you, that, notwithstanding I shall feel the utmost pain and reluctance in being compelled to use violent measures to preserve the persons and properties of his Majesty's subjects, yet I most assuredly shall, if it becomes necessary, use the most coercive measures in my power to suppress all unlawful combinations and persecutions within the province of Virginia.*[58]

Fortunately for all concerned, Captain Macartney had no cause to execute his threat to bombard Norfolk. Sprowle appeared before the committee, accompanied by Captain Macartney, on August 16th and explained that the soldiers who occupied his warehouse did so without his permission and that he had insisted to Lord Dunmore that they leave immediately.[59] Sprowle contended that the governor refused to move the troops until the ship that had been recently pressed into service for their barracks was ready to receive them.[60] This explanation seemed to satisfy the committee, who lightly reprimanded Sprowle for not informing them earlier of these events. The committee instead directed its displeasure at Lord Dunmore and Captain Squire of the *Otter* for harboring runaway servants and slaves aboard his ship:

---

[58] Ibid.
[59] Scribner, ed., "Norfolk County Committee, 16 August, 1775," *Revolutionary Virginia: The Road to Independence*, Vol. 3, 452
[60] Ibid.

> *Resolved, that it be recommended to the inhabitants*
> *of this county that they have no connections or*
> *dealings with LORD DUNMORE or CAPT. SQUIRE,*
> *and the other officers of the Otter sloop of war, as*
> *they have evinced on many occasions, the most*
> *unfriendly disposition to the liberties of this*
> *continent, in promoting a disaffection among the*
> *slaves, and concealing some of them for a*
> *considerable time on board their vessels.*[61]

Although Governor Dunmore and Captain Squire bore the brunt of the committee's anger, whatever goodwill Captain Macartney had earned with the inhabitants of Norfolk vanished after his threat to bombard the town. On August 21st, the Norfolk Common Hall (city council) blasted Macartney's threatening letter as disrespectful, indecent, and an unjustifiable intermeddling of civil matters.[62] The town council also declared that despite the, *"defenceless state of the Town,"* they would never, *"Tamely submit to the invasion of their priviledges…[or] desert the righteous cause of their Country"*[63] In the ensuing months, this bold pledge would be greatly tested.

---

[61] Ibid.

[62] Scribner, ed., "Proceedings of the Common Hall respecting Conduct of Captain John Macartney, 21 August, 1775," *Revolutionary Virginia: The Road to Independence*, Vol. 3, 473

[63] Ibid.

Chapter Seven

"Lord Dunmore may now see he has not cowards to deal with."

Fall: 1775

Over four months had passed since blood was shed at Lexington and Concord and although royal authority had collapsed in Virginia with the flight of Governor Dunmore, combat had yet to occur in the colony. Hundreds of Virginia riflemen had joined their fellow Virginian, General George Washington, in Massachusetts, and together they had seen combat outside of Boston, but the troops in Virginia had yet to fire a shot at each other.

This changed in the fall when a powerful hurricane swept into Virginia in early September and triggered a confrontation between Captain Matthew Squire of the *H.M.S. Otter* and the inhabitants of Hampton that ultimately led to armed conflict in October. The hurricane's fierce winds and strong tidal surge swept Dunmore's small fleet in the Elizabeth River and Hampton Roads close to shore where many vessels, including the 20 gun *H.M.S. Mercury,* were grounded. One of the *Otter's* tenders, a small sloop with Captain Squire aboard, was caught in the storm near Hampton (across the James River from Norfolk) and blown ashore near Back Creek. Most of the crew, including two runaway slaves, was taken into custody by the local militia and the ship's stores were seized before the vessel was burned, but Captain Squire managed to elude the militia and escape into the woods. Accounts of the incident appeared in the Virginia newspapers a few days after the storm:

> *Master Squires, the magnanimous commander of* [the H.M.S. Otter]...*was obliged to take shelter under the trees that* [dis]*agreeable night, and in the morning went in disguise to some negro's cabin, from whom he borrowed a canoe, by which he* [escaped].[1]

> *Capt. Squires....*[tender] *was burnt by the people thereabouts* [near Hampton] *in return for his harboring gentlemen's negroes, and suffering his sailors to steal poultry, hogs, etc. Two of the crew were runaway slaves...who were taken soon after they got ashore; and his pilot, a mulatto man,* [who escaped].[2]

These reports (and the accusations of plundering and thievery) angered Captain Squire and upon his return to the *Otter* he lashed out at John Holt, a Norfolk printer, with a threat:

> *You have in many papers lately taken the freedom to mention my name, and thereto added many falsities. I now declare, if I am ever again mentioned therein, with reflections on my character, I will most assuredly seize your person, and take you on board the Otter.*[3]

---

[1] Pinkney, *Virginia Gazette,* 7 September, 1775

[2] Purdie, *Virginia Gazette,* 8 September, 1775

[3] Clark, ed. "Captain Squire to John Hunter Holt," *Virginia Gazette,* in *Naval Documents of the American Revolution,* Vol. 2, 66

Captain Squire followed this public threat against Mr. Holt with a terse letter to the Hampton town committee demanding the return of the captured sloop and stores:

> *Whereas a sloop tender, manned and armed on his majesty's service, was on Saturday the 2d instant, in a violent gale of wind, cast onshore in Back river, Elizabeth county, having on board the under mentioned king's stores, which the inhabitants of Hampton thought proper to seize; I am therefore to desire that the king's sloop, with all the stores belonging to her, be immediately returned or the people of Hampton, who committed the outrage, must be answerable for the consequence.*[4]

The Hampton Committee forwarded Captain Squire's letter to Williamsburg and included a plea for assistance. One hundred volunteers marched to Hampton the next day to reinforce the local militia.[5]

The arrival of the reinforcements from Williamsburg bolstered the spirits of Hampton's inhabitants and prompted the town committee to belligerently respond to Captain Squire's threat on September 16th, with a taunt of its own:

---

[4] Clark, ed., "Captain Squire to the Hampton Town Committee, 10 September, 1775," *Naval Documents of the American Revolution,* Vol. 2, 74

Note: The king's stores that Captain Squires demanded be returned included: 6 swivel guns, 5 muskets, 5 cutlasses, 2 powder horns, 2 cartouch boxes, swivel shot; seine and rope, and an anchor. (Ibid.)

[5] Robert L. Scribner and Brent Tarter, ed., *Revolutionary Virginia: The Road to Independence,* Vol. 4, 96

The sloop, we apprehended, was not in his majesty's service, as we are well assured that you were on a pillaging or pleasuring party.... Neither the vessel or stores were seized by the inhabitants of Hampton. The threats of a person whose conduct hath evinced that he were not only capable, but desirous, of doing us, in our then defensless state, the greatest injustice, we confess, were somewhat alarming; but, with the greatest pleasure, we can inform you, our apprehensions are now removed.[6]

Captain Squire angrily responded by seizing any vessel that dared to sail out of Hampton. Squire's piratical actions were first reported in Holt's Virginia Gazette in mid-September:

We are informed from good authority that a system of justice similar to that adopted against the devoted town of Boston, is likely to be established in this colony, by the renowned Commodore of the Virginia fleet [Capt. Squire]. *He has, in the course of this week, as a reprisal for the loss of his tender, seized every vessel belonging to Hampton that came within his reach, and thereby rendered himself the terror of all the small craft and fishing boats in this river; especially the latter, having brought some of them under his stern, by a discharge of his cannon at them.*[7]

---

[6] Clark, ed., Hampton Committee to Captain Squire, 16 September, 1775, *Naval Documents of the American Revolution*, Vol. 2, 123

[7] Clark, ed. "Holt, *Virginia Gazette,* 20 September, 1775," *Naval Documents of the American Revolution,* Vol. 2, 167

The same letter in Holt's Gazette reported that Captain Squire had offered to cease his activities off of Hampton in exchange for the return of the seized stores. The Hampton Committee agreed to return the items, but only after Captain Squire hand over a runaway slave that was serving as a pilot aboard the *Otter*. Captain Squire refused and, *"swore he would make them no other reply than what his cannon could give them."*[8] Squire posted vessels at the mouth of Hampton's harbor and effectively blockaded the port. Lord Dunmore summarized the situation to his superior, Lord Dartmouth, in Britain:

We have demanded Satisfaction of the People at Hampton for the Sloop and desired that the King's Stores might be returned, to all which they have given us a positive refusal; their Port is now blocked up and we have taken two of their Boats and shall not permit a Vessell to pass or repass till they return the Stores etc, they have called to their assistance between two and three hundred of their Shirt men Alias Rebels.[9]

Norfolk is Chastised

The boldness displayed by the inhabitants of Hampton was not replicated in Norfolk when Captain Squire suddenly acted on his threat to stop John Holt from publishing his Virginia Gazette. An eyewitness to the September 30th incident in Norfolk described the lack of resistance offered by the town's residents to Captain Squire's daring move:

---

[8] Ibid.,

[9] Clark, ed., "Lord Dunmore to Lord Dartmouth, 5 October, 1775," *Naval Documents of the American Revolution*, Vol. 2, 317

Yesterday came ashore about 15 of the King's soldiers, and marched up to the printing-office, out of which they took all the types and part of the press and carried them on board the new ship Eilbeck, in presence, I suppose, of between two and three hundred spectators, without meeting with the least molestation; and upon the drums beating up and down the town, there were only about 35 men to arms....[10]

The poor showing of the local militia, most of who ignored the call to arms, was noted in another account of the incident:

A few spirited gentlemen in Norfolk, justly incensed at so flagrant a breach of good order and the constitution, and highly resenting the conduct of lord Dunmore and the navy gentry (who have now commenced downright pirates and banditti) ordered the drum to beat to arms, but were joined by few or none;[11]

The lack of opposition to Captain Squire's small landing party embarrassed Virginia's leaders and gave great delight to Lord Dunmore and his supporters. Norfolk's committee tried to salvage the town's tarnished reputation by complaining to Lord Dunmore about the, *"illegal and riotous,"* actions of his landing party but this charge provoked only derision from the

---

[10] Clark, ed., "Extract of a Letter from Norfolk, 1 October, 1775," *Naval Documents of the American Revolution*, Vol. 2, 267

[11] Clark, ed., Purdie, *Virginia Gazette, 7 October, 1775, Naval Documents* of the American Revolution, Vol. 2, 342-43

governor, who witnessed the entire incident from aboard his ship and mockingly replied to the committee that:

I was an Eye Witness to a Party belonging to the Otter Sloop of War landing at the time and place you mention, and did see them bring off two of the Printers Servants, together with his Printing Utensils, and I do really think they could not have rendered [Norfolk] or the Country adjacent to it, a more essential Service than [to] deprive them of the means of poisoning the minds of the People, and exciting in them a Spirit of Rebellion and Sedition, and by that means drawing inevitable ruin and destruction on themselves and Country.

As to the illegality of the Act, some of you [on the committee]…ought to blush when you make use of the expression, as you cannot but be Conscious that you have by every means in your power, totally subverted the Laws and Constitution, and have been the Aiders and Abettors in throwing off all Allegiance to that Majesty's Crown and Government to whom you profess yourselves faithful Subjects.[12]

Dunmore taunted the committee further with a stinging observation that its claim of self restraint in opposing the landing party was not due to choice, but rather, necessity:

---

[12] Clark, ed., "Common Hall of the Borough of Norfolk to Lord Dunmore, 30 September, 1775," and "Lord Dunmore to the Town Hall of the Borough of Norfolk, 30 September, 1775," *Naval Documents of the American Revolution*, Vol. 2, 258-60

Your not repelling the insult (as you call it) or taking prisoners the small party that was on Shore, I impute to some other reason (from your Drums beating to Arms, during the greatest part of the time which the party was on Shore) than to your peaceable intentions. [13]

He concluded with the assertion that

Every means in my power shall be employed, both with the Navy and Army, to preserve the peace, good order and happiness of the Inhabitants of...Norfolk, so long as they behave themselves as Faithful Subjects to His Majesty; and I expect at the same time, that, if an individual shall behave himself as your Printer has done by aspersing the Characters of His Majesty's Servants and others, in the most false and Scandalous manner, and being the instigator of Treason and Rebellion, and you do not take proper Steps to restrain such offenders, that you will not be surprised if the Military power interposes to prevent the total dissolution of all decency, Order and good Government. But I promise you on my Honor, that, if the Printer will put himself and Servants under my protection, that they shall not meet with the least insult, and shall be permitted to print every occurrence that happens during these unhappy disputes between the Mother Country and her Colonies, he confining himself to truth, and representing matters in a fair

---

[13] Clark, ed., "Lord Dunmore to the Town Hall of the Borough of Norfolk, 30 September, 1775," *Naval Documents of the American Revolution*, Vol. 2, 259

Candid impartial manner on both sides; this I hope will convince you that I had nothing more in view, when I requested Captain Squire to Seize the types, than, that the unhappy deluded Publick might no longer remain in the Dark concerning the present contest, but that they should be furnished with a fair representation of facts, which I know never would happen, if the Press was to remain under the Countrol of its present Dictators.[14]

Dunmore's Raids

Emboldened by the timid response of the residents of Norfolk, Lord Dunmore launched a series of raids in mid-October to seize arms and ammunition in the vicinity of Norfolk. Captain Samuel Leslie, the ranking officer of the 14th Regiment in Virginia, led the first raid on October 12th and recalled

I landed the 12th of [October] at 11 o'Clock at night about three miles from hence with Lieut. Lawrie, two Serjeants, & forty rank and file of the 14th Regiment, and after marching three miles into the country in search of Artillery we found in a wood nineteen pieces of cannon, some of them twelve, others nine, six & three pounders; seventeen of which we destroyed, & brought off two, and then returning to our boats we reimbarked without the least opposition. Lord Dunmore accompanied us upon this expedition.[15]

---

[14] Ibid., 259-60
[15] Clark, ed., "Captain Leslie to General Howe, 1 November, 1775," *Naval Documents of the American Revolution*, Vol. 2, 844-45

Dunmore described the next raid which occurred three days later:

> *On the 15th Instant, I landed with between 70 and 80 Men (which was all we could Spare to take with us) some little distance from [Norfolk] in the Night, and Marched about a Mile and a half up the Country, where we destroyed 17 pieces of Ordinance and brought off two more, that the Rebels had carried from...Norfolk, and concealed there.*[16]

Two days after this raid, Dunmore ordered another, led once again by Captain Leslie who recalled that

> *On the 17h of October his Lordship was informed, that there was a great quantity of Artillery, small arms and all sorts of ammunition, concealed in different stores at a place called Kemp's landing, in consequence of which, I, with [a few officers] & seventy rank & file of the 14th Regiment, Lieut Allen, one sergeant and twenty marines, some young gentlemen of the Navy & ten of twelve seamen, embarked at 2 o' Clock in the Afternoon in boats & a Schooner in which some Guns were mounted to cover our landing, and proceeded seven or eight miles up the eastern branch of Elizabeth river to Newtown, where we landed without opposition notwithstanding above two hundred of the rebels were at exercise near that place the same evening, and marching three or four miles through the Country we arrived at Kemp's landing a little after it was dark,*

[16] Clark, ed., "Lord Dunmore to Lord Dartmouth, 22 October, 1775," *Naval Documents of the American Revolution,* Vol. 2, 574-75

where we searched several stores and could discover nothing but a good many small arms, which we either brought off or destroyed; and returning pretty near the same road we went we reimbarked about 2 o'clock the next morning without interruption. We likewise took several prisoners one of whom was a Captain of Minutemen and another a Delegate to the Convention at Richmond.[17]

More raids followed, prompting Dunmore to brag on October 22nd that

On the 20th we landed again and brought off Six more Guns, and Yesterday we landed again and brought off Ten Guns and Two Cohorns, and between fifty and Sixty small Arms and a great quantity of Ball of all Sorts and Sizes, which I believe is all the Military Stores in this Neighborhood that could be of any Service to the Rebels....[18]

Dunmore also offered his assessment of the impact of the raids on both the rebels and the "friends of government".

I can assure your Lordship that landing in this manner has discouraged exceedingly the Rebels, and has raised the Spirits of the friends of Government so much that they are offering their Services from all quarters;[19]

---

[17] Clark, ed., "Captain Leslie to General Howe, 1 November, 1775," *Naval Documents of the American Revolution*, Vol. 2, 844-45

[18] Clark, ed., "Lord Dunmore to Lord Dartmouth, 22 October, 1775," *Naval Documents of the American Revolution*, Vol. 2, 574-75

[19] Ibid.

Captain Leslie offered an equally optimistic assessment of the situation in Virginia to General William Howe in Boston:

> *Many great guns, small arms, & other implements of war have been taken since by small parties, so that there has been in all at least seventy seven pieces of ordinance taken & destroyed since my Detachment arrived here without the smallest opposition, which is a proof that it would not require a very large force to subdue this Colony.*[20]

Battle of Hampton

The growing confidence and loyalist support generated by Lord Dunmore's successful raids was tempered by events across the James River in late October. While Dunmore had employed the 14th Regiment to seize arms and ammunition against virtually no opposition, Captain Matthew Squire's blockade of Hampton had continued into October and had expanded to include small landing parties that seized provisions, livestock, and occasionally slaves. The inhabitants of Hampton were furious but resolute in their refusal to return the seized military stores that Squire demanded and prepared for a possible attack on their town by partially blocking the harbor channel with scuttled vessels. Within Hampton, a mixed force of regulars, minute-men, and local militia waited to see if Captain Squire would act on his threat to punish the town. The answer arrived on Oct. 26th.

---

[20] Clark, ed., "Captain Leslie to General Howe, 1 November, 1775," *Naval Documents of the American Revolution*, Vol. 2, 844-45

On the evening of October 25th, one of Captain Squire's landing parties, supported by a small squadron of tenders consisting of a large schooner, two sloops and two pilot boats, came ashore near Hampton and "*robbed several houses on Mill Creek.*"[21] No opposition was offered by the local populace. In fact, most of Hampton was unaware of the raid until the next morning. One resident reported in Pickney's Gazette that

> *We heard of* [the raid] *the next morning, and observed the tenders at anchor, no great distance from the place where several vessels had been sunk in the channel of Hampton river to prevent their surprising us. The channel was not completely stopped, and we imagined, from their situation they intended to prevent our compleating the work, or perhaps might intend to land, to be at their old trade. However, to observe their motions particularly, captain Lyne, in the minute service, rode round nigh where the tenders lay, and left orders for his lieutenant (Mr. Smith) with 30 men, to come over to him, by crossing one of the branches of Hampton river.*[22]

---

[21] Pinkney, *Virginia Gazette,* 2 November, 1775
[22] Ibid.

Hampton Virginia

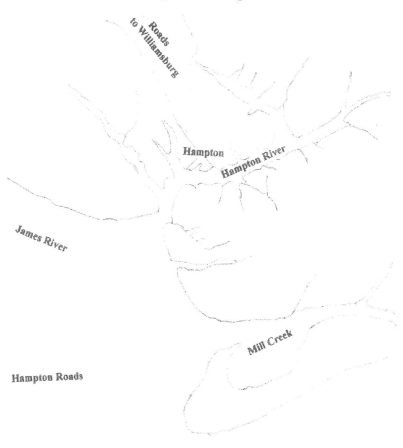

Roads to Williamsburg

Hampton

Hampton River

James River

Mill Creek

Hampton Roads

Chesapeake Bay

Another account in Dixon and Hunter's Gazette revealed Captain Squire's intentions to burn the town:

> [The] *next morning* [Oct. 26th] *there appeared off the mouth of Hampton river a large armed schooner, a sloop, and three tenders, with soldiers on board, and a message was received at Hampton, from Captain Squires, on board the schooner, that he would that day land and burn the town; on which a company of regulars and a company of minute-men, who had been placed there in consequence of former threats...against that place made the best disposition to prevent their landing, aided by a body of militia, who were suddenly called together on the occasion.*[23]

According to Lord Dunmore's account of the day's affair, gunfire erupted from the rebels onshore when Captain Squire's tenders approached Hampton harbor:

> *Some of the King's tenders went pretty close into Hampton Road. So soon as the rebels perceived them, they marched out against them and the moment they got within shot of our people, Mr. George Nicholas...who commanded a party of rebels at that time at Hampton, fired at one of the tenders, whose example was followed by his whole party. The tenders returned the fire but without the least effect.*[24]

---

[23] Dixon and Hunter, *Virginia Gazette,* 28 October, 1775

[24] Davis, ed., "Lord Dunmore to Lord Dartmouth, 6 December, 1775 through February, 1776," *Documents of the American Revolution,* Vol. 3, 58

Dunmore laid the blame for the first shot at Hampton (and thus the inauguration of warfare in Virginia) on Captain George Nicholas of the 2nd Virginia Regiment, but an American eyewitness saw the engagement differently. He reported that as the tenders approached Hampton

> *Two vollies of musquetry were discharged from the tenders, and answered by captain Lyne from his post by a rifle, which was answered by a four pounder from one of the tenders; then began a pretty warm fire from all the tenders. Captain Nicholas, observing this, soon joined about 25 of his men. The fire of our musquetry caused the tender nighest to us to sheer off some distance.*[25]

Captain Lyne of the minute company was identified in a second account as the one, "*who fired the first gun in the attack at the mouth of the river,* [and] *killed a man by that very fire.*"[26]

Whether this meant he fired the very first shot of the engagement is unclear. What is clear is that the two sides fired upon each other for over an hour with the tenders getting the worst of it. Unable to maneuver past the sunken vessels obstructing the harbor, the tenders were raked with rifle and musket fire from shore. Their crews responded with cannon, swivel, and musket fire, but it apparently had little effect on the Virginians, who were well sheltered on shore. One rebel combatant recalled that

---

[25] Clark, ed. "Pinkney, *Virginia Gazette,* 2 November, 1775," *Naval Documents of the American Revolution,* 842-43
[26] Pinkney, *Virginia Gazette,* 2 November, 1775

The fire [from the tenders] *consisted of 4 pounders, grape shot etc. for about an hour. Not a man of our's was hurt. Whether our men did any damage is uncertain. They could not get nigher than 300 yards. Some say they saw men fall in one of the tenders.*[27]

The confident rebels attempted to draw the enemy to shore, but Captain Squire would not take the bait:

After waiting under cover nigh the shore, and finding they would not land, the men were ordered to retreat to the woods, to try whether that would not induce them to land; but all in vain as long as we stayed. The men were then marched into Hampton about 5 o'clock in the afternoon.[28]

Pinkney's Virginia Gazette boasted of the bravery the Virginians displayed against Captain Squire's squadron:

No troops could shew more intrepidity than the raw, new raised men, under the command of captain Nicholas, of the second regiment, and captain Lyne, of the minute men, together with some of the country militia. These brave young officers, at the head of their men, without the least cover or breast-work, on the open shore, stood a discharge of 4 pounders, and other cannon, from a large schooner commanded by captain Squire himself, and from a sloop and two tenders, which played on them with all their guns,

---

[27] Clark, ed. "Pinkney, *Virginia Gazette*, 2 November, 1775," *Naval Documents of the American Revolution*, 842-43

[28] Ibid.

swivels, and muskets. They stood cooly till the vessels were near enough for them to do execution, when they began a brisk and well directed fire, which forced the little squadron to retire.[29]

Although nightfall ended the fighting, both sides remained active. Under cover of darkness and a driving rain the British returned to the sunken obstructions and worked to create a passage through the channel while the rebels strengthened their breastworks on the town wharf and anxiously waited for reinforcements from Williamsburg. Colonel William Woodford of the 2nd Virginia Regiment marched all night with a company of Culpeper Minutemen to reach Hampton by morning and assume command of the rebel forces. In a letter to his friend Thomas Jefferson, John Page, a prominent resident of nearby Gloucester County, gave a detailed account of the resumption of combat on October 27th:

Col. Woodford accompanied Captain Buford's rifle company through a heavy rain to Hampton and arrived about 7 a.m. When the Col. Entered the Town, having left the Rifle Men in the Church to dry themselves, he rode down to the River, took A view of the Town, and then seeing the Six Tenders at Anchor in the River went to Col. Cary's to dry himself and eat his Breakfast. But before he could do either the Tenders had cut their Way through the Vessel's Boltsprit which was sunk to impede their Passage and having a very fresh and fair Gale had anchored in the Creek and abreast of the Town.

[29] Clark, ed., "Pinkney, *Virginia Gazette,* 26 October, 1775," *Naval Documents of the American Revolution,* Vol. 2, 613-14

The People were so astonished at their unexpected and sudden Arrival that they stood staring at them and omitted to give the Col. the least Notice of their approach. The first Intelligence he had of this Affair was from the Discharge of a 4 Pounder. He mounted his Horse and riding down to the Warf found that the People of the Town had abandoned their Houses and riding down to the Militia had left the Breast Work which had been thrown up across the Wharf and street.

He returned to order down Captn. Nicholas's Company and Buford's and meeting Nicholas's, which had been encamped near Col. Cary's he lead them pulling down the Garden Pails [fence] through Jones's Garden under Cover of his House, and lodged them in the House directing them to fire from the Window which they did with great Spirit. He then returned and lead Buford's Company in the same manner under Cover of Houses on the other Side of the Street placing some in a House and others at a Breast work on the Shore.

Here he found the Militia had crowded in, and incommoded the Rifle men. He therefore ordered them off and stationed them with Captn. Lynes on the back of the Town to prevent a surprise, by an Attack of Regulars who it was said had landed at Back water. Captn. Barron with the Town Militia and Part of Nicholas's Company were stationed at the Breast Work on the Wharf and across the Street. The Fire was now general and constant on both Sides. Cannon Balls Grape Shot and Musket Balls whistled over the Heads of our Men, Whilst our Muskets and Rifles poured Showers of Balls into their Vessels and they were so well directed that the Men on Board the Schooner in which Captain Squires himself commanded were unable to stand to their 4 Pounders which were not sheltered by a Netting and gave but one Round of them but kept up an incessant firing of smaller Guns and swivels, as did 2 Sloops and 3 Boats for more than an Hour and ¼ when they slipt their Cables and towed out except the Hawk Tender a Pilot Boat they had taken some Time before from a Man of Hampton, which was [captured].

In her they found 3 wounded Men 6 Sailors and 2 Negroes. Lieut. Wright who commanded her had been forced to jump over Board and was attended to the Shore by 2 Negroes and a white Man, one of the Negroes was shot by a Rifle Man across the Creek at 400 yds. distance. If Col. Woodford's Men whom he had ordered round to the Creeks Mouth could have got there soon enough they would undoubtedly have taken the little Squadron, for the Sailors could not possibly have towed them through their Fire. Although the nearest of the Tenders was 3 Hundred Yds, and the farthest about 450 from our Men, yet our Fire was so well directed that the Sailors were not able to stand to their Guns and serve them properly but fired them at Random at an Unaccountable Degree of Elevation.[30]

[30] Clark, ed., "John Page to Thomas Jefferson, 11 November, 1775," *Naval Documents of the American Revolution*, Vol. 2, 991-92

Lord Dunmore confirmed much of Page's account in a report to Lord Dartmouth:

> [The] *next day* [Oct. 27ᵗʰ] *the tenders returned again to the creek and ran up very near to the town. The rebels, being reinforced and taking possession of the houses, made a very heavy fire upon them but only killed one or two of the men and wounded several others, took a pilot boat that the gentlemen of the navy had made a tender of, and made seven men prisoners belonging to the Otter that were in her. The loss of the rebels must have been very inconsiderable if they suffered at all. The tenders were towed out of the creek by the boats with some difficulty.*[31]

Both of these second hand accounts were supported by accounts that appeared in the different Virginia Gazettes.

One account printed in Dixon and Hunter's Gazette just a day after the engagement, reported that

> *The enemy had, in the night, cut through the boats sunk, and made a passage for their vessels, which were drawn up close to the town, and began to fire upon it soon after the arrival of the* [riflemen] *from Williamsburg; but as soon as our men were disposed as to give them a few shot, they went off so hastily that our people took a small tender with five white men, a woman, and two slaves, 6 swivels, 7 muskets,*

---

[31] Davis, ed., "Lord Dunmore to Lord Dartmouth, 6 December, 1775 through February, 1776," *Documents of the American Revolution,* Vol. 3, 58

some small arms and other things, a sword, pistols, and several papers belonging to a Lieutenant Wright, who made his escape by jumping overboard, and swimming away with Mr. King's Negro man, who are on shore, and a pursuit, it is hoped, may overtake them. There were in the vessel two men mortally wounded, one is since dead, and the other near his end; besides which, we are informed, nine men were seen to be thrown overboard from one of the vessels. We had not a man wounded. The vessels went over to Norfolk, and we are informed the whole force from thence is intended to visit Hampton to-day. If they come, we hope our brave troops are prepared for them, as we can with pleasure assure the public that every part of them behaved with spirit and bravery, and are wishing for another skirmish.[32]

Another report in Pinkney's Gazette a week after the engagement provided a similar account:

In the night they cut a passage through the vessels that were sunk, and the next morning, about 8 o' clock (which was about half an hour after colonel Woodford and captain Bluford arrived with a rifle company) 5 tenders, to wit, a large schooner, 2 sloops, and 2 pilot boats, passed the passage they had cleared, and drew up a-breast of the town; they then gave 3 cheers, and began a heavy fire.

Colonel Woodford immediately posted captain Nicholas with his company on one side of the main

---

[32] Clark, ed., "Dixon and Hunter, *Virginia Gazette,* 28 October, 1775," *Naval Documents of the American Revolution,* Vol. 2, 630

street, and captain Bluford with his riflemen on the other, who were joined by the town company of militia; captain Lyne with his company was ordered to march to the cross roads just out of town to sustain any attack that might come from James or Back river. The colonel had been informed that men were landed from both these rivers. The musquet and rifle balls soon began to fly so thick that few men were seen upon the decks. The engagement continued very warm for some time.

At length they began to cut and slip their cables, and all cleared themselves, except one, which was boarded and taken by some of our men. They took in her the gunner and 7 men, 3 of whom were wounded, 2 mortally (both since dead), 1 white woman, and 2 negro men' lieutenant Wright, who commanded the prize, after receiving a ball, jumped overboard, and it is thought he was not able to reach the tenders. Several more jumped overboard; but it is not known what is become of them, or what damage is done on board of the other tenders. In those 2 different actions, Mr. Printer, officers and soldiers of the regular, minute, and militia acted with a spirit becoming freemen and Americans, and must evince that Americans will die, or be free![33]

A third account of the battle boldly asserted that the defenders of Hampton were eager to face Dunmore's forces again:

---

[33] Clark, ed., "Pinkney *Virginia Gazette*, 2 November, 1775," *Naval Documents of the American Revolution*, Vol. 2, 842-43

The troops in town are in high spirits, and wish for an attack in this quarter; they are all excellent marksmen, and fine, bold fellows. After all the firing at the houses in Hampton, there were only a few windows broke, and a door panel. Lord Dunmore may now see he has not cowards to deal with.[34]

All of these accounts included bold expressions of confidence from the Virginians who clearly viewed the engagement as a victory. More importantly, the two day engagement marked the first spilling of blood between the two sides. A threshold was crossed at Hampton, one that had been crossed in Massachusetts six months earlier, and there was no stepping back from it. The Revolutionary War had reached Virginia and in the weeks that followed it only intensified.

---

[34] Pinkney *Virginia Gazette*, 2 November, 1775

Chapter Eight

"[Dunmore] has made a compleat Conquest of Princess Ann and Norfolk...."

November: 1775

In retrospect, the outbreak of combat in Virginia seemed almost inevitable and in fact, overdue. On the eve of the engagement at Hampton, the Virginia Committee of Safety, citing, *"degrading and mortifying accounts from Norfolk"* of the local populace *"tamely"* submitting to Dunmore, had ordered Colonel Woodford's 2nd Virginia Regiment and five companies of the Culpeper Minute Battalion to cross the James River and march to Norfolk.[1]

The committee ignored the criticism and complaints generated by its choice of Colonel Woodford rather than Colonel Henry (who as commander of the 1st regiment should have taken precedence). Determined to halt Dunmore's free reign over Norfolk and Princess Anne Counties, the committee justified its decision by specifying Dunmore's misdeeds:

Among other acts of violence...Lord Dunmore & the officers of the navy not only harboured [many runaway]

---

[1] Scribner and Tarter, ed., *Revolutionary Virginia: The Road to Independence,* Vol. 4, 294, 269

Note: The Committee of Safety was created by the 3rd Virginia Convention and served as the de-facto government when the Virginia Convention was not in session.

slaves…but had actually seized by force one Woman slave & various other private property, & seized & carried on board the ships of War several freemen….[2]

Colonel Woodford's departure was delayed by events in Hampton and he did not rejoin his regiment in Williamsburg until early November. When he finally returned, he set out with his unit to execute the Committee of Safety's instructions:

You are to use your best endeavors for protecting and defending the persons and properties of all friends to the cause of America, and to this end, to attack, kill, or captivate all such as you shall discover to be in arms for annoying of those persons, as far as you shall judge it prudent to engage them.[3]

Colonel Woodford was also instructed to sever all communication and supplies between Norfolk and the countryside and to be especially watchful for slaves who may attempt to join or serve under Dunmore.[4] Lastly, the committee advised Colonel Woodford on how to treat the local population:

There may be many persons in those towns, or near them, who may be afraid in their present situation, exposed to the vengeance of the Navy, to declare their real sentiments. We think, therefore, that all

---

[2] Ibid., 269
[3] Scribner and Tarter, ed., "Orders for Colonel William Woodford,"
Revolutionary Virginia: The Road to Independence, Vol. 4, 271
[4] Ibid.

those who will continue peaceable, giving no
assistance or intelligence to our enemies, nor
attempting to annoy your troops, or injure our
friends, may for the present remain unmolested;
those Tories and others who take an active part
against us, must be considered as enemies;[5]

Skirmishes along the James River

Brimming with confidence after his victory at Hampton, Colonel Woodford was eager to cross the James River and lead his regiment and the minutemen, totaling over 650 men, to Norfolk.[6] A shortage of tents and the sudden arrival of a portion of Dunmore's flotilla off of Burwell's Landing and Jamestown Island (which threatened Williamsburg and obstructed the ferry crossing over the river) delayed Woodford's crossing. Numerous skirmishes between Dunmore's ships and rebel parties onshore occurred and although they resulted in little loss for either side, they added to Colonel Woodford's delay. An account in Pinkney's gazette reported that

Last Tuesday night (Oct. 31) we were alarmed with a
report that the pirates were cannonading
Jamestown.... A party of our men were immediately
ordered to go to that place for its defense , when they
discovered two tenders, which, in the whole, fired 26
swivels, without doing any other injury than striking

[5] Ibid.

[6] Julian P. Boyd, ed., "Edmund Pendleton to Thomas Jefferson, 16 November, 1775," *The Papers of Thomas Jefferson*, Vol. 1, (Princeton, NJ: Princeton University Press, 1950), 260-61

the house (ferry house) of Mr. Lester with one ball only.[7]

Thomas Jefferson, who sat in Congress in Philadelphia, learned of the skirmishes through a letter from the President of the Committee of Safety, Edmund Pendleton:

The same Squadron [that attacked Hampton] *came up James River some Days after and attempted to land at Jas. Town but were prevented by* [some] *Rifle men and as many Country People who happened to be there.*[8]

Another letter from an unidentified writer reported that

Last Wednesday afternoon [November 8th] *two tenders came up James River and fired a considerable time upon Jamestown, and at the centinels placed there from the camp, but did no other damage than driving two or three small balls through the ferry-house.*[9]

Purdie's gazette included a detailed account of one of the engagements:

[7] Clark, ed., "Pinkney, *Virginia Gazette*, 2 November, 1775," *Naval Documents of the American Revolution*, Vol. 2, 863

[8] Clark, ed., "John Page to Thomas Jefferson, 11 November, 1775," *Naval Documents of the American Revolution,* Vol., 2 991-92

[9] Clark, ed. "Extract of a Letter from Williamsburg, 14 November, 1775," *Naval Documents of the American Revolution*, Vol. 2, 1024
Printed in the London Chronicle, Jan. 11 to Jan. 13, 1776

"Yesterday, about one o' clock the King-Fisher sloop of war, and 3 tenders, came up to Burwell's ferry, and sent off a boat to board a small vessel lying near the shore, who were fired upon by the rifle guard stationed at that place; upon which they immediately tacked about, and made for the ship. The ship and tenders then began a heavy cannonading, and one six-pounder went through the storehouse at the water-side; many of the shot likewise hit the ferry-house, in which was a large family. Providentially, however, no person was hurt, either then, or about three hours afterwards, when they began a second cannonading, and fired three or four broadsides. They now lie before the ferry, and have not dared since to come near the vessel in shore.[10]

Although the rebel troops guarding the shore lacked cannon to counteract Dunmore's naval guns, the accuracy of their rifles seemed an adequate alternative. John Page described the effectiveness of the riflemen against Dunmore's tenders in a letter to Thomas Jefferson:

I can assure you that about 20 Rifle Men have disputed with the Man of War and her Tenders for...2 Days and they have hitherto kept...the Ferry Boats safe, which it is supposed they wish to burn. It is incredible how much they dread a Rifle.[11]

---

[10] Clark, ed., "Purdie, 10 November, 1775," *Naval Documents of the American Revolution*, Vol. 2, 973

[11] Clark, ed., "John Page to Thomas Jefferson, 11 November, 1775, *Naval Documents of the American Revolution*, Vol. 2, 991-92

Edmund Pendleton also acknowledged the role of the riflemen in defending the shoreline:

> *The life and Soul of* [the troops guarding the shore] *is Capt. Green's Company of Riflemen from Culpeper, who in three Reliefs of about 22 at a time, scour the River, and have in various Attempts, prevented a landing of the enemy. Last week the King Fisher and four tenders full of men came up to Burwells Ferry and made several attempts to land during three days stay, but never came nearer than to receive a discharge of the Rifles, when they retired with great precipitation, and 'tis Supposed the loss of some men.*[12]

Pendleton included a somewhat humorous account of a contest between a party of riflemen on shore and Dunmore's vessels for control of a small boat. He recollected that the riflemen and ships had

> *a droll contest for a small Cyder boat with one man, who lay between them about 200 yds. from shore. He attempted to come on Shore, when a Cannon Ball from the Navy passed just over his head and deter'd him. He then set sail for them, when a Rifle brought him too; he gave a Signal to the Man of War, who sent a Boat full of men for him, but When near, a Volley of Rifle bullets hurried them back without*

---

[12] Boyd, "Edmund Pendleton to Thomas Jefferson, *The Papers of Thomas Jefferson*, Vol. 1, 260-61

their prize. This was several times repeated 'til the
Fleet moved up to James Town....[13]

Dunmore's effort to prevent the passage of rebel troops across the James River was not the only factor behind Colonel Woodford's lack of progress southward. His force was also plagued by supply shortages. John Page described the challenges that confronted Colonel Woodford and his men:

The Committee had resolved a Month ago to send down the 2d Regimt & the Culpeper Battalion of Minute Men to Norfolk – but for want of Arms, Tents &ct. they were unable to march, the whole of them til the Day before Yesterday [November 9th] – A Detachment passed Jas River about 10 days since under Major Spotswood -- & were ordered to halt at Cobham til joined by the Col. & Remainder of the Forces—This Junction was delayed several Days for want of Necessaries, & several more by high Winds & the Interposition of the King Fisher & several Tenders – which obliged our Men to cross the River higher up than was at first intended – This Delay for Want of proper Arms &c has been very mortifying to us, & has proved fatal to our Friends in the Neighborhood of Norfolk.[14]

---

[13] Ibid.

[14] Clark, ed., "John Page to Thomas Jefferson, 11 November, 1775, *Naval Documents of the American Revolution*, Vol. 2, 991-92

By mid-November, Colonel Woodford had gathered sufficient supplies to resume his movement to Norfolk and he led his troops upriver to cross the James River unmolested.[15]

Although concern remained about the supply situation, Colonel Woodford and his men were confident that they could handle what lay ahead. The Virginia Committee of Safety estimated Dunmore's force in mid-November at:

The Otter and [Kingfisher] *-- 20 guns & 170 men each; in this number however are included those which man Occasionally the Following tenders Vizt*

4 Schooners
3 Sloops
3 Pilot Boats

On board these Tenders are some 4 & 3 pounders, besides Swivels.[16]

The Committee added that three other ships completed Dunmore's flotilla, the *William* mounted 14 guns, the *Eilbeck*, pierced for 22 guns but apparently not equipped with them, and an unknown brig that had just arrived from New York with 500 muskets. The size of the crews for these vessels was unknown.

In addition to his small flotilla, it was estimated that Dunmore's ground forces amounted to only 300 men, about

---

[15] Clark, ed., "John Page to Congress, 17 Nov., 1775," *Naval Documents of the American Revolution,* Vol. 2, 1061
  Note: Page provided Congress with a detailed explanation for Woodford's delay in marching south. (See next page)

[16] Clark, ed., "Virginia Committee of Safety to Congress, 11 November, 1775," *Naval Documents of the American Revolution*, Vol. 2, 993-94

half of which were British regulars from the 14th Regiment. The committee was unable to determine the number of Tories in Norfolk as, *"they are mixed with our Friends, who do not choose to declare until Our Army is there to protect them."*[17] The number of runaway slaves who had escaped to and now served under Dunmore was also difficult to determine; *"some Accots make them about 100 Others less."*[18]

The committee sheepishly acknowledged, *"the disgraceful patience & Suffering of some of our people,"* in Norfolk and the surrounding area to Dunmore's rule, but maintained that, *the exposed Situation of their Families & property, the want of Arms & Ammunition & their intermixture with Torys, who instead of Assisting were ready every moment to betray them,* accounted for their lack of resistance and resolve.[19] The committee concluded with a confession regarding the vulnerable inhabitants of Norfolk and southern Virginia:

> *We could not protect them, We had men enough, but were left to ransack every corner of the Country for Arms, tents & other necessarys. The few we collected were unavoidably retained here for the protection of our Magazine, Treasury & Records;*[20]

Many believed that the presence of Colonel Woodford and his force would intimidate the supporters of Dunmore and encourage greater resistance or at least non-cooperation from the local populace. Thus, it was urgent that he arrive in the region as soon as possible.

---

[17] Ibid.
[18] Ibid.
[19] Ibid.
[20] Ibid.

News from Philadelphia and England

In the midst of Woodford's efforts to cross the river and march to Norfolk, Virginia was troubled by a series of reports from outside the colony. In early November, Virginians learned of the sudden death of Peyton Randolph, long-time Speaker of the House of Burgesses, President of the Continental Congress, and the most prominent man in Virginia. The distinguished Virginia gentlemen collapsed suddenly at a dinner party in Philadelphia on October 22nd and never regained consciousness.

A week after the shocking news of Randolph's death, two new reports from outside the colony generated more angst in Virginia. The first appeared on November 9th in Pinkney's gazette where Virginians learned of King George III's August 23rd proclamation for suppressing rebellion and sedition in the colonies. Although the King had, to date, consistently backed the Ministry's efforts against the colonies, many colonists, including a number of Virginians, had hoped that George III might be influenced by Congress's Olive Branch petition (sent to Britain in July) and intercede on their behalf. The King's new proclamation made it clear that he would not:

The Proclamation for Suppressing Rebellion and Sedition
(issued August 23, 1775)

Whereas many of our subjects, in [many] *parts of our colonies and plantations in North America, misled by dangerous and ill designing men, and forgetting the allegiance which they owe to the power that protected and sustained them, after various disorderly acts committed in disturbance of the public peace, to the obstruction of lawful commerce, and to the oppression of our lawful subjects carrying on the same, have at length proceeded to an open and avowed rebellion, by arraying themselves in hostile manner to withstand the execution of the law, and traitorously preparing, ordering and levying war against us; and whereas there is reason to apprehend that such rebellion hath been much promoted and encouraged by the traitorous correspondence, counsels, and comfort, of* [many] *wicked and desperate persons within this realm:"*

...we do accordingly strictly charge and command all our officers, as well civil as military, and all other obedient and loyal subjects, to use their utmost endeavours to withstand and suppress such rebellion, and to disclose and make known all treasons and traitorous conspiracies....[21]

Accompanying the proclamation was a report that the British government had no intention to consider or reply to Congress's Olive Branch petition, *"as it is thought beneath the dignity of government to treat with or acknowledge an assembly, which has no constitutional or legal existence."*[22]

Such a response ran the risk of driving Virginians to the ultimate act of rebellion -- independence. One writer to Purdie's gazette -- who styled himself, "A VIRGINIAN" -- justified the consideration of independence -- which had in fact been discussed by at least one member of Congress whose

---

[21] Pinkney, *Virginia Gazette,* 11 November, 1775, 3
[22] Ibid.

letters were intercepted and published by Tories as proof that the true aim of Congress was independence:

A VIRGINIAN argued that,

> *The Tories lay great stress on certain intercepted letters from a delegate, as containing full proof that the Congress are aiming at independence; but let any impartial person read their resolves and petitions, and judge whether they had any such views.* [23]

The writer quoted a long passage from the intercepted letter that admittedly justified separation from Great Britain:

> *If we entertain a wish to be unconnected with Great Britain, it is because we have been cruelly and inhumanly treated by her. Could any nation be more completely dependent on another, and retain even a shadow of freedom, than America was, and still consents to be, on Great Britain? Was Britain satisfied with this in the year 1763? She was. Did America ask for any immunities she did not then enjoy? She does not.... What then is the new claim that they charge us with demanding, and for which they are endeavouring to butcher our people, and to lay waste our coasts? The truth is, the ministry and parliament have made a new demand necessary, by new oppressions, by repeated and aggravated insults, and by unheard of cruelties. It is high time to look to ourselves, to take care of our extended coasts, "to form a connexion with some other powers," since*

---

[23] Purdie, *Virginia Gazette*, "A VIRGINIAN," 10 November, 1775, 3

Great Britain insultingly, wantonly, and cruelly, has spurned us from her, "and to think of laying the foundation of a great empire."

"A VIRGINIAN" contended that,

This is what the delegate said he had in contemplation, and this is what the British ministry have made necessary and this it must be the duty of the Congress to do, if the king refuses to hear their petition, and to redress our grievances.[24]

Yet, the writer insisted that he and his fellow colonists remained loyal to King George III and looked to him to protect his oppressed subjects in America:

We still love our fellow-subjects in Britain; we still wish to be connected with them. Although our king has hitherto refused us relief, and suffers us to be inhumanly treated, we have not, and wish not to withdraw our allegiance from him, and are willing to attribute all of the cruel oppression under which we labour to the baleful influence of certain men, who, unhappily, have gained the confidence of their prince, and who are deadly enemies to his family, and would wish to see him driven from the throne. But whatever may be their design, and however basely we may be misrepresented by our enemies, we call God to witness for the purity of our intentions, look up to him as the all-powerful protector of

---

[24] Ibid.

*injured innocence, and firmly rely on him as a shield
in the day of battle.*[25]

In other words, the colonists still wished to be loyal to the
King as well as Britain and looked to King George III to
intercede on their behalf.

Not every Virginian shared the same faith in their monarch.
Thomas Jefferson was more direct in his criticism of the King,
writing to his exiled friend and cousin, John Randolph, in late
November from Philadelphia that, "*It is an immense
misfortune to the whole empire to have a king of such a
disposition at such a time…we are told that…he is the bitterest
enemy we have.*"[26] Jefferson observed that the engagement in
Hampton, "*has raised our country into a perfect phrensy,*" and
he warned that

> *To undo his empire* [King George] *has but one truth
> more to learn, that after colonies have drawn the
> sword there is but one step more they can take.*[27]

Jefferson mused that the British government's actions
suggested that they desired confrontation and, "*That* [final]
*step is now pressed upon us by the measures adopted as if they
were afraid we would not take it.*"[28] He assured his cousin
that he still desired reconciliation with Britain, but not at any
price, and lamented that more bloodshed seemed inevitable.

---

[25] Ibid.
[26] Clark, ed., Thomas Jefferson to John Randolph, 29 November, 1775,
   Naval Documents of the American Revolution, Vol. 2, 1193
[27] Ibid.
[28] Ibid.

Believe me Dear Sir there is not in the British empire a man who more cordially loves a Union with Gr. Britain than I do. But by the god that made me I will cease to exist before I yield to a connection on such terms as the British parliament propose and in this I think I speak the sentiments of America. We want neither inducement nor power to declare and assert a separation. It is will alone which is wanting and that is growing apace under the fostering hand of our king. One bloody campaign will probably decide everlastingly our future course; I am sorry to find a bloody campaign is decided on. [29]

Jefferson concluded with a bold exclamation:

We must drub you soundly before the sceptered tryant will know we are not mere brutes, to crouch under his hand and kiss the rod with which he deigns to scourge us. [30]

Virginians were largely unaware of Jefferson's views of the conflict in November, but when they learned about the British navy's destruction of the seaport town of Falmouth, Massachusetts (present day Portland, Maine) through their weekly gazettes, the shocking news only confirmed charges of oppression and brutality leveled at the British government. The doomed town fell under the guns of a small British naval flotilla in mid-October commanded by Lieutenant Henry Mowat. Lieutenant Mowat's force had been sent from Boston to "chastise" the Massachusetts coastline. Unfortunately for

---

[29] Ibid.
[30] Ibid.

the inhabitants of Falmouth, they were the first (and as it turned out only) town that Mowat "chastized". When the townsfolk failed to comply with Mowat's demand to surrender their cannon and small arms, (and avoid the destruction of their town) Lieutenant Mowat commenced a bombardment. Purdie's gazette reported that

> *About half past 9 in the morning, he began to fire from the four armed vessels, and in five minutes set fire to several houses. He continued firing till after dark the same day, which destroyed the largest part of the town.*[31]

A week later, Purdie's November 17th edition of the gazette provided more detail of the bombardment and reported that over 400 buildings were destroyed. The account also included a warning to the rest of the colonists that they could be next:

> *In consequence of the barbarous proceedings of the enemy at Falmouth, vast numbers of men have been employed, for several days past, in fortifying the towns and harbours of Portsmouth, Newbury Port, Beverly, Salem, and Marblehead. We hope our southern brethren are also preparing for defence, as no mercy is to be expected from our savage enemies.*[32]

A day earlier, a letter from Nathaniel Greene, an officer in the continental army serving in Massachusetts, appeared in Pinkney's gazette. Greene provided additional details of the attack and a more explicit warning for all of the coastal towns of British North America:

---

[31] Purdie, *Virginia Gazette,* 10 November, 1775, 2

[32] Purdie, *Virginia Gazette,* 17 November, 1775, 2-3

By an express that arrived from Falmouth last night, we learn that the greatest part of the town is in ashes. The enemy fired about 3000 shot into it, and a large number of carcases and bombs, which set the town on fire. The enemy landed once or twice to set fire to the shore....no person killed or wounded during the whole time of their firing; the enemy produced orders from admiral Graves to burn all the towns from Boston to Halifax. Captain Mowat informed the committee at Falmouth that there had arrived orders from England, about 10 days since, to burn all the sea port towns on the continent, which would not lay down and deliver up their arms, and give hostages for their future good behavior.... By these accounts we may learn what we have to expect....[33]

Not all of the news in the gazettes was bad. Accounts of a possible accommodation between Parliament and the colonies appeared regularly in the gazettes as did numerous reports of American success in Canada, which suggested that it was only a matter of time before British troops were driven out of that province.

Concerned and interested as Virginians were with events outside the colony, they had little time to dwell on them as their own conflict with Lord Dunmore suddenly intensified in mid-November with a disastrous military clash at Kemp's Landing, a few miles east of Norfolk.

---

[33] Pinkney, *Virginia Gazette,* 16 November, 1775, 3

Kemp's Landing

Ever since the repulse of Captain Squire's squadron at Hampton, which Lord Dunmore viewed as an *"overt act of rebellion"* the governor longed for a chance to strike the rebels. The efforts of his naval squadron off of Jamestown proved ineffectual, and he grew more frustrated. On November 7th Dunmore vented some of his frustration in a written proclamation, but withheld its release out of concern over his shortage of arms, powder, and troops. Dunmore had confessed to Lord Dartmouth a month earlier that the primary cause of his reluctance to, "raise the King's standard" and declare that open rebellion existed in Virginia (as many loyal Virginians urged him to do) was that he did not have the means to defend his supporters or crush the rebels. He did not want his supporters, many of whom had remained quiet, placed in the position of declaring themselves for the King when they were still vulnerable to assault and abuse from the rebels.[34]

The situation seemingly improved for Dunmore in mid-October with his numerous successful raids around Norfolk, but the engagement at Hampton was a setback and Dunmore remained hesitant to declare Virginia in open rebellion. He needed a significant victory to seize upon and on November 14th he and his troops produced such a victory when they routed a detachment of rebel militia at Kemp's Landing. Dunmore described the engagement to Lord Dartmouth in a long letter in early December:

---

[34] Clark, ed., "Lord Dunmore to Lord Dartmouth, 5 October, 1775," *Naval Documents of the American Revolution,* Vol. 2, 316-17

"I was informed that a hundred and twenty or thirty North Carolina rebels had marched into this colony to a place called the Great Bridge, about ten miles from hence and a very strong post, in order to join some of ours assembled not far from thence. This I was determined not to suffer. I accordingly embarked in the night in boats with all of the 14th regiment that were able to do duty, to the amount of 109 rank and file, with 22 volunteers from Norfolk. The Carolina people had fled the evening before, but hearing at the Bridge that there were between three and four hundred of our rebels assembled at a place called Kemp's Landing nine or ten miles from the Bridge, I was then determined to disperse them if possible.[35]

Captain Samuel Leslie, who commanded the British regulars with Dunmore, described what followed:

After directions had been given to erect a kind of wooden fort to secure the pass [over the Great Bridge], we proceeded nine or ten miles farther to Kemp's landing where we were informed there were three or four hundred of the rebels ready to receive us, under the command of a Colonel Lawson. When we arrived within sight of Kemps landing our advance guard was twice fired upon by the rebels, who had concealed themselves in very thick woods on

---

[35] Davies, ed., "Lord Dunmore to Lord Dartmouth, 6 December through 18 February, 1776," *Documents of the American Revolution*, Vol. 12, 58-59

*the left of the road, but upon our rushing in among
them they were very soon totally routed.*[36]

The inexperienced and undoubtedly nervous rebels had
fired too soon, exposing their position without inflicting any
damage to Dunmore's advance guard. Dunmore
acknowledged that his troops were surprised by the ambush
but recovered quickly and routed the rebels:

About a mile from [Kemp's Landing] *our advanced
party was fired upon by the rebels from a thicket
before our people discovered them. I immediately
ordered the main body, who were within two or three
hundred paces, to advance and then detached a party
with the volunteers to outflank them. At the same
time the advanced guard with the grenadiers rushed
into the woods. The rebels fled on all quarters; we
pursued them above a mile, four of five were killed, a
good many wounded, and eighteen taken prisoners
on that and the following day....*[37]

Captain Leslie credited the militia's precipitous flight through
difficult terrain (which hampered pursuit) as the primary
reason most of them escaped:

*Their very precipitate flight and the closeness of the
woods prevented our giving a much better account of*

---

[36] Clark, ed., "Captain Samuel Leslie to General William Howe,
26 November, 1775," *Naval Documents of the American Revolution,*
Vol. 2, 1148

[37] Davies, ed., "Lord Dunmore to Lord Dartmouth, 6 December through
18 February, 1776," *Documents of the American Revolution,*
Vol. 12, 59

them. It is said that some of them ran away even before the firing began. However, five of the rebels, that we know of, were killed, two drowning in endeavouring to escape across a creek, and by all accounts a great many of them were wounded. We had only one Grenadier wounded in the knee. Colonel Hutchings and seven of the rebels were taken in the field, and Colonel Lawson & eight others were taken a day or two after.[38]

Initial accounts from the rebel side described a much different engagement, one in which the militia stood bravely, inflicted losses on the enemy, but were eventually overwhelmed and forced to retreat. An account in Purdie's gazette just days after the battle claimed, *"Our people fought a considerable time, and it is thought did great execution, but were at last over powered, and forced to retreat...."*[39] John Page, who was not at the battle, provided a similar account to Congress. *"[Dunmore's] Party came up with our Militia, who defended themselves with Bravery, but being overpower'd by Numbers were totally defeated."*[40]

Mr. Page's understanding of the battle changed considerably over the next week as more reliable reports reached him. On November 24th, Page sent his friend, Thomas Jefferson, a more accurate account of the battle that was highly critical of the militia's conduct:

---

[38] Clark, ed., "Captain Samuel Leslie to General William Howe, 26 November, 1775," *Naval Documents of the American Revolution,* Vol. 2, 1148

[39] Clark, ed., "Pinkney, Virginia Gazette, 17 November, 1775," *Naval Documents of the American Revolution,* Vol. 2, 1062

[40] Clark, ed., "John Page to Congress, 17 November, 1775," *Naval Documents of the American Revolution,* Vol. 2, 1061

Two hundred of the Militia of Pr. Ann were as judiciously disposed of in Ambush as could be, and the Ministerial Tools fell into it very completely, but were so faintly attacked, that although the advanced Guards were thrown into Confusions, They with little or no Loss gained a compleat Victory. Not a tenth Part of the Militia fired. They fled in a most dastardly manner. Col. Hutchings, who served in the Ranks as a common Soldier, and several others stood bravely, but being shamefully deserted were taken Prisoners.[41]

Dunmore's Proclamation

The Battle of Kemp's Landing was a humiliating defeat for the rebels and an important victory for Lord Dunmore; he seized upon his success to issue a proclamation. Like the King's proclamation published a week earlier, Virginians reacted to Dunmore's proclamation with disbelief and anger:

Dunmore's Proclamation

As I have ever entertained Hopes, that an Accommodation might have taken Place between Great Britain and this Colony, without being compelled by my Duty to this most disagreeable but now absolutely necessary Step, rendered so by a Body of armed Men unlawfully assembled, firing on His Majesty's Tenders, and the formation of an Army, and that Army now on their March to attack his Majesty's Troops and destroy the well disposed

[41] Boyd, ed., "John Page to Thomas Jefferson, 24 November, 1775," *The Papers of Thomas Jefferson*, Vol. 1, 264-65

Subjects of this Colony. To defeat such treasonable Purposes, and that all such Traitors, and their Abettors, may be brought to Justice, and that the Peace, and good Order of this Colony may be again restored, which the ordinary Course of the Civil Law is unable to effect; I have thought fit to issue this my Proclamation, hereby declaring, that until the aforesaid good Purposes can be obtained, I do in Virtue of the Power and Authority to ME given, by His Majesty, determine to execute Martial Law, and cause the same to be executed throughout this Colony: and to the end that Peace and good Order may the sooner be restored, I do require every Person capable of bearing Arms, to resort to His Majesty's STANDARD, or be looked upon as Traitors to His Majesty's Crown and Government, and thereby become liable to the Penalty the Law inflicts upon such Offences; such as forfeiture of Life, confiscation of Lands, &c. &c And I do hereby further declare all indentured Servants, Negroes, or others (appertaining to Rebels,) free that are able and willing to bear Arms, they joining His Majesty's Troops as soon as may be, for the more speedily reducing this Colony to a proper Sense of their Duty, to His Majesty's Crown and Dignity. I do further order, and require, all His Majesty's Leige Subjects, to retain their Quitrents, or any other Taxes due or that may become due, in their own Custody, till such Time as Peace may be again restored to this at present most unhappy Country, or demanded of them from their former salutary Purposes, by Officers properly authorized to receive the same.[42]

All three gazettes published a long reply to Dunmore's proclamation that blamed him for much of the conflict and challenged his true desire for a peaceful accommodation and reconciliation with the colonists:

Although lord Dunmore, in this proclamation, insidiously mentions his having till now entertained hopes of an accommodation, yet the whole tenour of his conduct, for many months past, has had the most direct and strongest tendency to widen the unhappy breach, and render a reconciliation more difficult. For what other purpose did he write his false and inflammatory letters to the ministers of state? Why did he, under cover of the night, take from us our powder, and render useless the arms of our publick magazine?... Why did he, secretly and treacherously lay snares for the lives of our unwary brethren [in the powder magazine]. *Why did he, under idle pretence, withdraw himself from the seat of government, where alone he could, had he been willing, have done effectual service to our country? Why, by his authority, have continual depredations been since made upon such of our countrymen as were situated within reach of ships of war and tenders? Why have our towns been attacked, and houses destroyed? Why have the persons of many of our most respectable brethren been seized upon, torn from all*

[42] Clark, ed., "Lord Dunmore's Proclamation," *Naval Documents of the American Revolution*, Vol. 2, 920

their connections, and confined on board of ships?
Was all this to bring about a reconciliation? Judge
for yourselves, whether the injuring of our persons
and properties be the readiest way to regain our
affections. After insulting our persons, he now
presumes to insult our understandings also. Do not
believe his words, when his actions so directly
contradict him, if he had a desire to restore peace
and order, as he professes, it was to be upon terms
which would have been disgraceful, and in the end
destructive of everything dear and valuable.[43]

The response went on to indict the British government for its
conduct and justify the actions of the colonists:

Consider again the many attempts which have been
made to enslave us. Nature gave us equal privileges
with the people of Great Britain...and we have never
resigned to them these rights, which we derived from
nature. But they have endeavoured, unjustly, to rob us
of them: They have made acts of parliament, in which
we in no manner concurred, which dispose of our
property; acts which abridge us of liberties we once
enjoyed, and which impose burthens and restraints upon
us too heavy to be born. Had we immediately taken up
arms to assert our rights, and to prevent the exercise of
unlawful power, though our cause would have been just,
yet our conduct would have been precipitate, and so far
blameable. We might then, with some shadow of justice,
have been charged with rebellion, or a disposition of

---

[43] Purdie, *Virginia Gazette*, 24 November, 1775, 2

rebel. But this was not the way we behaved. We petitioned once and again, in the most dutiful manner; we hoped that the righteousness of our cause would appear, that our complaints would be heard and attended to; we wished to avoid the horrours of a civil war, and so long proceeded in this fruitless track that our not adopting a more vigorous opposition seemed rather to proceed from a spirit of...fear than of peace and loyalty, and all that we gained was to be more grievously oppressed. At length, we resolved to withhold our commerce from Britain; and, by thus affecting her interest, oblige her to redress our grievances. But in this also we have been disappointed: Our associations have been deemed unlawful combination, and opposition to government; we have been entirely deprived of our trade to foreign countries, and...amongst ourselves, and fleets and armies have been sent to reduce us to a compliance with the unjust and arbitrary demands of the British minister, and corrupt parliament. Reduced to such circumstances, to what could we have recourse but to arms? Every other expedient having been tried, and found ineffectual, this alone was left; and this we have, at last, unwillingly adopted. If it be rebellion to take up arms in such a cause as this, rebellion then is not only a justifiable, but an honourable thing....[44.]

Virginians, both free and enslaved, were urged to reject Dunmore's call for support and warned that, "*the time will*

---

[44] Ibid.

*come when these invaders of the rights of human kind will
suffer the punishment due to their crimes.*"[45]

Dunmore's Force Grows

Hundreds of Virginians in Norfolk and Princess Anne
County ignored such appeals. *"The Whole Countys of Norfolk
and Princess Ann to a Man has come in to the Standard Which
is Now erected in Norfolk and taken the Oaths of Allegiance to
his Majesty,"* reported a inhabitant of Portsmouth.[46]   A
resident of Norfolk noted that

> *The day after* [Dunmore hoised the King's Standard]
> *the whole Country flocked to it, took the oath of
> allegiance...and declared their readiness to defend
> his Majesty's Crown & dignity.... I can assure you
> that L. Dunmore is so much admired in this part of
> the County that he might have 500 Volunteers to
> march with him to any part of Virginia.*"[47]

The swell of support for Dunmore alleviated some of the
concern residents of Norfolk felt for their city. Given the
contempt that many Virginians held for Norfolk (due to the
city's perceived lack of resistance to Dunmore) and aware of
the impending arrival of Colonel Woodford's troops, most of
the city's inhabitants feared that Norfolk was destined for

---

[45] Ibid.

[46] Scribner and Tarter, ed., "Robert Shedden, Portsmouth, VA to Mr. John
Shedden, In Glasgow: An Intercepted Letter, 20 November, 1775,"
Revolutionary Virginia, The Road to Independence, Vol. 4, 439

[47] Scribner and Tarter, ed., "John Brown, Virginia, to Mr. William Brown,
An Intercepted Letter, 21 November, 1775," *Revolutionary Virginia,
The Road to Independence*, Vol. 4, 445

destruction. The strong response to Dunmore's proclamation, however, caused at least one "rebel" in Norfolk to report that, *"The face of affairs* [in the city has entirely changed] *which encourages them to think they can with the assistance of the King's Ships and Forces here withstand the whole united Force of the rest of the Colony...."*[48]

Lord Dunmore appeared to share this new assessment of the situation and confidently informed General Howe that

> *Immediately on* [the victory at Kemp's Landing] *I issued the inclosed Proclamation which has had a Wonderful effect as there are not less than three thousand that have already taken and signed the inclosed Oath.*[49]

Dunmore was particularly pleased with the impact of the most controversial part of his proclamation, freedom for runaway servants and slaves of rebels who agreed to fight under the King's standard. Dunmore reported to General Howe that

> *The Negroes are flocking in also from all quarters which I hope will oblige the Rebels to disperse to take care of their families, and property, and had I but a few more men here I would March immediately to Williamsburg my former place of residence by which I should soon compel the whole Colony to Submit.*[50]

---

[48] Scribner and Tarter, ed., "Cary Mitchell, Norfolk, Directed to Colo. Cary Selden at Hampton: A Plea for Intervention, 23 November, 1775," *Revolutionary Virginia, The Road to Independence*, Vol. 4, 456

[49] Clark, ed., "Lord Dunmore to General William Howe, 30 November, 1775," *Naval Documents of the American Revolution*, Vol. 2, 1209-11

[50] Ibid.

Dunmore emphasized his need for arms and supplies, (two items he hoped General Howe might assist him with), and detailed his efforts to organize the large number of runaway slaves and servants and loyal Virginians who had answered his call to arms:

> *We are in great want of small Arms, and if two or three light field pieces and their Carriages could be Spared they would be of great Service to us, also some Cartridge paper of which not a Sheet is to be got here, and all our Cartridges expended.*
>
> *I have...ordered a Regiment (Called the Queens own Loyal Virginia Regiment) of 500 men to be raised immediately consisting...Ten Companys each of which is to consist...50 Privates.*
>
> *You may observe by my Proclamation that I offer freedom to the Slaves, (of all Rebels) that join me, in consequence of which there are between two and three hundred already come in and these I form into a Corps as fast as they come in giving them white Officers and Non Commissioned Officers in proportion....*[51]

Governor Dunmore's optimism carried into early December and was expressed in a report to Lord Dartmouth in which he acknowledged the significance of his victory at Kemp's Landing and the positive results of his proclamation:

> *The good effects of this most trifling success* [at Kemp's Landing] *was manifested strongly by the zeal which the people showed on this occasion to His Majesty's service when unawed by the opposite party.*

[51] Ibid.

I was immediately determined to run all risks for their support, and on that very day ordered the enclosed proclamation to be published, erected the King's standard (alias a pair of colours as I had no better), and the next day I suppose not less than a hundred of those very men who were forced into the field against me the day before came and took the enclosed oath.[52]

Dunmore added a cautionary note concerning the strength of his forces, citing the inexperience of most of his new volunteers, but concluded by asserting that he was making progress towards building an adequate naval and land force to challenge the rebels:

Your lordship may observe that about three thousand have taken that oath, but of this number not above three or four hundred at most are in any degree capable of bearing arms, and the greatest part of these hardly ever made use of the gun; but I hope a short time (if they are willing) will make them as good if not better than those who are come down to oppose them....

I am now endeavouring to raise two regiments, one of white people (called the Queen's Own Loyal Virginia Regiment), the other of Negroes called Lord Dunmore's Ethiopian Regiment. I wrote to your lordship in one of my former letters that I had taken ships into His Majesty's service, as also sloops and schooners as tenders, all of which I am now arming as well as I can;

---

[52] Davies, ed., "Lord Dunmore to Lord Dartmouth, 6 December through 18 February, 1776," *Documents of the American Revolution*, Vol. 12, 59

so your lordship sees I am equipping a fleet, raising an army, and all this without any order from your lordship or any other person....[53]

Dunmore's success was grudgingly acknowledged by his opponents. A week after the engagement, John Page wrote his friend, Thomas Jefferson, who was still in Philadelphia, and describe the impact of Dunmore's victory at Kemp's Landing:

Our late Governor...was so elated with this Victory, that he erected the Standard, published the Proclamation you will see in our Papers...and marched about making Prisoners of a Number of People, and administering an Oath of his own Framing, by which the Congress, Conventions, and Committees are utterly disclaimed and all obedience and Submission, I suppose promised to Acts of Parliament. In short he has made a compleat Conquest of Princess Ann and Norfolk and Numbers of Negroes, and Cowardly Scoundrels flock to his Standard.[54]

However, Page was not completely discouraged by the turn of events. He remained hopeful that Colonel Woodford and his force would soon turn the situation around for the rebels:

We hope soon to put a stop to his Career and recover all we have lost, for Col. Woodford after innumerable Delays for want of Arms &c. &c. is by this Time very near him with his Regiment and 250 Minute Men of the Culpeper Batalion and a Number of Volunteers....[55]

---

[53] Ibid.

[54] Boyd, ed., "John Page to Thomas Jefferson, 24 November, 1775," *The Papers of Thomas Jefferson*, Vol. 1, 264-65

[55] Ibid.

Great Bridge

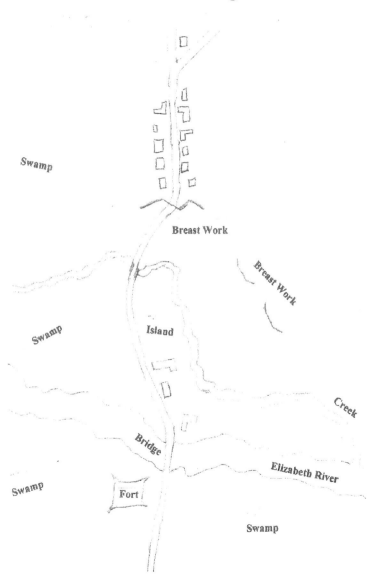

Swamp

Breast Work

Breast Work

Swamp

Island

Creek

Swamp

Bridge

Elizabeth River

Fort

Swamp

Swamp

Chapter Nine

Great Bridge

December: 1775

Colonel William Woodford's mixed force of 2nd Virginia regulars and Culpeper minutemen reached Suffolk, 15 miles southwest of Portsmouth, on November 25th.[1] A day earlier, Woodford had sent Charles Scott, now a Lieutenant Colonel in the 2nd Virginia Regiment, ahead towards the Great Bridge with over 200 troops to watch over the enemy. Ever the cautious officer, Woodford ordered Scott to, "*be safe kept 'till my arrival.*"[2]

The Great Bridge was actually a long, narrow, manmade causeway with multiple wooden bridges spanning the southern branch of the Elizabeth River and its tributaries and marshland. Norfolk lay eleven miles north of the main bridge span and since most of the terrain south of Norfolk was marsh and swamp, the Great Bridge road was the primary southern land route to Norfolk.

Lieutenant Colonel Scott was eager to confront Dunmore's small force of "*Tories and Blacks*" (who had removed the planks from the main bridge and were posted in a small wooden stockade fort on the north bank of the river adjacent to the dismantled bridge) but Colonel Woodford cautioned

---

[1] D.R. Anderson, ed., "Colonel Woodford to Edmund Pendleton, 26 November, 1775," in "The Letters of Colonel William Woodford, Colonel Robert Howe, and General Charles Lee to Edmund Pendleton," *Richmond College Historical Papers*, (June, 1915), 104

[2] Ibid.

against such a move.[3]   Woodford informed Scott that a severe shortage of ammunition and arms made it impossible for him to march to the Great Bridge until, "*a number of Ball is run, cartridges made, arms Repair'd &ct. &ct.*" [4] The best he could do to support Scott was to send him two more companies of regulars under Major Alexander Spotswood.

In Norfolk, Lord Dunmore and his force of British regulars, runaway slaves, and Tory volunteers, braced for the arrival of Woodford's troops. Word of their approach in late November had prompted Dunmore to withdraw the troops of the 14th Regiment from their quarters in Gosport – a village next to Portsmouth where they had spent much of the fall sheltered in Andrew Sprowles shipyard buildings -- and redeploy them across the Elizabeth River in Norfolk.[5]   Captain Samuel Leslie, the ranking officer of the 14th Regiment, informed General William Howe in Boston of their move and pledged to do everything possible to prevent the destruction of Norfolk:

> *We took possession of this town the 23d Inst and are now busy intrenching ourselves in the best manner we can, as a large body of the Rebels consisting of eight or nine hundred men are within ten or twelve miles of us. They marched from Williamsburg about a fortnight ago with an intention to pillage and burn this town, which however we shall do everything that is possible to prevent....*[6]

---

[3] Ibid.

[4] Ibid.

[5] Clark, ed., "Captain Samuel Leslie to General William Howe, 26 November, 1775," *Naval Documents of the American Revolution,* Vol. 2, 1148

[6] Ibid.

Lord Dunmore realized that to maintain his base of operation at Norfolk he had to prevent the rebels from gaining control of the Great Bridge. He explained the bridge's importance, and his efforts to defend it, to General Howe:

Having heard that a thousand chosen Men belonging to the Rebels, a great part of which were Rifle men, were on their March to attack us here so to cut off our provisions, I determined to take possession of the pass at the great Bridge which Secures us the greatest part of two Counties to supply us with provisions. I accordingly ordered a Stockade Fort to be erected there, which was done in a few days, and I put an Officer and Twenty five men to Garrison it, with some Volunteers and Negroes.[7]

Bloodshed and Stalemate at the Great Bridge

While Colonel Woodford hurried to make cartridges and equip his troops in Suffolk with functioning firearms, Lieutenant Colonel Scott's advance guard entrenched at the Great Bridge and skirmished with Dunmore's forces. A few days after their first clash, Scott reported that, *"We have been well informed that we killed 16 negroes and 5 white men the first day we got to this place."*[8] Although Dunmore's losses were likely much lighter, (he claimed that after a week of skirmishes he had only suffered one or two slightly wounded soldiers while the "rebels" had 15-20 soldiers killed) the

[7] Clark, ed., "Lord Dunmore to General William Howe, 30 November, 1775," *Naval Documents of the American Revolution*, Vol. 2, 1209-11

[8] Clark, ed., "Lt. Col. Charles Scott to a Williamsburg Correspondent, 4 December, 1775," *Naval Documents of the American Revolution*, Vol. 2, 1274-75

number of casualties that both sides claimed to have inflicted on the other suggest that the skirmish was heated.[9]

The bulk of Lieutenant Colonel Scott's force of nearly 200 men was posted behind hastily built breastworks on the southern edge of the causeway. Sentries were posted forward of the breastworks at night, on what was essentially an island, with the Elizabeth River to the north, a small creek to the south (fifty yards in front of the "rebel" breastworks), and marsh on either side of the causeway. Hidden amongst a few buildings and piles of debris close to the dismantled bridge and Dunmore's fort, Scott's sentries were positioned to alarm the "rebels" if the enemy approached at night. For their own safety, the sentinels were withdrawn back to the breastworks at dawn each day.

Scott also detached a party of about 40 troops five miles downriver to guard a crossing point and prevent a surprise from the enemy.[10] The day after they arrived, this detachment was attacked by Dunmore's troops. Lieutenant Colonel Scott reported that

> *Lieutenant Tibbs, who had the command of the boat guard, about 5 miles from this place, was attacked by a party of the king's troops, and several negroes, upon which some of our people gave ground; but mr. Tibbs, with 4 of his people, maintained his post until I reinforced him with 50 men under capt. [George] Nicholas, who were obliged to pass through a very*

---

[9] Clark, ed. "Lord Dunmore to Lord Dartmouth, 6 December through 18 February, 1776," *Documents of the American Revolution*, Vol. 12, 59

[10] Anderson, ed., "Colonel Woodford to Edmund Pendleton, 4 December, 1775," *Richmond College Historical Papers*, 106

heavy fire from the enemy. Before they got to the place, mr. Tibbs had beat off the enemy, and killed 7 of their men, amongst whom was the commander of the party.[11]

Although Lord Dunmore's account of the engagement suggests that Scott's casualty estimate was once again inflated, another heated engagement had obviously occurred between the two sides.

Colonel Woodford, with the main body of troops, reached the Great Bridge soon after this skirmish, on December 2nd. Woodford described the situation he found to Edmund Pendleton, President of the Committee of Safety:

I...found the Enemy Posted on the opposite side of the Bridge, in a Stockade Fort, with two four pounders, some swivels & wall pieces, with which they keep up a constant Fire, have done no other damage than kill'd Corpl Davis with a cannon ball....[12]

Woodford estimated that Dunmore's fort was defended by 250 men, most of who were escaped slaves commanded by sergeants of the 14th Regiment.[13] A handful of Tories also manned the fort. Woodford speculated that it might be possible to capture it, but the presence of cannon meant that its conquest would come at a very high cost in lives:

---

[11] Clark, ed., "Lt. Col. Charles Scott to a Williamsburg Correspondent, 4 December, 1775," *Naval Documents of the American Revolution,* Vol. 2, 1274-75

[12] Anderson, ed., "Colonel Woodford to Edmund Pendleton, 4 December, 1775," *Richmond College Historical Papers,* 106

[13] Ibid.

The Enemys Fort, I think, might have been taken, but not without the loss of many of our Men, their Situation is very advantageous, & no way to attack them, but by exposing most of the Troops to their Fire upon a large open Marsh.[14]

As for his own fortifications, Colonel Woodford reported that

We have raised a strong Breastwork upon the lower part of the street joining the Causeway, from which Centries are posted at some old Rubbish not far from the Bridge (which is mostly destroy'd).[15]

Although he believed that he held a strong position, Woodford was concerned about his limited supply of gunpowder and the lack of blankets and shoes for his men.

Our small stock of Ammunition will be soon expended, & I must request another supply; an additional Blanket to each soldier [will] *be very necessary, if to be had. The men are tolerably well at present, but the dampness of this Ground, without straw (which is not to be had) must soon lay many of them up, & Houses that are tolerably safe from the Enemy's Cannon, can only be procured for a few.*[16]

One officer who likely found shelter in one of the "safe" houses out of range (but not earshot) of Dunmore's guns was Lieutenant Colonel Scott. It had been over a week since he had led his detachment ahead of Woodford's main body to the

---

[14] Ibid., 107
[15] Ibid., 107
[16] Ibid., 108-09

Great Bridge and now that reinforcements had arrived Scott allowed himself to relax. He wrote to a friend that

> *Last night was the first of my pulling off my clothes for 12 nights successively. Believe me, my good friend, I never was so fatigued with duty in my whole life;* [17]

Despite the large number of reinforcements, it is likely that Lieutenant Colonel Scott still found it difficult to rest, "*We still keep up a pretty heavy fire between us, from light to light. We have only lost two men, and about half an hour ago one of our people was shot through the arm, which broke the bone near his hand.*"[18]

The skirmishing continued downriver as well. Within days of his arrival, Colonel Woodford sent a large detachment of troops under Colonel Edward Stevens of the Culpeper Minutemen across the river to encircle and surprise Dunmore's guard at the crossing. Woodford reported that

> *They crossed about midnight, & got to the Enemy's centinals without being discover'd, one of them challenged & not being answer'd, Fired at our party, the fire was returned by our men, & an over Eagerness at first, & rather a backwardness afterwards, occasion'd some confusion, & prevented the Colo's plan from being so well executed as he intended, however, he* [burned] *their Fortification & House, in which one negro perished, killed one dead upon the*

---

[17] Clark, ed., "Lt. Col. Charles Scott to a Williamsburg Correspondent, 4 December, 1775," *Naval Documents of the American Revolution*, Vol. 2, 1274-75

[18] Ibid.

spott, & took two others prisoners...this party (consisting of 26 Blacks & 9 Whites) escaped under the cover of night, he also took four new Muskets.[19]

Lieutenant Colonel Scott confirmed Woodford's account and reported that Colonel Stevens's force of 100 men faced about 30 and, *"being too eager, began the fire...without orders, and kept it up very hot for near 15 minutes."*[20]

Although the bulk of the enemy guard escaped, their post was destroyed. Discovered among the captured troops and abandoned equipment were altered musket balls designed to split into quarters upon impact. Colonel Woodford was outraged by the discovery and sent one to Williamsburg for the Committee of Safety and 4th Virginia Convention to see:

The bearer brings you one of the Balls taken out of the cartridges found upon the negro Prisoners, as they were extremely well made, & no doubt by some of the non comd. Officers of the Regulars, will submit it to the Convention, by who's orders this Horrid preparation was made for the Flesh of our Countrymen, the others are prepared in the same manner, likewise all that have been found in the Houses &ct; – I have never suffer'd a soldier of mine to do a thing of this kind – nor will I allow it to be done for the future, notwithstanding this provocation....[21]

[19] Anderson, ed., "Colonel Woodford to Edmund Pendleton, 5 December, 1775," *Richmond College Historical Papers*, 110
[20] Clark, ed., "Lt. Col. Charles Scott to a Williamsburg Correspondent, 5 December, 1775," *Naval Documents of the American Revolution*, Vol. 2, 1299
[21] Anderson, ed., "Colonel Woodford to Edmund Pendleton, 5 December, 1775," *Richmond College Historical Papers*, 112

Two nights later, the "rebels" struck again, attacking the same post – re-occupied and reinforced by Dunmore with 70 men. This time Lieutenant Colonel Scott led the attack with 150 men. Colonel Woodford described the engagement to Edmund Pendleton:

> *I have the pleasure to inform you...that my detachment last night under the Command of Lieut. Colo. Scott beat up the Quarters of the Enemys other party, who I inform'd you had again taken post opposite our Boat Guard, they killed one white man & three negro's, took three of the Latter Prisoners, two of which are wounded, one mortally, with six Muskets & 3 Bayonetts.*[22]

Woodford explained that bad luck prevented his troops from surprising the enemy:

> [Colonel Scott] *unluckily fell in with a cart coming from Norfolk, guarded by four men, some distance from the Enemy's post, who Fired upon our party & alarm'd them, otherways there is no doubt most of their men would have fallen into our Hands, their number 70, Scott's party, 150, who all escaped unhurt, one man only was grazed by a Ball in the Thumb.*[23]

---

[22] Anderson, ed., "Colonel Woodford to Edmund Pendleton,
7 December, 1775," *Richmond College Historical Papers*, 114
[23] Ibid.

Williamsburg Grows Anxious

Although Colonel Woodford's troops had successfully engaged Dunmore's forces in a number of skirmishes, apprehension grew among the leaders in Williamsburg that time was running out to drive Dunmore from Norfolk. Thomas Ludwell Lee of Stafford County summarized the concern of many in the 4th Virginia Convention and Committee of Safety:

> *Our Army has been for some time arrested in its march to Norfolk by a redoubt, or stockade, or hog pen, as they call it here, by way of derision, at the end of this bridge. Tho,' by the way, this hog pen seems filled with a parcel of wild-boars, which we appear not overfond to meddle with. My apprehension is that we shall be amused at this outpost, until Dunmore gets the lines at Norfolk finished; where he is now entrenching, & mounting cannon, some hundreds of negro's being employ'd in the work.*[24]

Another member of the Committee of Safety, John Page of Gloucester County, expressed a similar concern and declared that desperate measures might be necessary to dislodge Dunmore from Norfolk:

> *Col. Woodford with 600 Men has been hitherto prevented from passing the Great Bridge on his Way to Norfolk by a Body of Negroes headed by Scotch*

---

[24] Clark, ed., "Thomas Ludwell Lee to Richard Henry Lee, 9 December, 1775," *Naval Documents of the American Revolution*, Vol. 3, 26-27

Men [Tories] *& a few Regulars -- & I make no Doubt that before he can pass, Norfolk will be made impregnable by Land – it is capable of being strongly fortified on a small Neck of Land near the Church where it is said Ld D has for some Time past employd several hundred Negros – The only Way I conceive that Town can be taken without Cannon, must be, by taking Advantage of the Night & throwing into it by Water 3 or 400 resolute Fellows -- & make a bold push at the Sloops of War at the same Time.*[25]

Fortunately for the 'rebels", Page's dire assessment proved unnecessary; reinforcements from North Carolina, reportedly with cannon, were on the way.

Lieutenant Colonel Scott acknowledged as early as December 4th the arrival of a company of troops from North Carolina and reported that hundreds more (with artillery) were marching behind them:

The Carolina forces are joining us. One company came in yesterday, and we expect 8 or 900 of them by to-morrow, or next day at farthest, with several pieces of artillery, and plenty of ammunition and other warlike stores.[26]

---

[25] Clark, ed., "John Page to Richard Henry Lee, 9 December, 1775," *Naval Documents of the American Revolution*, Vol. 3, 25-26

[26] Clark, ed., "Lt. Col. Charles Scott to a Williamsburg Correspondent, 4 December, 1775," *Naval Documents of the American Revolution*, Vol. 2, 1274-75

On the same day that Scott mentioned the reinforcements, Colonel Woodford also revealed his expectation of reinforcements with cannon from North Carolina:

> *They inform me I might expect 4 or 500 men with some Cannon & ammunition at this place tonight, & that they had 900 men at different places in Motion to join us.*[27]

Colonel Woodford also reported that his troops

> *Were now making the necessary preparations to raise Batterys for these Cannon upon the most advantageous Ground to play upon their Fort & send a large detachment at the same time to intercept their Retreat.*[28]

Even Lord Dunmore believed that a large reinforcement of rebel troops were on their way to the Great Bridge and this belief helped spur him to action:

> *The Rebels had procured some Cannon from North Carolina,* [which were expected to arrive any day] *and that they were also to be reinforced from Williamsburg, and knowing that our little Fort was not in a Condition to withstand anything heavier than Musquet Shot, I thought it advisable to risqué Something to save the Fort.*[29]

---

[27] Anderson, ed., "Colonel Woodford to Edmund Pendleton, 4 December, 1775," *Richmond College Historical Papers*, 108

[28] Ibid.

[29] Clark, ed., "Lord Dunmore to Lord Dartmouth, 13 December, 1775," *Naval Documents of the American Revolution*, Vol. 3, 140-41

Dunmore Decides to Attack

A significant factor behind Lord Dunmore's ill fated decision to attack Colonel Woodford's breastworks on December 9th was inaccurate information he reportedly received from a deserter from the rebel camp. Colonel Woodford reported after the battle that

> *A servant belonging to major* [Thomas] *Marshal, who deserted the other night from col.* [Charles] *Scott's party, has completely taken his lordship in. Lieutenant* [John] *Batut...informs, that this fellow told them not more than 300 shirtmen were here; and that imprudent man* [Dunmore] *catched at the bait, dispatching capt. Leslie with all the regulars (about 200) who arrived at the bridge about 3 o'clock in the morning.*[30]

It remains uncertain whether the deserter purposefully or accidently misled Dunmore about Woodford's troop strength, but it appears likely that Dunmore viewed the report of such a small number of rebels across the causeway as an opportunity that would soon disappear when the expected reinforcements arrived. As a result, on the evening of December 8th,

---

[30] Clark, ed., "Colonel Woodford to Edmund Pendleton, 9 December, 1775," *Naval Documents of the American Revolution*, Vol. 3, 28

Note: Colonel Woodford repeated this account in a second letter to Edmund Pendleton the next day. A similar account was included in the *Annual Register for the Year 1776*, p. 29
"It has been said, that we were led into this unfortunate affair, through the designed false intelligence of a pretended deserter, who was tutored for the purpose."

Dunmore rushed his own reinforcements, including most of the regulars of the 14th Regiment (approximately 120 under Captain Leslie) as well as a detachment of sailors (to help man the fort's cannon) and about 60 Tory volunteers, from Norfolk to the fort at the Great Bridge. A British midshipman from the *HMS Otter* participated in the battle recalled that

> *Our troops, with about sixty Townsmen from Norfolk, and a detachment of Sailors from the ships, among whom I had the honour to march, set out from Norfolk to attack once more the Rebels at the great bridge....We arrived at the Fort half an hour after three in the morning, and, after refreshing ourselves, prepared to attack the Rebels in their intrenchments.*[31]

These reinforcements joined the garrison of Tories, runaway slaves, and handful of regulars already at the fort early in the morning of December 9th.

Dunmore's Plan

Worried that his small wooden fort would not hold against an assault by the soon to be reinforced rebels, Lord Dunmore chose to strike preemptively. In his report to Lord Dartmouth after the battle, Dunmore explained that his plan called for,

---

[31] Clark, ed., "Letter from a Midshipman on Board H.M. Sloop Otter, 9 December, 1775," *Naval Documents of the American Revolution,* Vol. 3, 29

Two Companies of Negroes to make a detour, [cross the river] *and fall in behind the Rebels a little before break of Day in the morning, and just as Day began to break, to fall upon the rear of the Rebels, which* [Dummore] *expected would draw their attention, and make them leave the breast work they had made near the Fort,* [Captain Leslie] *was then with the Regulars, the Volunteers and some recruits to sally out of the Fort, and attack* [the rebel] *breast work....*[32]

Dunmore hoped that the distraction caused by his black troops would allow his main force under Captain Samuel Leslie to cross the Elizabeth River and narrow causeway and storm the rebel breastworks against limited opposition. Unfortunately for Dunmore, miscommunication, or perhaps a misunderstanding of orders, prevented the diversionary attack from occurring. Dunmore noted after the battle that

The Negroes by some mistake were sent out of the Fort to guard a pass, where it was thought the Rebels might attempt to pass, and where in fact some of them had Crossed a Night or two before, burnt a house or two, and returned; Captain Leslie not finding the Negroes there, imprudently Sallied out of the Fort at break of Day in the morning....[33]

---

[32] Clark, ed., "Lord Dunmore to Lord Dartmouth, 6 December through 18 February, 1776," *Naval Documents of the American Revolution,* Vol. 3, 141

[33] Ibid.
   Note: Lord Dunmore claimed in this letter that he left the discretion of whether to actually launch the attack with Captain Leslie.

The Attack

Under cover of the dim light of dawn Captain Leslie's force of approximately 350 men advanced from their fort and hastily re-laid the bridge planks that had been removed weeks earlier.[34]   If the handful of sleepy rebel pickets sheltered by the buildings on the island initially failed to notice the activity at the bridge, the discharge of the fort's cannon undoubtedly drew their attention that way.   Startled at what they saw, the rebel sentries opened fire upon Dunmore's troops.   One rebel account of the battle included high praise for the sentries:

> *The conduct of our sentinels I cannot pass over in silence. Before they quitted their stations they fired at least three rounds as the enemy were crossing the bridge, and one of them, who was posted behind some shingles, kept his ground till he had fired eight times, and after receiving a whole platoon, made his escape over the causeway into our breast works.*[35]

As the handful of sentinels scurried back to the rebel earthworks 150 yards to the rear, their comrades behind the breastwork began to stir, realizing that the gunfire they heard was not the normal morning salute of the past few days.

Four hundred yards south of the earthworks at the main rebel encampment, however, few of Colonel Woodford's

---

[34] Clark, ed., "Letter to John Pinkney, 20 December, 1775,"
Naval Documents of the American Revolution, Vol. 3, 186-89
[35] Ibid.
> Note: The brave sentinel who stood his ground for so long was twenty year old Billy Flora, a free born black volunteer from Norfolk.

troops, who had just been awakened by reveille, took notice of the distant gunfire. Major Thomas Spotswood recalled

> *We were alarmed this morning by the firing of some guns after reveille beating, which, as the enemy had paid us this compliment several times before, we at first concluded to be nothing but a morning salute.*[36]

Colonel Woodford had a similar reaction:

> *After reveille beating, two or three great guns, and some musquetry were discharged from the enemy's fort, which, as it was not an unusual thing, was but little regarded.*[37]

The situation was much different at the rebel breastworks. Realizing that they were under attack, the commander of the guard, Lieutenant Edward Travis ordered his small detachment of approximately sixty men, *"to reserve their fire till the enemy came within the distance of fifty yards."*[38] A small stream lay about 50 yards in front of the rebel breastworks and served as an excellent range marker for the rebels. To their front across the narrow 150 yard causeway were more than five times their number of enemy troops with two cannon that one rebel recalled were, *"planted on the edge*

---

[36] Peter Force, ed., "Major Spotswood to a Friend in Williamsburgh, 9 December, 1775," *American Archives*, Vol. 4, 224

[37] Clark, ed., "Col. Woodford to Edmund Pendleton, 10 December, 1775," *Naval Documents of the American Revolution*, Vol. 3, 39-40

[38] Force, ed., "Major Spotswood to a Friend in Williamsburgh, 9 December, 1775," *American Archives*, Vol. 4, 224 and Clark, "Letter to Pinkney, 20 December, 1775", *Naval Documents of the American Revolution*, Vol. 3, 186-89

of the island, facing the left of our breast-work, [and] *played briskly...upon us."*[39]

Joining the cannon at the edge of the island were the Tory and Black soldiers of Dunmore, over 200 strong. Behind them rose the smoke of several buildings -- formerly the outposts of the rebel sentries but now torched by Dunmore's troops. Captain Leslie remained on the island with the Tory and Black troops while Captain Charles Fordyce led the British regulars of the 14th Regiment, 120 strong in a column six abreast, across the narrow causeway to storm the rebel earthworks.[40]

Back in the main "rebel" camp, the gravity of the situation had finally become apparent. Major Spotswood recalled

> *I heard Adjutant Blackburn call out, Boys! stand to your arms! Colonel Woodford and myself immediately got equipped, and ran out; the Colonel pressed down to the breastwork in our front, and my alarm-post being two hundred and fifty yards in another quarter, I ran to it as fast as I could, and by the time I had made all ready for engaging, a very heavy fire ensued at the breastwork, in which were not more than sixty men;*[41]

The heavy fire that Major Spotswood heard came from Lieutenant Travis's guard detail and a few brave reinforcements who had rushed forward at the first alarm.

---

[39] Clark, "Letter to Pinkney, 20 December, 1775," *Naval Documents of the American Revolution,* Vol. 3, 186-89

[40] Clark, "Letter from a Midshipman on Board H.M. Sloop Otter, 9 December, 1775" *Naval Documents of the American Revolution,* Vol. 3, 29

[41] Force, ed., "Major Spotswood to a Friend in Williamsburgh, 9 December, 1775," *American Archives,* Vol. 4, 224

Lieutenant John Marshall of the Culpeper Minutemen (and future Chief Justice of the Supreme Court) was at Great Bridge and remembered

> *As is the practice with raw troops, the bravest rushed to the works, where, regardless of order, they kept up a heavy fire on the front of the British column.*[42]

The valor of some of the rebels was also acknowledged by Major Spotswood, who proudly noted in a letter immediately after the engagement that as the redcoats approached the breastworks with fixed bayonets, "*Our young troops received them with firmness, and behaved as well as it was possible for soldiers to do.*"[43] In his own letter after the battle, Colonel Woodford also commented on the rebel fire from the breastwork, writing that, "*perhaps a hotter fire never happened, or a greater carnage, for the number of troops.*"[44]

The hot fire delivered upon the British originated not only from the breastworks directly in front of them, but also from breastworks on a small island west of the causeway. Riflemen from the Culpeper Minute Battalion manned this position and poured deadly enfilade fire into the British column's right flank.[45] According to one American account, the intense rebel small arms fire from both positions

---

[42] John Marshall, *The Life of George Washington*, Vol. 2, (Fredericksburg, VA: The Citizens Guild of Washington's Boyhood Home, 1926), 132

[43] Force, ed., "Major Spotswood to a Friend in Williamsburgh, 9 December, 1775," *American Archives*, Vol. 4, 224

[44] Clark, ed., "Col. Woodford to Edmund Pendleton, 10 December, 1775," *Naval Documents of the American Revolution*, Vol. 3, 39-49

[45] *The Annual Register for the Year 1776*, 4th ed. 29

Threw [the advancing British regulars] *into some confusion, but they were instantly rallied by a Captain Fordyce, and advanced along the causeway with great resolution, keeping up a constant and heavy fire as they approached. The brave Fordyce exerted himself to keep up their spirits, reminded them of their ancient glory, and waving his hat over his head, encouragingly told them the day was their own. Thus pressing forward, he fell within fifteen steps to the breast-work. His wounds were many, and his death would have been that of a hero, had he met it in a better cause.*[46]

A British participant in the battle noted that

[The rebel] *fire was so heavy, that, had we not retreated as we did, we should every one have been cut off. Figure to yourself a strong breast-work built across a causeway, on which six men only could advance a-breast; a large swamp almost surrounding them, at the back of which were two small breast-works to flank us in our attack on their intrenchments. Under these disadvantages it was impossible to succeed; yet our men were so enraged, that all the intreaties, and scarcely the threats of their Officers, could prevail on them to retreat; which at last they did.*[47]

---

[46] Clark, "Letter to Pinkney, 20 December, 1775", *Naval Documents of the American Revolution*, Vol. 3, 186-89

[47] Clark, "Letter from a Midshipman on Board H.M. Sloop Otter, 9 December, 1775," *Naval Documents of the American Revolution*, Vol. 3, 29

Captain Fordyce, riddled with buck and ball, was one of many redcoats to fall before the American earthworks. Strewn about the ground just a few paces from the Virginians were over thirty British dead and wounded. One rebel officer described a scene of bloody carnage before the breastworks:

The scene, when the dead and wounded were bro't off, was too much; I then saw the horrors of war in perfection, worse than can be imagin'd; 10 and 12 bullets thro' many; limbs broke in 2 or 3 places; brains turning out. Good God, what a sight![48]

Captain Fordyce and twelve British privates lay dead in front of the breastworks and nearly a score of wounded redcoats, including Lieutenant John Batut, who led the British advance guard, were taken prisoner. An American observer noted that

The progress of the enemy was now at an end; [the survivors] *retreated over the causeway with precipitation, and were dreadfully galled in their rear. Hitherto, on our side only the guard, consisting of twenty five, and some others, upon the whole, amounting to not more than ninety, had been engaged. Only the regulars of the 14th regiment, in number one hundred and twenty, had advanced upon the causeway, and about two hundred and thirty tories and negroes had, after crossing the bridge, continued upon the island.*[49]

---

[48] Charles Campbell, ed., "Richard Kidder Meade to Theodorick Bland Jr., 18 December, 1775" *The Bland Papers*, Vol. 1, (1840) 38-39

[49] Clark, "Letter to Pinkney, 20 December, 1775," *Naval Documents of the American Revolution*, Vol. 3, 186-89

Although the British assault had been repulsed, the battle was yet over, for Captain Leslie rallied his men on the island:

> *The regulars, after retreating along the causeway, were again rallied by captain Leslie, and the two field pieces continued to play upon our men.*[50]

While Dunmore's troops re-grouped around their cannon, Colonel Woodford led troops from the main camp through heavy artillery fire to reinforce the breastworks:

> *It was at this time that colonel Woodford was advancing down the street to the breast-work with the main body, and against him was now directed the whole fire of the enemy. Never were cannon better served, but yet in the face of them and the musquetry, which kept up a continual blaze, our men marched on with the utmost intrepidity.*[51]

Major Spotswood also noted the severity of the enemy cannon fire:

> *The* [enemy] *field pieces raked the whole length of the street, and absolutely threw double-headed shot at far as the church, and afterwords, as our troops approached, cannonaded them heavily with grapeshot.*[52]

---

[50] Ibid.

[51] Ibid.

[52] Force, ed., "Major Spotswood to a Friend in Williamsburgh, 9 December, 1775," *American Archives*, Vol. 4, 224

Spotswood credited divine providence for protecting all but one man, who was wounded in the hand, from the intense artillery barrage.[53]

With Dunmore's battered troops stubbornly remaining on the island, Colonel Woodford sent Colonel Edward Stevens with the Culpeper minutemen to reinforce the riflemen on the left flank. The rebel militia poured more deadly enfilade fire from their rifles upon Captain Leslie's troops. The accurate American rifle fire finally prompted Captain Leslie, who was dismayed at his losses (especially that of his nephew, Lieutenant Peter Leslie) to withdraw to the fort. One "rebel" noted that

> *The enemy fled into their fort, leaving behind them the two field pieces, which, however, they took care to spike up with nails. Many were killed and wounded in the flight, but colonel Woodford very prudently restrained his troops from urging their pursuit too far. From the beginning of the attack till the repulse from the breast work might be about fourteen or fifteen minutes; till the total defeat upwards of half an hour. It is said that some of the enemy preferred death to captivity, from fear of being scalped, which lord Dunmore inhumanly told them would be their fate should they be taken alive. Thirty one, killed and wounded, fell into our hands, and the number borne off was much greater.* [54]

---

[53] Ibid.

[54] Clark, "Letter to Pinkney, 20 December, 1775," *Naval Documents of the American Revolution*, Vol. 3, 186-89

Aftermath

The Battle of Great Bridge was a decisive victory for the Virginians. Colonel Woodford proudly described it as, "*a second Bunker's Hill affair, in miniature; with this difference, that we kept our post, and had only one man wounded in the hand.*"[55] More than one observer attributed the lack of rebel casualties to providence (divine intervention). The British 14th Regiment of Foot, on the other hand, was shattered in the attack. Their brave, bold assault on the rebel breastworks cost them half their men. Colonel Woodford initially estimated Dunmore's losses at 50 men, noting that some of their dead and wounded were taken back to the fort. He reported that

> *We buried 12, besides...*[Captain Fordyce] *(him with all the military honors due to his rank) and have prisoners lieutenant Batut, and 16 privates; all wounded; 35 stands of arms and accoutrements, 3 officers* [fusils], *powder, ball, and cartridges, with sundry other things, have likewise fallen into our hands.*[56]

Dunmore's report on the 14th Regiment's losses (which was presumably more accurate) claimed 3 officers and 17 men killed and 1 officer and 43 men wounded.[57] The number of casualties among Dunmore's Tory and black soldiers is unknown.

---

[55] Clark, ed., "Colonel Woodford to Edmund Pendleton, 10 December, 1775," *Naval Documents of the American Revolution*, Vol. 3, 39-40
[56] Ibid.
[57] Clark, ed., "Lord Dunmore to Lord Dartmouth, 13 December, 1775" *Naval Documents of the American Revolution*, Vol. 3, 141

Calm settled over the causeway soon after the battle as Colonel Woodford dispatched an officer under a flag of truce to allow Captain Leslie to collect his dead and wounded from the battlefield.[58] One observer reported that

> *The work of death being over, every one's attention was directed to the succor* [assistance] *of the unhappy sufferers, and it is an undoubted fact, that captain Leslie was so affected with the tenderness of our troops towards those who were yet capable of assistance, that he gave signs from the fort of his thankfulness for it.*[59]

With both sides secure behind their fortifications the sun set with no more fighting. Captain Leslie abandoned the fort shortly after dark and marched the entire garrison to Norfolk. Lord Dunmore explained Captain Leslie's decision in a letter a few days later:

> *This loss having so much weakened our before but very weak Corps, and Captain Leslie being much depressed by the loss of Lieutenant Leslie, his Nephew, and thinking that the Enemy elated with this little advantage they had gained over us, might force their way across the branch, either above, or below, and by that means, Cut off the Communication between us, determined to evacuate the Fort, and accordingly left it soon after it was dark, and returned with the whole to*

---

[58] Clark, ed., "Colonel Woodford to Edmund Pendleton, 9 December, 1775," *Naval Documents of the American Revolution*, Vol. 3, 28

[59] Clark, "Letter to Pinkney, 20 December, 1775," *Naval Documents of the American Revolution*, Vol. 3, 186-89

this place [Norfolk]; *The Rebels however remained at the Bridge for a day or two.*[60]

Colonel Woodford's troops took possession of the abandoned fort in the morning and found it in disarray. Woodford reported that

We have taken possession of [the fort] *this morning, and found therein the stores mentioned in the enclosed list, to wit, 7 guns, 4 of them sorry, 1 bayonet, 29 spades, 2 shovels, 6 cannon, a few shot, some bedding, a part of a hogshead of rum, two or more barrels, the contents unknown, but supposed to be rum, 2 barrels of bread, about 20 quarters of beef, half a box of candles, 4 or 5 dozen of quart bottles , 4 or 5 iron pots, a few axes and old lumber; the spikes, I find, cannot be got out of the cannon without drilling.*[61]

Woodford made another observation that led him to believe the enemy had suffered much greater than he realized:

From the vast effusion of blood on the bridge, and in the fort, from the accounts of the sentries, who saw many bodies carried out of the fort to be interred and other circumstances, I conceive their loss to be much greater than I thought it yesterday, and the victory to be complete.[62]

---

[60] Clark, ed., "Lord Dunmore to Lord Dartmouth, 13 December, 1775," *Naval Documents of the American Revolution,* Vol. 3, 140-41

[61] Clark, ed., "Colonel Woodford to Edmund Pendleton, 10 December, 1775," *Naval Documents of the American Revolution,* Vol. 3, 40-41

[62] Ibid.

The 14th Regiment's heavy losses apparently had a strong impact on Captain Leslie. The Virginia Committee of Safety in Williamsburg gleefully reported a few days after the battle that

> *The Regulars, disgusted, refused to fight in junction with Blacks; and Captain Leslie, we are told, declared no more of his troops should be sacrificed to whims, and put them on board the ships, in consequence of which Norfolk is abandoned, and we expect is now occupied by our troops, who were on their march there when our last account was dispatched. Many Tories are come to us, and their cases now under consideration. More notorious ones are gone on board the vessels, which have in them very valuable cargoes.*[63]

Norfolk Abandoned

Whether Captain Leslie refused to cooperate further with Lord Dunmore (as the committee's account suggests) is unclear, but it does appear that Leslie had had enough of the land campaign. Upon his midnight arrival in Norfolk, he immediately placed his troops onboard two ships anchored off of the city.[64] The condition of his force, combined with the accounts of the battle, greatly unsettled the Tory and black troops who had worked so diligently constructing entrenchments on the edge of town. One Tory, who sought refuge aboard the H.M.S. *Kingfisher*, noted that

---

[63] Clark, ed., "Letter from the Virginia Committee of Safety, 16 December, 1775," *Naval Documents of the American Revolution*, Vol. 3, 132

[64] Clark, "Letter from a Midshipman on Board H.M. Sloop Otter, 9 December, 1775," *Naval Documents of the American Revolution*, Vol. 3, 29 and "Thomas Macknight to Rev. Macknight, 26 December, 1775," *Naval Documents of the American Revolution*, Vol. 3, 260-61

This unfortunate attack [at the Great Bridge] *which was made in the morning about sunrise dispirited most people.... All thoughts of defending the Town were given up. The Soldiers are gone on board two Transports and those who have dared to be active in supporting Government are under the necessity also of taking refuge in vessels. Such as had not that in their power are left to the mercy of the Rebels who have taken possession of the Town – a single regiment a few weeks ago would have reduced this colony to a sense of its duty. God only knows when it will be done, now....*[65]

Dunmore lamented the panic of his supporters and their abandonment of the trenches protecting the city, but speculated to Lord Dartmouth that they might be convinced to return if only reinforcements were sent to him:

This Town standing on a Neck of Land and by that means pretty easily made defensible against an undisciplined Army [prompted] *the few remaining Inhabitants (most of whom are Natives of Great Britain) to throw up a breast work and to defend themselves, for which I had supplied them with the few Arms I had, but this work not being quite finished the News of this little advantage the Enemy had gained,* [at the Great Bridge] *threw them all into despair, and they at present give themselves up as lost, but their transitions from hope to despair are very quick, should any assistance (which God grant) they possibly may be*

---

[65] Clark, ed., "Thomas Macknight to Reverend Macknight, 26 December, 1775," *Naval Documents of the American Revolution*, Vol. 3, 260-61

induced to return to their Trenches, when they may soon put themselves in such a Situation as will make it very difficult for the Enemy to force them.[66]

Dunmore's speculation proved to be wishful thinking for no assistance was coming, at least for him. Instead, Colonel Woodford's force was reinforced by hundreds of North Carolinians under Colonel Robert Howe. Together they led their troops northward from Great Bridge to Norfolk, occupying the abandoned city on December 14th. Offshore, the harbor was filled with desperate families fearful of retribution for their support of Dunmore. The governor described the bleak scene to Lord Dartmouth:

All who were friends of Government took refuge on board of the Ships, with their whole families, and their most valuable Effects, some in the Men of War, some in their own Vessels, others have chartered such as were here, so that our Fleet is at present Numerous tho' not very powerful. I do assure your Lordship it is a most melancholy sight to see the Numbers of Gentlemen of very large property with their Ladies and whole families obliged to betake themselves on board of Ships, at the Season of the year, hardly with the common necessarys of Life, and great numbers of poor people without even these, who must have perished had I not been able to supply them with some flour, which I purchased from His Majesty's service some time ago....[67]

---

[66] Clark, ed., "Lord Dunmore to Lord Dartmouth, 13 December, 1775," *Naval Documents of the American Revolution*, Vol. 3, 141-42

[67] Ibid. 142

Onshore, the streets of Norfolk were full of "rebel" troops. With the arrival of Colonel Robert Howe and his North Carolina troops, the "rebel" force had swelled to well over a thousand men. While most encamped out of range of the naval cannon, guard detachments were posted along the shore to observe Dunmore's activities and warn of a possible attack. Some of the sentries succumbed to the temptation to take pot shots at Dunmore's ships, especially the *Otter*, and frequent flags of truce went back and forth between the two sides concerning the issue of whether the sporadic gunfire from shore was authorized:

Norfolk Dec. 15, 1775
Captain Squire's compliments to the commanding officer, informs him that several musquet balls were last night fired at the king's ship from some people at Norfolk. Captain Squire did not return the fire, from a supposition it was done out of wantonness. Captain Squire does not mean to fire on the town of Norfolk unless first fired at; must beg to know if any hostile intention was meant to his Otter sloop....

The Virginia Officers' Reply
Colonel Howe's and colonel Woodford's compliments to captain Squire, and assure him they gave no orders to fire upon the Otter, and conceive the musquet balls mentioned in captain Squire's message to have come from our guard, who fired by mistake upon one of our own parties.[68]

---

[68] Clark, ed., "Captain Matthew Squire R.N., to the Officer Commanding at Norfolk, 15 December, 1775," *Naval Documents of the American Revolution*, Vol. 3, 119

In another message delivered by a midshipman aboard the Otter, Captain Squire threatened, *" that if another shot was fired at the Otter*, [the rebels] *must expect the town to be knocked about their ears."*[69]

Oddly enough, despite all of the bloodshed and confrontation over the past month, both sides remained civil, to the point that Lord Dunmore had the audacity to inquire (through Captain Squires) whether the navy and army would be allowed to obtain fresh provisions and water from shore.[70] Colonel Woodford shared the reply that he and Colonel Howe (who was the ranking colonel) sent back:

> *Col. Howe and col. Woodford's compliments to capt. Squire, and return him for answer to his message, that as his majesty's troops and ships of war have long since committed hostilities upon the persons and property of the good people of this colony, and have actually taken and imprisoned several private gentlemen, and others, who did not bear arms at the time, our express orders are, to prevent, to the utmost of our power, any communication whatever between the said troops and ships of war and this town, or any part of this Colony.*[71]

---

[69] Clark, ed., "Letter from a Midshipman on board H.M. Sloop Otter, 14 December, 1775," *Naval Documents of the American Revolution*, Vol. 3, 103

[70] Clark, ed., "Lord Dunmore to Lord Dartmouth, 13 December, 1775," *Naval Documents of the American Revolution*, Vol. 3, 142

[71] Clark, ed., "Colonel Woodford to Edmund Pendleton, 17 December, 1775," *Naval Documents of the American Revolution*, Vol. 3, 140

Interestingly, when Captain Henry Bellew of the H.M.S. *Liverpool* (mounting 28 guns) arrived in Norfolk in mid-December and posed a similar request for fresh provisions, Colonel Howe referred the request to Edmund Pendleton and the Committee of Safety:

Yesterday, by a flag of truce, I received a letter from capt. Bellew.... Though col. Woodford and myself were sensible it was our duty to withhold from him...those supplies he wishes to obtain, yet the moderate conduct he has pursued, and the sentiments of humanity by which he seems to be actuated, induced us to delay an answer till to-day, and to couch it in terms which cannot but show him, that occasion, not inclination, had influence upon our conduct. Capt. Bellew's letter was brought to us by one of his lieutenants; he expressed for himself, and every officer on board, the reluctance they should feel, if compelled by necessity, they should be obliged by marauding parties to snatch from the indigent farmers of this colony those provisions they were so willing to purchase..... Col. Woodford and myself beg leave to submit it to the consideration of your Honourable Board, whether we are to show any indulgence to those people, and, if we are, to what bounds we are to extend it. [72]

While Colonel Howe waited for a reply, news from across Hampton Roads bolstered the "rebels" already high spirits.

---

[72] Clark, ed., "Extract of a Letter from Col. Robert Howe to Edmund Pendleton, 25 December, 1775," *Naval Documents of the American Revolution*, Vol. 3, 244

Chapter Ten

"Let our countrymen view and contemplate the scene!"

Norfolk is Destroyed

January: 1776

Virginians were excited to learn in late December that their success against Dunmore extended beyond land engagements. In the days following the Battle of Great Bridge, Captain James Barron of Hampton scored a small naval victory over one of Dunmore's tenders off of Hampton (capturing its crew of 17) and also seized two vessels loaded with salt, a commodity that was in desperately short supply in Virginia.[1] Barron's efforts attracted the praise of the Committee of Safety, who highlighted the captain's accomplishments in a letter to Maryland's Congressional delegates:

There is a Captain Barron, a brave, experienced seaman, whose company of Militia, being also stationed [at Hampton] *has been very active in small excursions of vessels, in Hampton Roads, from which he has brought in several vessels belonging to Tories, protected others, the property of friends, from falling into the enemy's hands,*

---

[1] Clark, ed., "Pinkney, *Virginia Gazette*, 23 December, 1775," *Naval Documents of the American Revolution*, Vol. 3, 220

and has taken two tenders, on their way to the Eastern-Shore for provisions, manned with Americans and slaves.[2]

The Committee of Safety was so impressed with Captain Barron that it announced that it had, *"strengthened his hands, by empowering him to fit out three armed vessels, to be employed in this way, and have great confidence in his prudence and valor."*[3]

Fostering a fledging navy was not the only thing Virginia's leaders in Williamsburg had done to strengthen their military capabilities. In mid-December the 4th Virginia Convention, meeting in Williamsburg, expanded the colony's infantry forces from two regiments of regulars to nine and increased the length of service for the 700 plus officers and men of each regiment to two years.[4]

The Convention also issued a stinging reply to Dunmore's November proclamation of martial law, asserting that he had assumed powers, *"which the king himself cannot exercise,"* had no real interest in reconciling with the colonies, and was, *"one of the principal causes of the misfortunes under which we now labour."*[5] The Convention indicted Dunmore as a, *"rigid executioner"* of *"that system of tyranny adopted by the ministry and parliament,"* and proclaimed that Dunmore, *"ever zealous in support of tyranny...hath broken the bonds of society, and trampled justice under his feet."*[6] In addition to

---

[2] Clark, ed., "Virginia Committee of Safety to Maryland Delegates in Congress, 29 December, 1775," *Naval Documents of the American Revolution*, Vol. 3, 296-97

[3] Ibid.

[4] Scribner and Tarter, ed., *Revolutionary Virginia, The Road to Independence*, Vol. 5, 125-128

[5] Ibid.

[6] Ibid.

the long standing charges against Dunmore of pillaging, plundering, and illegal seizure of property and slaves, was a new accusation. The Convention accused Dunmore of devising a scheme with his aide, Dr. John Connolly, to encourage the Indians in the west to enter the conflict as Dunmore's ally and sweep down upon northern Virginia in April to unite with Dunmore in Alexandria.[7] Connolly's capture by Maryland authorities in the fall of 1775 ended this scheme, but the fact that Dunmore was willing to employ Indians (on top of runaway slaves) against the colonists was one more reason many Virginians wished the governor harm.

Even General Washington, stuck in the siege lines outside of Boston, recognized the danger of allowing Dunmore to continue to operate in Virginia. In a letter to Richard Henry Lee written the day after Christmas, Washington candidly shared his views on what should happen to Lord Dunmore:

> *If, my Dear Sir, that Man* [Dunmore] *is not crushed before Spring, he will become the most formidable Enemy America has – his strength will Increase as a Snow ball by Rolling; and faster, if some expedient cannot be hit upon to convince the Slaves and Servants of the Impotencey of His designs...I do not think that forcing his Lordship on Ship board is sufficient; nothing less than depriving him of life or liberty will secure peace to Virginia.*[8]

---

[7] Scribner and Tarter, ed., "Major John Connolly to General Thomas Gage: Captured Proposals," *Revolutionary Virginia,* The Road to Independence Vol. 4, 82-83

Printed in Purdie's Virginia Gazette on December 22, 1775

[8] Chase and Runge, "George Washington to Richard Henry Lee, 26 December, 1775," *The Papers of George Washington,* Vol. 2, 611

For the time being, Lord Dunmore was safe, protected in Norfolk harbor by the guns of the British navy, specifically, the 36 gun *Liverpool*, 18 gun *King Fisher*, 16 gun *Otter*, a sloop with 8 guns, the *Dunmore* (formerly Eilbeck, number of guns unknown) and 6 or 7 tenders armed with a few 3 and 4 pound cannon and swivel guns. Scores of other vessels were also anchored in the harbor, sheltering Tory refugees who had nowhere else to go.[9]

Destruction of Norfolk

Like Lord Dunmore and the miserable inhabitants of the floating Tory town in the harbor, Captain Bellew of the *Liverpool* and Captain Squire of the *Otter*, were increasingly annoyed by the daily harassment of the "shirtmen" (in the form of random small-arms fire at the ships and daily formations and sentinels in full view of the harbor). Numerous warnings to curtail the provocations were sent ashore under flags of truce, but the conduct continued. Finally, in late December, Captain Bellew issued an ultimatum:

Captain Bellew to Colonel Howe, Dec. 30, 1775

As I hold it incompatible with the Honor of my Commission to suffer Men in Arms against their Sovereign and the Laws, to appear before His Majesty's Ships I desire you will cause your Centinels in the Town of Norfolk to avoid being seen, that Women and Children may not feel the effects of

---

[9] Clark, ed., "Ships in Norfolk and Hampton Roads, 30 December, 1775, *Naval Documents of the American Revolution*, Vol. 3, 309-310

their Audacity, and it would not be imprudent if both were to leave the Town.[10]

Captain Bellew's request, and his threat, was clear.   Rebel sentinels onshore had chided, insulted, and fired upon the ships in the harbor long enough.   Either the harassment stopped, or Norfolk would be bombarded.

Colonel Howe replied immediately to Captain Bellew's ultimatum with an assurance that the sentinels had been instructed to avoid any insulting behavior and if any were guilty of such conduct, he agreed that they should be punished for it. But, continued Colonel Howe, *"if...you feel it your duty to make your resentment extend farther than merely as to them, we should wish that the Inhabitants of this Town, who have nothing to do in this matter, may have time to remove with their Effects which to Night they have not...."*[11]

The next day -- the last of 1775 -- passed incident free, but on New Year's Day rebel sentinels paraded before the harbor with their hats on their bayonets, taunting the British.[12] Captain Bellew, aboard the *Liverpool*, responded:

On the 1ˢᵗ Janry at 3 o'Clock in the Afternoon...their Centinels, came to the Wharf very near me, from their Guard House, which was close to it, and used every mark of insult; I then ordered three Guns to be fired

---

[10] Clark, ed., "Captain Henry Bellow to Colonel Robert Howe, 30 December, 1775," *Naval Documents of the American Revolution*, Vol. 3, 310

[11] Clark, ed., "Colonel Robert Howe to Captain Henry Bellew, 30 December, 1775," *Naval Documents of the American Revolution*, Vol. 3, 315

[12] Clark, ed., "A Letter from a Midshipman aboard the Liverpool, 4 January, 1776," *Naval Documents of the American Revolution*, Vol. 3, 621-22

into the House, it had its effect by setting them running; my Lord Dunmore sent (under those Guns) his Boats Arm'd to fetch off a Long boat they had taken from him, whose People set fire to some Store houses, which burnt a good number of Houses, the Rebels have since destroyed the greatest part of the Town.[13]

Lord Dunmore provided a similar account:

Captain Bellow discovering the Rebels parading in the Streets, sent a few Cannon Shot amongst them, his example was immediately followed by all of us, and under Cover of the Cannon, I sent some boats on Shore to burn some detached Warehouses on the lower part of the Wharfs (from whence they used to annoy our boats as they passed) I, at the same time hailed Captain Bellew to beg he would send his boats to burn the Brig with the Salt, which he did immediately.[14]

Colonel Howe's account of the bombardment was similar to his adversaries, except he placed the blame for the destruction of the city upon the British:

The cannonade of the town began about a quarter after three yesterday, from upwards of one hundred pieces of cannon, and continued till near ten at night, without intermission; it then abated a little, and

---

[13] Clark, ed., "Captain Bellew to Philip Stephens, 11 January, 1776," *Naval Documents of the American Revolution*, Vol. 3, 737

[14] Clark, ed., "Lord Dunmore to Lord Dartmouth, Aboard the Dunmore off Norfolk, 4 January, 1776," *Naval Documents of the American Revolution*, Vol. 3, 617-18

continued till two this morning. Under cover of their guns they landed and set fire to the town in several places near the water, though our men strove to prevent them all in their power; but the houses near the water being chiefly of wood, they took fire immediately, and the fire spread with amazing rapidity. It is now become general, and the whole town will, I doubt not, be consumed in a day or two.... The burning of the town has made several avenues, which yesterday they had [not], so that they now may fire with greater effect. The tide is now rising and we expect at high water another cannonade. I have only to wish it may be as ineffectual as the last; for we have not one man killed, and but a few wounded. I cannot enter into the melancholy consideration of the women and children running through a crowd of shot to get out of the town, some of them with children at their breasts, a few have, I hear, been killed.[15]

In Colonel Howe's account, the fire that destroyed Norfolk was set, "*in several places near the water,*" and spread rapidly because of all of the wooden structures. A number of other accounts from both sides of the engagement suggest that the fires set by Dunmore's men quickly spread throughout the city, but Lord Dunmore claimed that the offshore wind, (which blew towards the water) prevented the fires set along

---

[15] Clark, ed., "Colonel Howe to the Virginia Convention, 2 January, 1776," *Naval Documents of the American Revolution*, Vol. 3, 579-80

the shore from spreading to the rest of the city and placed the blame for the destruction of Norfolk upon the rebels:

The Vessels from the Fleet to shew their Zeal for His Majesty's Service, sent great Numbers of Boats on Shore, by which means the fire soon became general on the Wharfs, the wind rather blowing off Shore would have prevented the fire from reaching any farther than the Wharfs, but the Rebels so soon as the Men of War ceased firing, and our People came off, put the finishing Stroke to it, by Setting fire to every House, which has given them employment for these two days past, they have also burnt many houses on both sides of the River, the property of individuals who have never taken any part in this contest, in Short from every transaction they appear to me to have nothing more at heart, than the utter destruction of this once most flourishing Country, Conscious I suppose that they cannot long enjoy it themselves, they wish to make it of as little use as possible to others;[16]

Dunmore's claim that the "rebels" actually burned the bulk of Norfolk was dismissed by most Virginians as a lie, but an official inquiry of the incident in 1777 (which was not made public for over sixty years) concluded that Dunmore's claim was correct:

---

[16] Clark, ed., "Lord Dunmore to Lord Dartmouth, Aboard the Dunmore off Norfolk, 4 January, 1776," *Naval Documents of the American Revolution*, Vol. 3, 617-18

Upon an inspection of the schedule, and the depositions which have been taken, it will appear that very few of the houses were destroyed by the enemy, either from their cannonade or by the parties they landed on the wharves; indeed, the efforts of these latter were so feeble that we are induced to believe most of the houses which they did set fire to might have been saved had a disposition of that kind prevailed among the soldiery, but they [the troops under Colonel Howe and Colonel Woodford] *appear to have had no such intentions; on the contrary, they most wantonly set fire to the greater part of the houses within the town, where the enemy never attempted to approach, and where it would have been impossible for them to have penetrated.*[17]

Months of anger at the residents of Norfolk for their cooperation with and in many cases outright support for Dunmore erupted into a combustible fury, and although no one admitted it publicly, Norfolk was looted and burned to the ground by the soldiers under Colonel Howe and Woodford, some of who shouted, "*Keep up the Jigg! Keep up the Jigg!*" as they torched building after building.[18]   Nearly 900 structures were destroyed over three days and the destruction spread across the river to Andrew Sprowles shipyard and warehouses in Gosport.[19]   Colonel Woodford confirmed the

---

[17] Journal of the House of Delegates, 1835-36, Doc. No. 43, Richmond, 1835, Virginia State Library, 16

[18] Scribner and Tarter, *Revolutionary Virginia: Road to Independence*, Vol. 5, 16

[19] Ibid.

extent of damage, reporting that nine tenths of Norfolk was destroyed.[20]

Unfortunately for Lord Dunmore, the accounts of the devastation that appeared in the gazettes laid the blame upon the governor and his naval lackeys:

> *"It was a shocking scene to see the poor women and children, running about through the fire, and exposed to the guns from the ships, and some of them with children at their breasts. Let our countrymen view and contemplate the scene!...The cannonade had lasted twenty five hours when the express came away, and the flames were raging (it being impossible to extinguish them on account of the heavy fire from the ships) and had consumed two thirds of the town.... It is affirmed that one hundred cannon played on the town almost incessantly for twenty five hours....*[21]

Another account from an observer with the "rebels" painted a desolate picture of Norfolk:

> *I doubt not you have heard before this of the furious cannonade with which the enemy opened the year. They began about 3 in the afternoon of new year's day, and continued, with very little intermission, for 9 hours. Everything that could carry a gun, from a frigate to a boat, played against us. Under the cover of their cannon, they set fire to the town in four*

---

[20] Clark, ed., "Colonel William Woodford to Thomas Elliot, 4 January, 1776," *Naval Documents of the American Revolution*, Vol. 3, 617

[21] Clark, ed., "Pinkney Virginia Gazette, Account of the Burning of Norfolk, 6 January, 1776," *Naval Documents of the American Revolution*, Vol. 3, 661

different places, and made several attempts to land field pieces, but were repulsed with loss. The horror of the night exceeds description, and gives fresh occasion to lament the consequences of civil war.

The thunder of artillery, the crash of falling houses, the roar of devouring flames, added to the piteous moans and piercing shrieks, of the few remaining wretched, ruined inhabitants, form the outlines of a picture too distressing to behold without a tear. I pray God I may never see the like again.... In short, desolation and ruin have overspread the face of the country, and the once populous town of Norfolk now resembles, in miniature the ruins of Palmyra![22]

The destruction of Norfolk did not mean an end to the fighting. The combatants remained where they were, Lord Dunmore's force onboard ships just offshore from the smoldering ruins of Norfolk, and Colonel Howe's troops on the outskirts and amongst the ruins of the city. Heated skirmishes occasionally erupted whenever Dunmore sent landing parties ashore and both sides suffered casualties, but for most of January the two sides shared the common misery of a winter encampment -- wet, cold weather, and limited provisions and supplies.

---

[22] Clark, ed., "Extract of a Letter from a Gentleman at Norfolk, 7 January, 1776," *Naval Documents of the American Revolution*, Vol. 3, 673 Printed in Pinkney's Virginia Gazette, 20 January, 1776

Norfolk is Abandoned

It was no secret that Colonel Howe and Colonel Woodford wanted to abandon Norfolk and in doing so, burn what was left of the city to deny its use to Dunmore. Both officers argued (before and after Norfolk was burned) that it was dangerous for their force to remain at Norfolk; they ran the risk of being cut off by British reinforcements.[23] Colonel Howe went to Williamsburg in mid-January to report to the Convention and gain their approval to withdraw from Norfolk. On January 15th, the Virginia Convention relented, recommending that Norfolk be evacuated.[24] The rebels departed on February 6th, the bulk heading to Suffolk with detachments posted at Kemp's Landing and Great Bridge to block access and provisions from reaching Dunmore.[25] Before the troops left, they torched the remaining buildings of Norfolk, over 400 of them.[26]

Within a week, Lord Dunmore, covered by the 44 gun frigate *H.M.S. Roebuck* (which sailed into Norfolk harbor three days after the "shirtmen" marched to Suffolk), landed troops onto Tucker's Point (adjacent to Portsmouth and across

---

[23] Anderson, ed., "Colonel Robert Howe to Edmund Pendleton, 22 December, 1775," and 2 January, 1776, and Colonel William Woodford to Edmund Pendleton, 22 December, 1775," *Richmond College Historical Papers*, 136-39, 148

[24] Scribner and Tarter, ed., "Proceedings of the 4th Virginia Convention, 15 January, 1776," *Revolutionary Virginia, Road to Independence*, Vol. 5, 405

[25] Clark, ed., "Purdie Virginia Gazette, 9 February, 1776," and "Letter in London Chronicle, ," *Naval Documents of the American Revolution*, Vol. 3, 1187 and Vol. 4, 23

[26] Journal of the House of Delegates, 1835-36, Doc. No. 43, Richmond, 1835, Virginia State Library, 16

the river from Norfolk). They immediately began digging wells to replenish their critically low supply of fresh water. A windmill and a few buildings stood on the point, damaged, but not destroyed in all of the conflict, and Dunmore converted some of them to barracks to house his growing number of smallpox cases.[27] Earthworks were erected to, *"Secure the Watering Place from the Depredations of the Rebels,"* and ovens were built to supply bread.[28] It was clear that Lord Dunmore, the most despised man in Virginia, had no intention of leaving the colony.

---

[27] Selby, 86

[28] Clark, ed., "Journal of HMS Liverpool, 13-14 February, 1776," *Naval Documents of the American Revolution*, Vol. 3, 1293 and Selby, 86

Norfolk and Portsmouth

A PLAN of PORTSMOUTH HARBOUR in the PROVINCE of VIRGINIA Shewing the WORKS erected by the BRITISH FORCES for its DEFENCE 1781

NORTH BRANCH

Gosport

Portsmouth

EAST BRANCH

Norfolk

Tucker's Point

ELIZABETH

RIVER

Chapter Eleven

"All hopes of Reconciliation seem at an end."

Winter and Spring: 1776

The destruction of Norfolk had a significant impact on the views of many colonists, most particularly Virginians. Convinced that Lord Dunmore was responsible for the destruction of Virginia's largest town, many repeated the question asked by Colonel Howe, "*Does* [Norfolk's destruction] *not call for vengeance, both from God and men?*"[1] A frequent essayist to Virginia's gazettes who styled himself, "An American", asserted that the burning of Norfolk served

> *No other purpose than to give the world specimens of British cruelty, and American fortitude, unless it be to force us to lay aside that childish fondness for Britain, and that foolish dependence on her.*[2]

The writer exclaimed what a growing number of colonists were thinking, that it was, "*time to cut the "Gordian Knot" that binds us with Britain*".[3]

---

[1] Clark, ed., "Colonel Howe to the Virginia Convention, 2 January, 1776, *Naval Documents of the American Revolution*, Vol. 3, 579

[2] Purdie, *Virginia Gazette*, "An American," 5 January, 1776, 2

[3] Ibid.

Colonists outside of Virginia like Samuel Adams of Massachusetts recognized the significance of Norfolk's demise and predicted that the news of it, *"will prevail more than a long Train of Reasoning to accomplish a Confederation,"* of the colonies. General Washington agreed, writing to an aide that

> *I hope...that the destruction of Norfolk, and the threatened devastation of other places, will have no other effect, than to unite the whole country in one indissoluble band against a nation* [Britain] *which seems to be lost to every sense of virtue.....*[4]

Washington included a prediction and subtle endorsement for independence in his letter:

> *A few more of such flaming arguments, as were exhibited at Falmouth and Norfolk, added to the sound doctrine and unanswerable reasoning contained in the pamphlet "Common Sense," will not leave numbers at a loss to decide upon the propriety of a separation.*[5]

Although General Washington was correct to credit Thomas Paine's pamphlet, *Common Sense*, for convincing many colonists to support independence, another significant event grabbed the attention of Virginians a few weeks before they learned of Mr. Paine's writings.

---

[4] John C. Fitzpatrick, ed., "General Washington to Joseph Reed, 31 January, 1776," *The Writings of George Washington,* Vol. 4, 297
[5] Ibid.

King George III's Speech

On January 19th and 20th all three Virginia gazettes in Williamsburg published King George III's October 27th, 1775 speech to Parliament. It was essentially a declaration of war on the colonists. King George began by specifying the traitorous acts of rebellious colonial leaders:

> *Those who have long too successfully labored to inflame my people in America, by gross misrepresentations, and to infuse into their minds a system of opinions repugnant to the true constitutions of the colonies, and to their subordinate relation to Great Britain, now openly avow their revolt, hostility, and rebellion. They have raised troops, and are collecting a naval force; they have seized the public revenue, and assumed to themselves legislative, executive, and judicial powers, which they already exercise, in the most arbitrary manner, over the persons and properties of their fellow-subjects.[6]*

The King claimed that many colonists desired to remain loyal, but fear and intimidation compelled them to submit to the policies of their rebellious brethren.[7] King George scoffed at repeated declarations from colonial leaders that professed their attachment to Britain. Instead, the King speculated on their true objective:

---

[6] Purdie, *Virginia Gazette*, 19 January, 1776, 2
[7] Ibid.

They meant only to amuse by vague expressions of attachment to the parent state, and the strongest protestations of loyalty to me, whilst they were preparing for a general revolt.[8]

King George maintained that he and Parliament had sought reconciliation with the colonists a number of times, but to no avail.[9] At the very least, continued the King, he had hoped that such reconciliation efforts would convince most colonists to reject, *"the traitorous views of their leaders,"* but instead

The rebellious war now levied is become more general, and is manifestly carried on for the purpose of establishing an independent empire....[10]

The King's stunning contention, that independence was the colonists' objective, (and had been since the start of the dispute years earlier) held sway with many members of Parliament in 1775. With the stability of the empire at stake, the King asserted that he and Parliament had no choice but to suppress the growing rebellion in North America:

The object is too important, the spirit of the British nation too high, the resources with which GOD has blessed her too numerous, to give up so many colonies, which she has planted with great industry, nursed with great tenderness, encouraged with many

---

[8] Ibid.
[9] Ibid.
[10] Ibid.

commercial advantages, and protected and defended at much expense of blood and treasure.

It is now become the part of wisdom, and (in its effects) of clemency, to put a speedy end to these disorders, by the most decisive exertions. For this purpose, I have increased my naval establishment, and greatly augmented my land forces....I have also the satisfaction to inform you, that I have received the most friendly offers of foreign assistance....[11]

King George concluded his speech with a gesture of forgiveness towards the colonists that suggested he was confident that his military would soon end this unhappy conflict in his favor:

When the unhappy and deluded multitude, against whom this force will be directed, shall become sensible of their error, I shall be ready to receive the misled with tenderness and mercy;[12]

Colonial Reaction to the King's Speech

The reaction among many members of Congress who learned of the speech in early January was one of anger and disillusionment with the king and resignation about the conflict. A number of delegates, for the first time, directly blamed the King for the crisis. Samuel Ward of Rhode Island informed his daughter that, *"Thus you see my...Sentiments are confirmed that the* [King] *ever meant to make himself an absolute despotic Tyrant...Every Idea of Peace is now*

---

[11] Ibid.
[12] Ibid.

over…"[13] Eliphalet Dyer of Connecticut declared, *"From the Appearance of the Kings Speech All hopes of Reconciliation seem at an end; therefore Nothing remains on our part but the most Vigorous preparations & Exertions."*[14] Samuel Adams of Massachusetts mocked the speech and asked an important question:

> *You have seen the most gracious Speech – Most Gracious! … It* [reveals], *to be sure, the most "benevolent" & "humane" Feelings of its Author. I have heard that he is his own Minister – that he follows the Dictates of his own Heart. If so, why should we cast the odium of distressing Mankind upon his Minions & Flatterers only. Guilt must lie at his Door….*[15]

In Virginia, the writer, "An American", once again expressed the view of many Virginians with a long reply to the King's speech:

> *Can any American read the King's Speech without feeling the utmost indignation? Good God! What must we think of the king of Great Britain when we read his assertions from the Throne, that we meant only to amuse, by vague expressions of attachment to*

---

[13] Smith, ed., "Samuel Ward to his Daughter, 8 January, 1776," *Letters to the Delegates to Congress: 1774-1789*, Vol. 3, 61

[14] Smith, ed., "Eliphalet Dyer to Joseph Trumbull, 15 January, 1776," *Letters to the Delegates to Congress: 1774-1789*, Vol. 3, 95

[15] Smith, ed., "Samuel Adams to John Pitts, 12 January, 1776," *Letters to the Delegates to Congress: 1774-1789*, Vol. 3, 84

the parent state, and protestations of loyalty whilst
we were preparing for a general revolt.[16]

"Would to God this had been the case," continued "An American" because the colonies would be better prepared to resist! The author challenged the King's claim that he and his ministers had been moderate and restrained in their conduct towards the colonies and offered a list of offenses they had committed against the colonists:

But, let the wanton butchery at Concord and Lexington, and the savage destruction of Charlestown, and of our other towns now in ashes, let the bloody plot which was to have been executed by 30,000 Canadians, let the destruction of thousands of innocent and helpless women and children on our frontiers, which was meditated and was to have been carried into execution by all the tribes of savages, which Carleton, a Johnson, a Dunmore, or a Connolly could stir up against us; and, above all, let the horrid massacre which, for ought he knew, might have followed the insurrections which his tools have labored to excite, be told throughout the world, and let them judge of the truth of this royal declaration....[17]

With faith in and support of the King rapidly evaporating among the colonists, hope for reconciliation faded fast. The colonists had long ago come to view the British Ministry and Parliament as their enemy and now the King fell squarely into

---

[16] Purdie, *Virginia Gazette*, 26 January, 1776, 3
[17] Ibid.

that category too. With little reason to expect the English people to intervene on their behalf, more and more colonists, (and Virginians) seriously considered independence.

Thomas Paine's *Common Sense*

It was at this moment that a pamphlet written by a recently arrived Scottish radical named Thomas Paine, appeared in print and became a sensation. Extracts of the pamphlet appeared in the Virginia gazettes in early February, but other Virginians became aware of Paine's work even earlier. Nicholas Cresswell, the loyalist Englishman still stranded in Virginia, observed from Leesburg in mid-January that

> *A pamphlet called "Commonsense: makes a great noise. One of the vilest things that ever was published to the world. Full of false representation, lies, calumny, and treason, whose principles are to subvert all Kingly Governments and erect an Independent Republic.... The sentiments are adopted by a great number of people who are indebted to Great Britain.*[18]

Cresswell complained that, *"Nothing But Independence* [is] *talked off...The Devil is in the people."*[19]

Josiah Bartlett, a Congressional delegate from New Hampshire, wrote home in mid-January about the strong interest in Philadelphia for Paine's work. *"This week a*

---

[18] Cresswell Journal, 19 January, 1776, 136
[19] Cresswell Journal, "22 and 26 January, 1776," 136

pamphlet on [independence] *was printed here, and greedily bought up and read by all ranks of people.*"[20]

With the devastation of Norfolk and accounts of the King's speech weighing on their minds, Virginians read extracts of Paine's work in the gazettes that proclaimed

> *Everything that is right, or reasonable, pleads for separation. The blood of the slain, the weeping voice of nature, cries, It is time to part.*[21]

Paine challenged, "*the warmest advocate for reconciliation to show a single advantage that this continent can reap by being connected with Great Britain.*"[22] As he believed there were none, he concluded with the assertion that

> *Reconciliation is now a fallacious dream...As Milton wisely expresses, Never can true reconcilement grow where wounds of deadly hate have pierced so deep.*[23]

Within a month, the influence of Paine's pamphlet on the minds of Virginians was clear. George Washington's brother-in-law, Fielding Lewis reported that

> *The opinion for independence seems to be gaining ground, indeed most of those who have read the Pamphlet Common Sense say its unanswerable.*[24]

---

[20] Smith, ed., "Josiah Bartlett to John Langdon, 13 January, 1776," *Letters to the Delegates to Congress: 1774-1789*, Vol. 3, 88

[21] Purdie, *Virginia Gazette*, 2 February, 1776, 1

[22] Ibid.

[23] Ibid.

[24] Chase, "Fielding Lewis to George Washington, 6 March, 1776," *The Papers of George Washington, Vol. 3*, 418-419

Another unidentified Virginian, whose letter was printed in a Pennsylvania gazette, claimed

> *Common Sense has gained a number of disciples*
> *here. Indeed, I know of none who disapprove, save a*
> *few dastard souls.*[25]

One Last Reconciliation Rumor

In the same gazettes that printed excerpts of Paine's *Common Sense* appeared a report from England that Lord North had offered

> *To repeal all of the American acts and give up the*
> *point of taxation, provided the Americans will lay*
> *down their arms, and that they shall be placed in the*
> *same situation as they were in the year 1763.*[26]

There was little truth to this report, but it was the sort of news that moderate and conservative colonists would have seized upon a year earlier to push for reconciliation. Now, in the late winter of 1776, most colonists dismissed the report (as well as another that announced that Parliament was sending peace commissioners to negotiate with the colonies.) Joseph Hewes, a Congressional delegate from North Carolina, expressed the view of many colonists:

---

[25] Scribner and Tarter, *Revolutionary Virginia, Road to Independence,* Vol. 6, 284

[26] Pinkney, *Virginia Gazette*, 3 February, 1776, 2

It is hinted in the papers that persons will be sent from England to Negotiate with the Colonies. Many people do not believe it, those who do have but little expectation from it. They are to treat under the influence of a mighty Fleet & Army. What are we to expect from the mouth of a Cannon or the point of a Bayonet.[27]

Oliver Walcott, another delegate from Connecticut, agreed. *"All this news makes no impression on firm whigs. It is considered as an insidious manoeuvre."*[28]

A writer to Purdie's Virginia Gazette expressed similar skepticism of reconciliation efforts in early February:

I am astonished that any American should be pleased at the late accounts from England, of lord North's declaration that he would agree to a repeal of the detestable acts we complain of, provided we will first lay down our arms...for who is so mad as to believe that America, after such cruel persecution, can be long at peace with her persecutors, or that England will not lay hold on some opportunity to be revenged...for her disgrace and disappointment? ... Who can rely on the promise of a minister, and of a Prince who has already deceived us, by the like promise?[29]

---

[27] Smith, ed., "Joseph Hewes to Samuel Johnston, 13 February, 1776," *Letters to the Delegates to Congress: 1774-1789*, Vol. 3, 247

[28] Smith, ed., "Oliver Walcott to Samuel Lyman, 19 February, 1776," *Letters to the Delegates to Congress: 1774-1789*, Vol. 3, 286

[29] Purdie, Virginia Gazette, Supplement, 2 February, 1776, 2

John Adams would have been very pleased with the views of this Virginia writer. In a letter to his wife, Abigail, he subtly criticized the southern colonists for what he believed (mistakenly) was their lack of awareness of the true nature of the crisis:

Reconciliation if practicable and Peace if attainable, you very well know would be as agreeable to my Inclinations and as advantageous to my Interest, as to any Man's. But I see no Prospect, no Probability, no Possibility. And I cannot but despise the Understanding, which sincerely expects an honourable Peace, for its Credulity, and detest the hypocritical Heart, which pretends to expect it, when in Truth it does not. The News Papers here are full of free Speculations.... The Writers reason from Topicks which have been long in Contemplation, and fully understood by the People at large in New England, but have been attended to in the southern Colonies only be Gentlemen of free Spirits and liberal Minds, who are very few.[30]

Mr. Adams's fellow congressional delegate from Virginia, Thomas Nelson of Yorktown, would have strongly objected to the contention that the southern colonists did not fully contemplate the long standing crisis with Britain. And yet, Nelson was just as frustrated with the views of some of his fellow delegates in Congress, both north and south of Virginia. He complained to John Page in mid-February that

---

[30] Smith, ed., "John Adams to Abigail Adams, 19 February, 1776," *Letters to the Delegates to Congress: 1774-1789*, Vol. 3, 271

> *Independence, Confederation & foreign alliance are*
> *as formidable to some of the Congress, I fear to a*
> *majority, as an apparition to a weak enervated*
> *Woman. These subjects have been gently touch'd*
> *upon. Would you* [believe] *that we have some among*
> *us, who still expect honourable proposals from* [the]
> *administration.*[31]

One of the delegates whom Nelson might have had in mind was Robert Livingston of New York. Recent newspaper reports of growing public support in England for the colonies prompted Livingston to express his expectation for a last minute resolution to the long dispute with Britain:

> *I can not help thinking from the late advices from*
> *England on the increase of our Friends there that we*
> *shall before long be enable to carry our great points*
> *and that they are already prepared to give up the*
> *right of taxation and I can hardly think they will*
> *deem* [Congress] *of sufficient consequence to make it*
> *the subject of war.*[32]

Livingston's hope for a resolution was fueled by new reports of last ditch reconciliation efforts that appeared in the gazettes and in letters from Britain. One such letter, printed in Purdie's gazette in mid-February, reported that

---

[31] Smith, ed., "Thomas Nelson to John Page,13 February, 1776,"
  Letters to the Delegates to Congress: 1774-1789, Vol. 3, 249
[32] Smith, ed., "Robert Livingston to James Duane, 16 February, 1776,"
  Letters to the Delegates to Congress: 1774-1789, Vol. 3, 265

The general cry of [England] *was for PEACE...our friends in* [Parliament] *were exerting themselves to bring about a happy reconciliation... Which GOD grant...this unnatural contest may be settled to the satisfaction of both countries, upon a solid and permanent foundation.*[33]

Reconciliation, however, was destined to elude the two sides. The British Ministry's insistence to negotiate only with the "legitimate", governing body of each colony (not the Continental Congress) assured that such negotiations were a non-starter. Virginia, like her sister colonies, was committed to continental unity and had long ago acknowledged the Continental Congress as the sole arbiter for the colonies. If Congress were not involved in the negotiations, there would be no negotiations.

Another factor that undermined colonial hope for reconciliation was that for every positive report from England about such efforts, there were two others that commented on Britain's military preparations against the colonies. In late February, Virginians learned that Britain had "hired" 4,000 German soldiers to replace 4,000 troops that were sailing from Ireland to America.[34] Three weeks later, two reports appeared in the gazettes that stated the British army was to increase to 20,000 troops, and that 5,000 of them were destined for Virginia.[35]

---

[33] Purdie, *Virginia Gazette*, 16 February, 1776, 3
[34] Purdie, *Virginia Gazette*, 23 February, 1776, 3
[35] Purdie, *Virginia Gazette*, 15 March, 1776, 2 and
Purdie *Virginia Gazette,* Supplement, 15 March, 1776, 1

Military Affairs in Virginia

While fighting between Virginia's military forces south of the James River and Lord Dunmore's forces at Tucker's Point had subsided with the withdrawal of "rebel" troops to Suffolk in early February, a great deal of military activity continued into the spring in Virginia. The arrival of General Henry Clinton with 1,200 British troops aboard transport ships on February 9th, had momentarily encouraged Lord Dunmore, but his optimism soon turned to disappointment when he learned that Clinton had orders to continue on to the Carolinas.

Dunmore was dumbfounded that troops he desperately needed to regain control of Virginia, the largest and most significant colony in North America, were instead ordered to the relatively insignificant colony of North Carolina. Try as he might to convince General Clinton to alter his plans, the British force that sailed into the Elizabeth River in mid-February, sailed south just two weeks later after repairs were completed to some of the ships.

Dunmore was left with a force of runaway slaves, bolstered by a handful of Tories, British regulars, and British marines, plus the cannon of a few British warships to maintain royal authority in Virginia (at Tucker's Point). To make matters worse, illness swept through Dunmore's ranks, prompting a number of desertions and killing over 150 black soldiers.[36] The governor described his difficult situation to the new Secretary of State, Lord George Germain, in late March:

---

[36] Purdie, *Virginia Gazette*, 8 March, 1776, 2-3

Your Lordship will observe...that I have been endeavouring to raise two Regiments here, one of White People, the other of Black. The former goes on very slowly, but the latter very well, and would have been in great forwardness, had not a fever crept in amongst them which carried off a great many very fine fellows.[37]

In contrast to Dunmore's struggles, recruitment among the Virginia regiments of regulars went well. The Virginia Committee of Safety, recognizing that Virginia's many rivers left the colony vulnerable to Britain's naval forces, stationed the newly raised regiments near the James, York, Rappahannock, and Potomac Rivers. The 1st and 6th Regiments were stationed at Williamsburg, the 3rd Regiment was posted at Dumfries, the 5th Regiment at Richmond (county) Courthouse, and the 7th Regiment at Gloucester Courthouse. Colonel Woodford's 2nd Regiment remained at Suffolk, keeping a close watch on Dunmore and was reinforced by the 4th and 8th Regiments.[38]

Over the course of the spring, companies of recruits (68 men strong) were raised in their respective counties and when complete, reported to their assigned regiments at their muster stations. Each regiment was allotted ten companies so when they reached full strength, each regiment numbered around 700 men. Of course, illness, desertion, and detached service typically lowered that number. Nonetheless, Virginia had

---

[37] Clark, ed., "Lord Dunmore to Lord Germain, 30 March, 1776," *Naval Documents of the American Revolution*, Vol. 4, 585

[38] Scribner and Tarter, ed. "Proceedings of the Virginia Committee of Safety, 10 February, 1776," *Revolutionary Virginia: Road to Independence*, Vol. 6, 85

successfully raised an impressive military force in the spring of 1776, one that appeared perfectly capable of subduing Lord Dunmore.

One of the biggest challenges that faced Virginia's military forces in 1776 was not attracting recruits, but rather equipping, training, and disciplining them once they enlisted. Linen hunting shirts continued to serve as the uniform of Virginia's troops and they were relatively easy to supply, but firearms were another matter. Authorities scrambled to procure muskets and rifles for the regulars, often at the expense of the militia, who went without weapons. Thirteen foot long spears were distributed to two companies of each regiment for a short time as the search for more firearms continued.[39]

As for training and drill, few Virginians had military experience beyond occasional militia service, and it showed in camp and on the parade ground. The orderly books of the 5th and 6th Virginia Regiments for the spring of 1776 reveal the constant struggle commanders experienced in their efforts to properly train their troops:

5th Regiment Orderly Book, March 20, 1776

> *The Brigadier-General...expects that the Soldiers will Pay the Strictest attention to their Duty and Exert themselves to Learn that Discipline so Necessary to their own Honor and Safety, that they will behave with Decency to their Fellow Citizen Whose Persons and Property they were ordained to Protect and Defend, and that they will not by any*

---

[39] Chase, ed., "General Charles Lee to General George Washington, 10 May, 1776," *The Papers of George Washington*, Vol. 4, 258

unworthy Conduct Disgrace the Honorable Profession of a Soldier.[40]

6th Regiment Orderly Book, March 28, 1776

I am sorry to see so little regard paid to Orders, for not withstanding I expressly ordered the awkward Squad (aptly named for their need of more drill) to be out at 7 o' clock in the morning & 3 in the afternoon [for two hours of drill each session], *to my great Surprize this morning on going to the Parade not one was to be found....*[41]

Along with the daily struggle to maintain order and discipline among the ranks of newly recruited citizen-soldiers, two incidents in particular highlighted the challenge of raising the new army.

Colonel Henry's Resignation

Although Patrick Henry was the most popular public figure in Virginia in 1776, many political leaders continued to question his selection as colonel of the 1st Virginia Regiment and commander-in-chief of Virginia's military forces. They believed that his lack of military experience and his well known political abilities, made him much better suited for politics than the military.

---

[40] R.A. Brock, ed., "Orderly Book of the Company of Captain George Stubblefield, 5th Virginia Regiment: From March 3, 1776 to July 10, 1776, Inclusive," *Virginia Historical Society Collections,* New Series 6, (1887)

[41] Charles Campbell, ed. *The Orderly Book of that Portion of the American Army Stationed at or near Williamsburg* (6th Regiment)...*from March 18, 1776 to August 28, 1776,* (Richmond, 1860), 8

The Virginia Committee of Safety, headed by one of Henry's most frequent opponents, moderate Edmund Pendleton of Caroline County, held authority over the military when the Convention was not in session. When the committee decided in November 1775 to send troops to Norfolk to limit Lord Dunmore's activities, it selected the 2nd Virginia Regiment and Colonel William Woodford to lead the force. The committee's slight to Henry was compounded by Colonel Woodford, who often communicated directly to the Committee of Safety instead of through Colonel Henry, the de facto commander-in-chief of Virginia and Woodford's superior officer.

Denied any chance of military glory in southern Virginia, Henry bristled further when three of his eight companies were detached from his regiment and sent to reinforce Colonel Woodford. The final insult for Henry occurred in late February when the Continental Congress appointed Andrew Lewis, the experienced commander of Lord Dunmore's expedition against the Shawnee in 1774, as Brigadier General of Virginia's continental forces, making Henry, who remained colonel of the 1st Virginia Regiment, subordinate to Lewis. This blow to Henry's pride, which he believed occurred with the blessing of the Committee of Safety, was too much for Henry to accept, and he resigned his commission.

The news of Henry's resignation prompted a near mutiny in the ranks of the 1st Virginia; they went into, "*deep mourning*" and gathered, under arms at Henry's lodging to address him.[42] Expressing their, "*sincere thanks*," for his leadership and "*poignant sorrow*" at his resignation, the troops praised Henry's, "*spirited resentment to the most glaring*

---

[42] Purdie, *Virginia Gazette*, 1 March, 1776, 3

indignity," of Congress.[43]   Henry graciously thanked those assembled for their support and then attended a farewell dinner at the Raliegh Tavern in his honor. He was forced to postpone his departure from the capital, however, when word spread of, "*some uneasiness getting among the soldiery, who assembled in a tumultuous manner, and demanded their discharge, declaring their unwillingness to serve under any other commander.*"[44] Henry spent most of the evening with the troops, "*visiting the several barracks, and* [using] *every argument in his power with the soldiery to lay aside their imprudent resolution, and continue in the service...*"[45] His efforts succeeded and the disgruntled troops eventually settled down.

Mutiny of Gibson's Lambs

About two weeks after Henry's departure, the ranking officer in Williamsburg, Colonel Hugh Mercer of the 3rd Regiment, citing a mutinous spirit among Captain George Gibson's company of 1st Virginia riflemen, confiscated their weapons and placed them on fatigue duty under armed guards. The guards were instructed that, "*if any obstruction arise from the same Mutinous Disposition, the Guard is to fire on the offenders With such Effect as to kill them if possible.*"[46] This harsh directive was challenged by the officers of the company and Mercer eventually relented, publically acknowledging that he had, "*exceeded the line of duty,*" in his

---

[43] Ibid.
[44] Ibid.
[45] Ibid.
[46] Scribner and Tarter, ed. *Revolutionary Virginia: Road to Independence,* Vol. 6, 197-98 note 7

treatment of Captain Gibson's company."[47]   The fact that
Mercer felt compelled to go to such extremes to enforce
discipline, however, demonstrated the challenges that faced
Virginia's commanders.

General Charles Lee Arrives

The arrival of General Charles Lee in Williamsburg in late
March offered a solution to the discipline dilemma. Lee, a
former British officer with extensive military service in
Europe, held the rank of Major-General in the Continental
army and served with General Washington in Massachusetts
in 1775. Although he was a native of Britain and had only
arrived in the colonies in 1773, Lee had earned the trust and
admiration of many in Congress and held the third highest
rank in the continental army. He was the most militarily
experienced and knowledgeable officer in the army and was
highly esteemed throughout the colonies.

Reports of planned British military operations in the
southern colonies prompted Congress to send General Lee
southward in March to oversee the region's defense.   He
arrived in Williamsburg on March 29th and informed General
Washington of the situation in Virginia a week later:

> *The Regiments in general are very compleat in numbers,
> the Men (those that I have seen) fine – but a most horrid
> deficiency of Arms – no entrenching tools, no* [effective
> cannon] *(although the Province is pretty well stockd)...I
> have order'd...the Artificers to work night and day....*[48]

---

[47] Ibid.

[48] Chase, ed., "General Charles Lee to General George Washington,
5 April, 1776," *The Papers of George Washington*, Vol. 4, 43

Lee speculated that the unrealistic hope for reconciliation among some and a degree of apathy among others had caused Virginians to procrastinate on important military preparations. He also criticized the scattered deployment of the colony's regiments, noting sarcastically that, *"They have distributed their Troops in so ingenious a manner, as to render every active offensive operation impossible."*[49]

General Lee acted quickly to rectify the situation. He ordered the 5th Regiment and half of the 7th Regiment to march from their duty stations in Richmond Courthouse and Gloucester Courthouse to Williamsburg (to join the 1st and 6th regiments who were already in the capital).[50] He commenced work on fortifications for Jamestown, Burwell's Ferry, Yorktown, and Williamsburg and publically urged Virginia's young gentlemen (in the gazettes) to voluntarily form companies of light dragoons, something the convention had failed to do because of the expense.[51] When a shortage of muskets left many of the troops unarmed, Lee resorted to the use of spears, arming two companies of the tallest and strongest men of each regiment with them:[52]

> *They were formed something like the Triarii of the Romans,* [reported Lee to Richard Henry Lee] *in the rear of the battalions, occasionally either to throw themselves into the intervals of the line, or to form a third, second, or front rank in close order. It has a*

[49] Ibid.

[50] Schribner and Tarter, ed. *Revolutionary Virginia, Road to Independence*, Vol. 6, 277

[51] Ibid., 278 and Purdie, *Virginia Gazette*, 26 April, 1776, 1

[52] Chase, ed., "General Charles Lee to General George Washington, 10 May, 1776, *The Papers of George Washington*, Vol. 4, 258

fine effect to the eye, and the men in general seemed convinced of the utility of the arrangement.[53]

As for the discipline and quality of the troops, General Lee informed Richard Henry Lee that

My opinion of your troops and officers is, thank God, so good, as to put me entirely at my ease with respect to action, corps to corps.[54]

While General Lee and the troops prepared for battle, a growing number of Virginians, encouraged by numerous writings in the weekly gazettes as well as developments both abroad and in Virginia, seriously considered independence.

Support for Independence Grows

By the spring of 1776, public support for independence in Virginia was widespread. One writer to Purdie's gazette in March justified his support for it and asked readers to

Consider the great preparations England is making for war, the arrival of [warships]...that lord Dunmore is actually entrenching on Tucker's Mills, that he is daily recruiting his army of slaves, that there has been a dangerous commotion in North Carolina, and that the English commander in Detroit has instigated some Indians to make an attack on our frontier.... I say, whoever knows or considers these

---

[53] "General Charles Lee to Richard Henry Lee, 12 April, 1776, *The Lee Papers*, Vol. 1, (Collections of the New York Historical Society, 1871), 417

[54] Ibid., 416

*things must see that the story of commissioners,
repeal, accommodation, was intended but to lull us
into security, or to insult and mock us. It is therefore
high time to look to ourselves, and if we cannot enjoy
the privileges of Englishmen...let us instantly break
off those [chains] of affection which have hitherto
bound us to them; and if England calls in foreign
assistance, let us follow the wisdom of her example,
and do so likewise.*[55]

The assistance of European nations and establishment of foreign trade became important arguments of many pro-independence writers. Influenced no doubt by the writing of Thomas Paine in *Common Sense*, writers like, "An American" argued in the gazettes that since Britain had sought the assistance of, "*Russians, Hanoverians, Canadians, Indians, and Negro slaves...she deserved that we should declare ourselves independent of her, and call into our assistance the French and Spaniards.*"[56]

Prohibitory Act

While accounts of Britain's plans to broaden its military activities in the colonies certainly disturbed the colonists, they were outraged to learn in March about a new parliamentary act approved by the King. The Prohibitory Act, which was passed by Parliament in December 1775, sought to isolate and economically strangle the colonies and declared all American vessels and property subject to seizure and forfeiture. Described by Whig opponents in Parliament as, "*a cruel*

---

[55] Purdie, *Virginia Gazette*, 8 March, 1776, 3
[56] Purdie, *Virginia Gazette*, 29 March, 1776, 1

declaration of war against the Americans," the act specifically prohibited all manner of American trade and commerce and authorized the seizure of ships, personnel, and property engaged in such activities.[57]

As this act placed all of the colonists of British North America outside of the King's protection, some colonists wryly argued that Parliament and the King had essentially expelled the colonies from the empire, making a declaration of independence by Congress, unnecessary. John Adams, who was a strong advocate for a separation from Britain well before the Prohibitory Act was passed, declared that the measure should be known as the Act of Independency, "*for King, Lords, and Commons have united in Sundering this Country...forever.*"[58] Adams went on to assert that

> *It is a compleat Dismemberment of the British Empire. It throws thirteen Colonies out of the Royal Protection, levels all Distinctions and makes us independent in Spite of all our supplications and Entreaties.*[59]

Adams added that

> *It might be fortunate that the Act of Independency should come from the British Parliament, rather than the American Congress: But it is very odd that Americans should hesitate at accepting Such a Gift from them.*"[60]

---

[57] Purdie, *Virginia Gazette*, 15 March, 1776, 2

[58] Smith, ed., "John Adams to Horatio Gates, 23 March, 1776," *Letters of Delegates to Congress*, Vol. 3, 431

[59] Ibid.

[60] Ibid.

The hesitancy to embrace independence, an act that Adams claimed many colonists still feared as if it were, "*a Hobgoblin,*" was a great frustration to Adams and those who thought as he did on the issue.[61] Yet, many colonists had taken great strides towards independence. The number who supported it in Virginia, (which was few before 1776) increased sharply in the winter and spring of 1776. Some, like Francis Lightfoot Lee and Richard Henry Lee (future signers of the Declaration of Independence and brothers from Virginia) agreed with John Adams and asserted privately that the Prohibitory Act had already decided the issue by casting the colonists out of the King's protection:

Our late King & his Parliament having declared us Rebels & Enemies, confiscated our property, as far as they were likely to lay hands on it; have effectually decided the question for us, whether or not we shou'd be independent.[62]

--- Francis Lightfoot Lee

It is curious to observe, that whilst people here [in Philadelphia] *are disputing and hesitating about independency, the Court by one bold Act of Parliament* [the Prohibitory Act] *and by a conduct the most extensively hostile, have already put the two Countries asunder.*[63]

--- Richard Henry Lee

---

[61] Ibid.

[62] Smith, ed., "Francis Lightfoot Lee to Landon Carter, 19 March, 1776," *Letters of Delegates to Congress,* Vol. 3, 407

[63] Ballagh, ed., "Richard Henry Lee to Landon Carter, 1 April, 1776," *The Letters of Richard Henry Lee,* Vol. 1, 173

Support in Virginia for independence received another boost in early April when intercepted letters from the British Ministry to Governor Robert Eden of Maryland were published in the Virginia gazettes. Unlike Lord Dunmore, Governor Eden had managed to avoid direct confrontation with the colonists of Maryland, but this changed in early April when Captain James Barron of Hampton seized a British tender bearing letters from Lord North, (the new British Secretary of State) to Governor Eden. The letters revealed Eden's support for the suppression of the colonies and more importantly, announced the imminent arrival of a large British military force in the southern colonies:

> An armament consisting of seven regiments, with a fleet of frigates and small ships, is now in readiness to proceed to the southern colonies, in order to attempt the restoration of legal government in that part of America. It will proceed, in the first place, to North Carolina, and from thence either to South Carolina or Virginia....[64]

The Virginia Committee of Safety sent copies of the letters to the Maryland Committee of Safety and to the Continental Congress, who requested that Maryland officials seize the governor if possible.

With renewed fighting and bloodshed seemingly imminent in Virginia, an unidentified supporter of independence asked readers of Alexander Purdie's gazette a series of pointed questions on the anniversary of Lexington and Concord that indicted the King, Parliament and the British people:

---

[64] Purdie, *Virginia Gazette*, 12 April, 1776, 2

Is it your intention to be freemen or slaves? ... Is it not manifest that you have sinned beyond forgiveness in the eye of the accursed ministry of Great Britain, and of that more accursed tyrant [the King], *who will employ no ministry unless they previously stipulate to work your ruin? Is there any circumstance in the whole life or character of this tyrant which gives you reason to think that he will relent? Was he ever known to forgive those that he had once oppressed or injured? Is there any symptom of virtue in ...Parliament which can flatter you that they will check the disposition of their masters? Is there any appearance of vigour and spirit in the people of Great Britain which can open a prospect of relief? Is it probable that a people who have suffered their own most sacred laws to be baffled, violated, and trampled upon with impunity, should rouse themselves in the cause of others, who are removed three thousand miles distant from them?*

On the contrary, is it not plain that they are scarcely less hostile to your rights and happiness than the tyrant himself? ... Have not your fields been laid waste, your property confiscated, your citizens butchered, and your cities reduced to ashes? Have not the savages been tampered with to deluge your frontiers with blood and slaughter? Have not your slaves been instigated to murder you, and your wives and children? Are not these things...notorious? But in what manner have they affected the people of England? Have they shewn the least resentment, indignation, or even compassion? Have they not, on the contrary, voted or suffered their representatives to vote, fresh means of prosecuting the diabolical plan?

Will you suffer a few coward hearts, contemptible, confused heads, or perhaps treacherous [individuals] *to keep you fascinated in a state of torpor,* [about possible reconciliation] *till the chain is fixed about your necks...? Are your liberties to be risked on the chance of a die, merely through compliance to the fears, if not the treachery, of the most despicable and worthless part of the community? ... Who, what are these men thus sobbing and whining after their darling dependence* [on Britain]. *... Are they not the very men who, from the beginning, have either openly opposed, or thrown obstacles in the way of, every spirited measure of resistance? In short, are they not men of suspected principles...?*[65]

The writer insisted that foreign assistance was essential and would only be granted if independence was declared:

For Heaven's sake, why, wherefore, do you hesitate? The pusillanimous mortals who labor to raise spectres in your imaginations, similar to those which dance before their own, know very well that reconciliation and reunion with your butchers are impossible.... Will you stake the liberties of yourselves and posterity, on hazard and fortune, merely in complacency to the fears of a few timid, or perhaps to the designs of a few disaffected men? Or

---

[65] Purdie, *Virginia Gazette*, 19 April, 1776, 3

will you, by a brave, spirited, and manly injunction on your servants in Congress, to declare you A FREE AND INDEPENDENT PEOPLE, bring the calamities of war to a shorter issue, and fix your liberties on a firm and durable foundation?[66]

The question of independence from Great Britain was the dominant issue in county elections for delegates to the 5th Virginia Convention in April. Anxiety over reports of British military plans for the southern colonies created a sense of urgency that pushed many Virginians to support independence. The swelling sentiment for independence in Virginia was revealed in the correspondence of Richard Henry Lee. John Lee of Essex County informed Lee on April 2nd that, *"Independence is now the Topic here, and I think I am not mistaken when I say, it will (if not already) be very soon a Favorite Child."*[67] Two weeks later, William Aylett of King William County announced to Lee that, *"The People of this County almost unanimously cry aloud for independence..."*[68] It was soon evident that King William County was not the only place in Virginia where support for independence was nearly unanimous.

---

[66] Ibid.

[67] Schribner and Tarter, ed., *Revolutionary Virginia: Road to Independence*, Vol. 6, 285

[68] Ibid.

Chapter Twelve

"[Dissolve] the connexion between America and Great Britain."

April-May : 1776

The selection of delegates in April to the 5th Virginia Convention (which was to convene in early May in Williamsburg) involved a surprising number of contested elections. Many long serving county leaders were challenged at the polls and in some cases, defeated. Notable delegates like Edmund Pendleton and George Mason survived close elections, but others, like Carter Braxton and Francis Lightfoot Lee (who was a delegate to the Continental Congress) lost their seats.[1] In fact, over one third of the delegates to the 4th Virginia Convention failed to return to the 5th Convention.[2] Not all were turned away at the polls, some chose military service (making them ineligible to serve in the convention) and others opted not to seek re-election. Nonetheless, an inordinately large number of seats for the 5th Virginia Convention were hotly contested, despite the fact that nearly all of the candidates supported independence.[3]

Some of the county committees sent instructions with their convention delegates to emphasize their support for

---

[1] Schribner and Tarter, ed., *Revolutionary Virginia: Road to Independence*, Vol. 6, 285
[2] Ibid.
[3] Ibid., 289

independence from Great Britain. Cumberland County, in central Virginia, declared on April 22nd, that

> *When the King of Great Britain, deaf to all the humiliating and well intentioned Petitions from his once loyal Subjects...changes his Justice to Severity...; When his Majesty...has ordered his Governour, Lord Dunmore, to arm our Slaves against us...; when a uniform System through all of the Acts of Parliament...tending evidently to the total Destruction of American Liberty, leaves no other Alternative than a base Submission, to their inhuman, impolitic and oppressive Measures, or Independency; ...We think ourselves indispensably obliged to declare boldly for the latter. We therefore, your Constituents instruct you positively to declare for an Independency; that you solemnly abjure any Allegiance to his Britannick Majesty, and bid him a good Night forever....*[4]

Charlotte County issued similar instructions to its delegates the following day:

> *When we consider the despotick plan adopted by the king, ministry, and parliament of Great Britain, insidiously pursued these twelve years past to enslave America; when we consider that they have turned a deaf ear to the repeated petitions, and remonstrances of this and our sister colonies, and that they have*

---

[4] Schribner and Tarter, ed., "Cumberland County Committee Instructions, 22 April, 1776," *Revolutionary Virginia: Road to Independence*, Vol. 6, 433

been equally inattentive to the rights of freemen and the British constitution; and when we consider that they have for some time been endeavouring to enforce their arbitrary mandates by fire and sword, and likewise encouraging, by every means in their power, our savage neighbours, and our more savage domesticks, to spill the blood of our wives and children; and...they have added insult to their injustice and cruelty, by repeatedly pretending to hold out the olive branch of peace [although] *they intended for us the most abject slavery; Of this we can no longer doubt, since we have* [discovered the] *late letter from the secretary of state to governor Eden, and the late act of parliament for seizing and confiscating all our ships and property that may fall into their hands. Therefore, despairing of any redress of grievances from the king and parliament of Great Britain, and all hopes of a reconciliation between her and the United Colonies being now at an end...we advise and instruct you cheerfully to...push to the utmost a war offensive and defensive...* [and] *to use your best endeavours that the delegates which are sent to the General Congress be instructed immediately to cast off the British yoke, and to enter into a commercial alliance with any nation, or nations, friendly with our cause.*[5]

---

[5] Schribner and Tarter, ed., "Charlotte County Committee Instructions, 23 April, 1776," *Revolutionary Virginia: Road to Independence*, Vol. 6, 447-48

Charlotte County's instructions included a reference to the British peace commissioners but offered little hope or expectation that it would meet with success.[6]

Closer to Williamsburg, the freeholders of James City County issued equally forceful instructions, but included a stipulation which voided them if the King offered, *"just and honorable terms"* to the colonies at the last minute:

> *Reason, drawn from justice, policy and necessity, are everywhere at hand for a radical separation from Great Britain. From justice; for the blood of those who have fallen in our cause cries aloud, "it is time to part." From necessity; because she hath, of herself, repudiated us, by a rapid succession of insult, injury, robbery, murder, and a formal declaration of war.... We, therefore...do request and instruct you, our delegates (provided no just and honourable terms are offered by the king) to exert your utmost ability, in next Convention, towards dissolving the connexion between America and Great Britain, totally, finally, and irrevocably.*[7]

Such instructions placed Robert Carter Nicholas, the colony's treasurer and one of James City County's two delegates to the convention, in a difficult position. Although he, like all of the delegates, acknowledged that the colonists' rights had been grievously violated by Britain and that the possibility of reconciliation was virtually non-existent, Nicholas worried that a declaration of independence was

---

[6] Ibid.

[7] Schribner and Tarter, ed., "Freeholders of James City County to Delegates Robert Carter Nicholas and William Norvell, 24 April, 1776," *Revolutionary Virginia: Road to Independence*, Vol. 6, 458

premature and that the colonies were not strong enough to win a war with Britain.[8] Nicholas was not alone in this concern.

Even Patrick Henry acknowledged the necessity of gaining foreign assistance if the colonies wished to prevail against Britain. Just a month before the convention, Henry expressed reservations to General Charles Lee about declaring independence before foreign alliances were secured.[9] Henry set aside his reservations at the convention, however, and drafted one of the three resolutions on independence debated by the delegates.

5th Virginia Convention

The 5th Virginia Convention assembled in the capitol on May 6th and selected Edmund Pendleton to chair the assembly as president. Although the primary issue on everyone's mind was independence, a week's worth of other business superseded consideration of that issue. Much of what occurred in the first week of the convention was routine: appointments to and reports from committees, petitions from counties and individuals, appeals for payment for items supplied to the troops or losses suffered in the conflict with Dunmore. General Lee's request to forcibly relocate all of the inhabitants and livestock in Norfolk and Prince Anne Counties within reach of Dunmore at Tucker's Point (estimated to be many thousands of people) generated much debate before it was approved.[10] Time was also spent in the convention

---

[8] Brent Tarter, ed. *Revolutionary Virginia: Road to Independence,* Vol. 7, Part 1, 4

[9] Ibid.

[10] Tarter, ed., "Proceedings of the Sixth Day of the Virginia Convention," 11 May, 1776, *Revolutionary Virginia: Road to*

discussing a response to an appeal for military assistance from the Carolinas. On May 10th, the Convention ordered 1150 minute-men from sixteen counties to accompany the 8th Virginia Regiment and General Lee to the South.[11] It was not until the eighth day of the convention (May 14th) that the issue of independence was considered.

On this day the Convention resolved itself into a Committee of the State of the Colony, chaired by Archibald Cary of Chesterfield County, and considered three resolutions on independence. One was offered by Bartholomew Dandridge of New Kent County. He declared that since the British Parliament had usurped unlimited authority over the colonies, the British Ministry had executed many tyrannical acts upon the colonies, the King had withdrawn his protection of the colonies, and all three had initiated a barbarous war against the colonies

> *The Union that has hitherto subsisted between Great Britain and the American Colonies is hearby totally dissolved, and that the Inhabitants of America are discharged from any Allegiance to the Crown of Great Britain.*[12]

The resolution was clear and bold, but many delegates were uncomfortable with Dandridge's proposal that the Convention

---

Independence, Vol. 7, part 1, 96

[11] Tarter, ed., "Proceedings of the Fifth Day of the Virginia Convention," 10 May, 1776, *Revolutionary Virginia: Road to Independence*, Vol. 7, part 1, 88

[12] Tarter, ed., "Proceedings of the Ninth Day of the Virginia Convention," 15 May, 1776, *Revolutionary Virginia: Road to Independence*, Vol. 7, part 1, Note 8, 145

proclaim independence for all thirteen colonies; they preferred that Congress take on that responsibility itself.

Another resolution, offered by Meriwether Smith of Essex County, also began with a list of grievances against the British Parliament and King:

> *Whereas Lord Dunmore hath assumed a Power of suspending, by Proclamation, the Laws of this Colony, which supported by a late Act of the British Parliament, declaring the Colonies in North America to be in actual Rebellion and out of the King's Protection, confiscating our Property wherever found on Water, and legalizing every Seizure, Robbery & Rapine, that their People have heretofore committed on us....*[13]

Smith's resolution called for the dissolution of the colonial government, "*hitherto exercised under the Crown of Great Britain.*" Smith also called for the adoption of a Declaration of Rights and a new plan of government, "*as shall be judged most proper to maintain Peace & Order in this Colony & secure substantial & equal Liberty to the People.*"[14] No direction was given to Virginia's delegation in Congress, it appeared that Smith viewed independence as a decision to be left up to each colony.

A third resolution proposed to the convention was drafted by Patrick Henry but introduced by Thomas Nelson of Yorktown. It was the most comprehensive of the three, both in terms of its list of grievances and its call to action. Henry noted the contempt that Parliament long held for the colonists'

---

[13] Ibid.
[14] Ibid.

many petitions and its recent passage of [the Prohibitory Act], *"approving of the ravages that have been committed upon our coasts."*[15] Henry's resolution continued

> *As they are not only making every preparation to crush us, which the internal strength of the nation and its alliances with foreign powers afford them, but are using every art to draw the savage Indians upon our frontiers, and are even encouraging insurrection among our slaves, many of whom are now actually in arms against us. And as the King of G.B. by a long series of oppressive acts has proved himself the tyrant instead of the protector of his people, We...do declare, that we hold ourselves absolved of our allegiance to the crown of G.B...and as a full declaration of independency appears to us to be the only hounourable means under Heaven of obtaining that happiness, and of restoring us again to a tranquil and prosperous situation;*
> *Resolved, That our delegates in Congress be enjoined in the strongest and most positive manner to exert their ability in procuring an immediate, clear, and full Declaration of Independency.*[16]

Despite the fact that nearly every delegate supported independence, debate over the resolutions lasted two days. Robert Carter Nicholas apparently stood alone in his public opposition to independence, asserting that it was premature and that the colonies were too feeble, militarily and

---

[15] Ibid.
[16] Ibid., 146

economically, to succeed against Britain.[17]   A few other delegates may have agreed with Nicholas, but there is no record of anyone else speaking against the resolutions.

It fell to the convention's president, Edmund Pendleton, to draft a compromise resolution that incorporated portions of all three resolutions. The bulk of Pendleton's draft came from Henry's resolution. The preamble, which comprised nearly half of Pendleton's final draft, re-stated the grievances of all three resolutions, particularly Patrick Henry's detailed list. Henry's proposal to instruct Virginia's congressional delegates in Philadelphia to procure from Congress, *"an immediate, clear, and full Declaration of Independency,"* was also included in Pendleton's draft.[18]   Meriwether Smith's proposal that the Convention adopt a Declaration of Rights and new plan of government to replace the government they had just cast off was incorporated into Pendleton's resolution and Pendleton added his own proposal for Congress to pursue foreign alliances and a confederation of the colonies. Pendleton's compromise resolution was introduced to the Convention on May 15th, 1776:

Forasmuch as all endeavours of the United Colonies by the most decent representations and petitions to the king and parliament of Great Britain to restore peace and Security to America under the British government and a re-union with that people upon just and liberal terms instead of a redress of grievances have produced from an imperious and vindictive administration increased insult oppression and a vigorous attempt to

---

[17] Ibid.
[18] Ibid.

effect our total destruction. By a late act all these colonies are declared to be in rebellion and out of the protection of the British crown, our properties subjected to confiscation, our people when captivated compelled to join in the murder and plunder of their relations and countrymen and all former rapine and oppression of Americans declared legal and just. Fleets and armies are raised and the aid of foreign troops engaged to assist these destructive purposes. The kings representative in this Colony [Dunmore] *hath not only withheld all the powers of government from operating for our safety but having retired on board an armed ship is carrying on a piratical and savage war against us tempting our Slaves by every artifice to resort to him and training and employing them against their masters. In this state of extreme danger we have no alternative left but an abject submission to the will of those over-bearing tyrants, or a total separation from the crown and government of Great Britain uniting and exerting the strengths of all America for defence and forming alliances with foreign powers for commerce and aid in War:*

Wherefore appealing to the Searcher of Hearts for the sincerity of former declarations, expressing our desire to preserve the connection with that nation and that we are driven from that inclination by their wicked councils and the eternal laws of self-preservation,

Resolved unanimously that the delegates appointed to represent this colony in General Congress be instructed to propose to that respectable body to declare the United Colonies free and independent upon the crown or parliament of Great Britain and that they give the assent of this Colony to such declaration and to whatever measures may be thought proper and necessary by the Congress for forming foreign alliances and a confederation of the Colonies at such time and in the manner as to them shall seem best: Provided that the power of forming government for and the regulation of the internal concerns of each colony be left to the respective colonial legislatures.

Resolved unanimously that a Committee ought to prepare a Declaration of Rights and such a plan of government as will be most likely to maintain peace and order in this colony and secure substantial and equal liberty to the people.[19]

There was apparently little debate or discussion on Pendleton's revised resolutions, the delegates were resolved to vote for independence. Those few in the convention who may have opposed them remained silent and the resolutions were approved by a unanimous voice vote of the 112 delegates.[20] Virginia's leaders had taken an irrevocable step, publically declaring their support for independence from Great Britain. It remained to be seen whether Congress and the other colonies would follow Virginia's lead.

---

[19] Tarter, ed., "Proceedings of the Ninth Day of the Virginia Convention," 15 May, 1776, *Revolutionary Virginia: Road to Independence*, Vol. 7, part 1, 142-43

[20] Ibid., 142

Chapter Thirteen

"These United Colonies are... Free and Independent States."

June-July 1776

On the same day that the 5th Virginia Convention approved its resolution on independence, Congress took its own giant stride towards independence and finalized a resolution that called on all the colonies to establish new governments to replace the royal colonial governments. Congress had actually adopted the resolution five days earlier on May 10th, but after much debate and a close vote, a preamble that justified the bold action was added to the resolution:

> *Whereas his Britannic Majesty, in conjunction with the lords and commons of Great Britain, has, by a late act of Parliament, excluded the inhabitants of these United Colonies from the protection of his crown; And whereas, no answer, whatever, to the humble petitions of the colonies for redress of grievances and reconciliation with Great Britain, has been or is likely to be given; but, the whole force of that kingdom, aided by foreign mercenaries, is to be exerted for the destruction of the good people of these colonies; And whereas, it appears absolutely irreconcileable to reason and good Conscience, for the people of these colonies now to take the oaths and*

affirmations necessary for the support of any government under the crown of Great Britain, and it is necessary that the...authority [of] the...crown should be totally suppressed, and all the powers of government exerted, under the authority of the people of the colonies, for the preservation of internal peace, virtue, and good order, as well as for the defence of their lives, liberties, and properties, against the hostile invasions and cruel depredations of their enemies; therefore,

Resolved, That it be recommended to the respective assemblies and conventions of the United Colonies...to adopt such government as shall, in the opinion of the representatives of the people, best conduce to the happiness and safety of their constituents in particular, and America in general.[1]

John Adams was thrilled with the resolution, announcing to Joseph Palmer that, "*Yesterday, the Gordian Knot was cut asunder.*"[2] He was more specific with his wife, Abigail:

G. B. has at last driven America, to the last Step, a compleat Seperation from her, a total absolute Independence, not only of her Parliament but of her Crown, for such is the Amount of the Resolve of the 15th.[3]

---

[1] Journals of the Continental Congress, "May 10 and May 15, 1776," (accessed online at www.loc.gov)

[2] Smith, "John Adams to Joseph Palmer 16 May, 1776," *Letters of Delegates to Congress*, Vol. 4, 3

[3] Smith, "John Adams to Abigail Adams, 17 May, 1776," *Letters of Delegates to Congress*, Vol. 4, 17

Not everyone agreed with Adams that the resolution signified absolute independence from Great Britain. James Duane, a delegate from New York, doubted whether Maryland or Pennsylvania will, *"listen to a Recommendation the preamble of which so openly avows Independence & Seperation."*[4] Duane had strongly objected to the preamble as too hasty and now informed his fellow New York delegate, John Jay, that there was no reason for New York to, *"be too precipitate in changing the present mode of Government."*[5] Duane wanted to see how the middle colonies reacted to the resolution and wanted to gauge the opinion of his fellow New Yorkers on the issue of independence. *"Let them* [the people] *be rather followed than driven on an Occasion of such momentuous Concern,"* he declared.[6] To John Adams's great frustration, Duane was not alone in his caution.

Virginia Declaration of Rights and Constitution

In Virginia, the 5th Convention paused one day to participate in ceremonies to mark its historic vote. Troops were paraded in Waller's Grove (within sight of the capitol) to hear Virginia's resolution read aloud and receive the admiration of much of Williamsburg. Toasts to the independent American states, the Grand Congress, General Washington, and victory for American arms were offered, each toast saluted by volleys from the troops. The soldiers were treated to refreshments compliments of a number of gentlemen of the convention and the evening concluded with

---

[4] Smith, "James Duane to John Jay, 18 May, 1776," *Letters of Delegates to Congress*, Vol. 4, 34
[5] Ibid.
[6] Ibid.

illuminations and other demonstrations of joy. Purdie's gazette reported that

> *Everyone seeming pleased that the domination of Great Britain was now at an end, so wickedly and tyrannically exercised for these twelve or thirteen years past, notwithstanding our repeated prayers and remonstrances for redress."*[7]

The Convention addressed the challenge of forming a new government with the formation of a constitutional committee under Archibald Cary of Richmond. The committee undertook two enormous challenges, first to create a Declaration of Rights that outlined Virginia's basis of government, and second to create a constitution, or actual plan of government. George Mason quickly rose to the forefront of the committee. He recognized the difficult task at hand and wrote to his friend Richard Henry Lee in Philadelphia for assistance:

> *We are now going upon the most important of all Subjects – Government: The Committee appointed to prepare a plan is, according to Custom, overcharged with useless members...We shall, in all probability have a thousand ridiculous and impracticable proposals & of Course, a Plan form'd of hetrogenious, jarring & unintelligible Ingredients; this can be prevented only by a few Men of Integrity & Abilitys...I need not tell you how much you will be wanted here on this Occasion...We can not do without you—Mr*

---

[7] Purdie, *Virginia Gazette*, 17 May, 1776, 3

*[Thomas] Nelson is now on his Way to Philadelphia;
& will supply your place in Congress....*[8]

Lee was unable to return to Virginia in time to help draft
the Declaration of Rights, which were introduced to the 5th
Virginia Convention on May 27th, 1776. The document was
largely the product of George Mason and asserted:

> *That all men are born equally free and independent,
> and have certain inherent natural rights...among
> which are, the enjoyment of life and liberty, with the
> means of acquiring and possessing property, and
> pursuing and obtaining happiness and safety...*
> *That all power is vested in, and consequently derived
> from, the people...That government is, or ought to be,
> instituted for the common benefit....*[9]

The Declaration of Rights also called for religious toleration,
trial by jury, freedom of the press, and protection from
excessive bail and cruel and unusual punishment.[10] Two
weeks of debate ensued in the convention before a final
version was adopted on June 12th. The Convention then
turned its attention towards adopting a constitution to establish
Virginia's new government.

While the 5th Virginia Convention wrestled with these
weighty issues in Williamsburg, Virginia's representatives in
Philadelphia prepared to introduce the Convention's resolution
on independence to the Continental Congress.

---

[8] Rutland, "George Mason to Richard Henry Lee, 18 May, 1776,"
The Papers of George Mason, Vol. 1, 271

[9] Tarter, ed., "5th Virginia Convention, 27 May, 1776," *Revolutionary
Virginia,* Vol. 7 part 2, 271

[10] Selby, 102

Independence Proposed in Philadelphia

On June 7th, 1776 Richard Henry Lee stood before the Continental Congress in Philadelphia and announced that

> *These United Colonies are, and of right ought to be, free and independent States, that they are absolved from all allegiance to the British Crown, and that all political connection between them and the State of Great Britain is, and ought to be, totally dissolved.*[11]

The resolution Lee introduced on behalf of Virginia also called on Congress to pursue foreign alliances and draft a plan of confederation to better govern the new states. Virginia had thrown down the gauntlet; it was time for the Continental Congress to address the issue of American independence.

Debate on Lee's resolution commenced the following day. John Dickinson and James Wilson of Pennsylvania, Robert Livingston of New York, and Edward Rutledge of South Carolina, were the most vocal opponents of the resolution.[12] They argued that although the prospect of separation from Great Britain was probably irreversible (given the events of the past year) the arrival of a huge British invasion force off of New York made a declaration of independence extremely dangerous and tenuous. This was not the time, argued Dickinson and the other opponents to the resolution, to antagonize Britain with such a declaration.[13]

---

[11] *Journals of the Continental Congress*, "June 7, 1776," (accessed online at www.loc.gov)

[12] Smith, "Thomas Jefferson's Notes on the Proceedings of Congress, June 8, 1776," *Letters of Delegates to Congress*, Vol. 4, 160

[13] Ibid., 163

Besides, they asserted, Virginia's resolution was too hasty and rash. The driving force of independence needed to come from the people, not a handful of delegates in Congress. *"The people of the middle colonies...,"* argued those opposed to the resolution, *were not yet ripe for bidding adieu to the British connection but they were fast ripening."*[14] Opponents added that while Congress debated Lee's resolution in Philadelphia, meetings were being held in all the middle colonies to, *"take up the question of Independence".*[15] Why not await the outcome of those meetings, asked the opposition? The wise policy, Dickinson and the others argued, was to avoid any decisive step, *"till the voice of the people drove us to it."*[16] To do otherwise would risk disunity and dissention between the colonies.

The resolution's supporters, however, were exasperated at the thought of more delay. Representatives from New England as well as Georgia and Virginia, led by John Adams, Richard Henry Lee and George Wythe, (of Virginia), forcefully argued that it was fruitless to wait any longer for perfect unanimity (among Congress or the people), *"The people wait for us to lead the way."*[17] Besides, they argued, the bond of allegiance to the King

Was now dissolved by his assent to the late act of parliament, [Prohibitory Act] *by which he declares us out of his protection, and by his levying war on us...; allegiance & protection are reciprocal, the one ceasing when the other is withdrawn....*

---

[14] Ibid., 160
[15] Ibid.
[16] Ibid.
[17] Ibid., 162

[So as a result] *the question was not whether, by a declaration of independence, we should make ourselves what we are not; but whether we should declare a fact which already exists.*[18]

After two days of heated debate it was clear that opposition to independence was too great to call for a vote, so it was agreed to postpone the vote for three weeks to allow the representatives (especially those from the middle colonies) to consult with their assemblies and conventions. Thomas Jefferson observed that

It appearing in the course of these debates that the colonies of N. York, New Jersey, Pennsylvania, Delaware, Maryland, & South Carolina were not yet matured for falling from the parent stem, but that they were fast advancing to that state, it was thought most prudent to wait a while for them, and to postpone the final decision to July 1.[19]

Committees were formed to draft a plan for a confederation of states, propose foreign alliances, and draft a declaration of independence, should these be necessary as everyone expected they would be. Thomas Jefferson was tapped by the committee charged with writing a declaration of independence to compose a first draft. While he worked on this document, his fellow Virginians in Williamsburg, much to Jefferson's chagrin (for he desired to be in Virginia with them) drafted Virginia's first state constitution.

---

[18] Ibid., 161
[19] Ibid., 163

The 5th Virginia Convention Adopts a Constitution

Since there were few examples of republican governments on which to model Virginia's state constitution, the 5th Virginia Convention relied mostly on the political theories of Enlightenment era philosophers and the brilliance of George Mason.

Under Mason's proposals, legislative responsibilities of the new government were handled by a General Assembly, consisting of a House of Delegates and a Senate. Judicial affairs were handled by judges, who were appointed by the General Assembly to fixed terms. Executive affairs were the responsibility of a Governor who was elected annually by the General Assembly. A proposal to give the governor veto power over legislation was rejected by the convention.[20]

The will of the people was best expressed through the elected legislature. Free, white, male, landowners, over twenty-one years of age voted for members of the General Assembly. Representatives served two year terms in the House of Delegates and four year terms in the Senate.

On June 29th, the Virginia Convention adopted the constitution and elected Patrick Henry as Virginia's first state governor. Over the next week the delegates also selected a Council of State, created legislative districts, scheduled elections for the summer, and passed laws that gave additional authority to county sheriffs and justices of the peace.[22] The Convention concluded it deliberations in early July and transferred governing authority to the Governor and the soon to be elected General Assembly.

---

[20] Tarter, ed., *Revolutionary Virginia,* Vol. 7 part 1, 12-13

[22] Selby, 121

Declaration of Independence

In Philadelphia, the committee formed to compose a declaration of American independence (which included John Adams and Benjamin Franklin) met in mid-June to consider Thomas Jefferson's first draft. The document was favorably received by the committee members (who offered mostly stylistic changes.) Whether Jefferson's draft would be embraced by the rest of Congress remained to be seen.

A week before the formal vote on independence (scheduled for July 1st), John Adams acknowledged the challenge that faced supporters of Virginia's resolution.

> *That we are divorced...is to me, very clear. The only Question is, concerning the proper Time for making an explicit Declaration in Words. Some People must have Time to look around them, before, behind, on the right hand, and on the left, then to think, and after all this to resolve . Others see at one intuitive Glance into the past and the future, and judge with Precision at once. But remember you cant make thirteen Clocks strike precisely alike, at the same second.*[23]

Although Adams's comments to Benjamin Kent revealed an awareness of the difficulty in securing a unanimous vote for independence, Adams also expressed deep frustration in a second letter with one particular colony for its reluctance to take a position on the issue either way.

---

[23] Smith, "John Adams to Benjamin Kent, June 22, 1776," *Letters of Delegates to Congress*, Vol. 4, 290

What is the Reason that New York must continue to embarrass the Continent, Must it be so forever? What is the Cause of it? Have they no Politicians, capable of instructing and forming the Sentiments of their People? Or are they People incapable of seeing and feeling like other Men. One would think that their Proximity to New England would assimilate their opinions and Principles....[24]

Adams followed this letter on June 22nd, with yet another the next day that was a bit more optimistic but still highly critical of New York. Noting that Pennsylvania and New Jersey were quickly turning "patriotic" and Maryland would soon come around to support Virginia's resolution on independence, Adams once again blasted New York for its indecision:

New York still acts in Character, like a People without Courage or sense, or Spirit, or in short any one Virtue or Ability. There is neither Spunk nor Gumption, in that Province as a Body. Individuals are very clever. But it is the weakest Province in point of Intellect, Valour, public Spirit, or anything else that is great and good upon the Continent. It is incapable of doing Us much good, or much Hurt, but from its local situation. The low Cunning of Individuals, and their Prostitution plagues Us, the Virtues of a few Individuals is of some Serve to Us. But as a Province it will be a dead Weight upon any side, ours or that of our Enemies.[25]

---

[24] Smith, "John Adams to Samuel Parsons, June 22, 1776," *Letters of Delegates to Congress*, Vol. 4, 292

[25] Smith, "John Adams to Cotton Tufts, June 23, 1776," *Letters of Delegates to Congress*, Vol. 4, 298

New York was not alone in its hesitancy to support independence. South Carolina voted against Virginia's resolution when it came up for a procedural vote on July 1st. South Carolina's opposition was joined not by Delaware (whose delegation was deadlocked 1-1) or New York, which abstained from the vote, but by Pennsylvania, who, led by John Dickinson, also voted against independence.

It was Dickinson, the strongest and most vocal opponent to independence in Congress, who tried one last time to persuade the delegates to reject Virginia's resolution. Dickenson acknowledged that his opposition to independence, which was clearly in the minority of Congress and, most likely, the people, would, *"Give the finishing Blow to my once too great and...now too diminish'd Popularity,"* but he refused to suppress his belief that independence would be a disaster for the colonies.[26]

At the request of Edward Rutledge, the final vote on independence was pushed back to July 2nd. Pressure on the two dissenting colonies, South Carolina and Pennsylvania, was enormous and when the vote was taken the next day, the proponents of independence were pleasantly surprised.

South Carolina had changed its mind and voted yes (for the sake of unanimity) and John Dickinson and another Pennsylvania delegate (Robert Morris) grudgingly abstained from the vote. This allowed the remainder of the Pennsylvania delegation to vote, 3-2 in favor of independence. The arrival of an ailing Caesar Rodney broke the tie in the Delaware delegation, and suddenly, Virginia's resolution on

---

[26] Smith, "John Dickinson's Notes for a Speech in Congress, July 1, 1776," *Letters of Delegates to Congress*, Vol. 4, 352

independence had twelve affirmative votes. Only New York remained intransigent, abstaining once again from the final vote. (A week later New York's leaders signaled their approval of independence as well.) The 2nd Continental Congress had finally acted; it had approved a resolution that proclaimed the colonies independent from British rule. The British yoke was officially cast off and the American states were now free and independent.

Two days of debate over the wording of Jefferson's Declaration of Independence followed the historic vote. For many of the delegates, Jefferson's declaration was a mere formality, a justification (after the fact) for their vote on independence. John Adams expressed the view of nearly all the delegates in a letter to his wife, Abigail the day after Virginia's resolution was adopted:

The Second Day of July 1776 will be the most memorable Epocha, in the History of America. I am apt to believe that it will be celebrated, by succeeding Generations, as the great anniversary Festival. It ought to be commemorated, as the Day of Deliverance by solemn Acts of Devotion to God Almighty. It ought to be solemnized with Pomp and Parade, with Shews, Games, Sports, Guns, Bells, Bonfires and Illuminations from one End of this Continental to the other from this Time forward forever more.[27]

---

[27] Smith, ed., "John Adams to Abigail Adams, July 3, 1776," *Letters of Delegates to Congress*, Vol. 4, 376

Although Adams was thrilled with the outcome of the vote, he included words of caution, along with hope, in his letter.

> *You will think me transported with Enthusiasm but I am not. I am well aware of the Toil and Blood and Treasure, that it will cost Us to maintain this Declaration and support and defend these States. Yet through all the Gloom I can see the Rays of ravishing Light and Glory. I can see that the End is more than worth all the Means. And that Posterity will triumph in that Days Transaction even [if] We should rue it, which I trust in God We shall not.*[28]

Virginians learned about Congress's vote and subsequent Declaration of Independence in mid-July. The Council of State, filling in for a gravely ill Governor Patrick Henry, ordered Virginia's gazettes to publish the Declaration in their next editions and the county sheriffs were ordered to proclaim the Declarations from their county courthouses at their next court day.[29] In Williamsburg, "*amidst the acclamation of the people*," the Declaration was proclaimed at the courthouse, the capitol, and the palace.[30]

---

[28] Ibid.

[29] Purdie, *Virginia Gazette*, July 26, 1776, 1

[30] Ibid., 2

The long struggle to preserve their rights as free men had ended in a way that few colonists (now Americans) would have imagined a decade earlier. To those who just years before had been immensely proud of their connection with Great Britain, separation from the mother country was not taken lightly. Most concluded, however, that they no longer had any other choice. If they were to keep their God-given rights, they had to go it alone.

To many people, the Declaration of Independence represents the culmination of America's long's dispute with Great Britain, a dispute that emerged with the passage of the Stamp Act in 1765 and steadily escalated over the next decade. Although Virginians had embraced independence two months before the Declaration of Independence was adopted by the Continental Congress, they were well aware that proclaiming their independence did not insure that they were to have it. The dispute with Britain had merely entered a new phase. It was now a struggle to insure and maintain American independence, and like the fight leading up to the historic July 2nd vote for independence, the thirteen new American states would have to remain united if they had any chance of success.

Bibliography

Abbot, W.W., and Dorothy Twohig, eds. *The Papers of George Washington: Colonial Series,* Vol. 7. Charlottesville: University Press of Virginia, 1990.

Albion Robert and Leonidas Dodson, eds. *Philip Vickers Fithian: Journal, 1775-1776, Written on the Virginia-Pennsylvania Frontier and in the Army Around New York.* Princeton: Princeton University Press, 1934.

Anderson, D. R. ed., "The Letters of Colonel William Woodford, Colonel Robert Howe, and General Charles Lee to Edmund Pendleton," *Richmond College Historical Papers,* June, 1915.

Archer, Richard. *As If an Enemy's Country: The British Occupation of Boston and the Origins of Revolution.* Oxford University Press, 2010

Ballagh, James C., ed., *The Letters of Richard Henry Lee,* Vol. 1, NY: Macmillan Co., 1911.

Boyd, Julian P. ed., *The Papers of Thomas Jefferson,* Vol. 1. Princeton, NJ: Princeton University Press, 1950.

Brock, R.A. ed., "Orderly Book of the Company of Captain George Stubblefield, 5th Virginia Regiment: From March 3, 1776 to July 10, 1776, Inclusive," *Virginia Historical Society Collections,* New Series 6, 1887.

Brock, R.A. ed., "Papers Military and Political, 1775-1778 of George Gilmer, M.D. of Pen Park, Albemarle Co., VA," *Miscellaneous Papers 1672-1865 Now First Printed from the Manuscripts in the Virginia Historical Society*. Richmond, VA, 1937.

Calloway, Colin G. The Scratch of a Pen: 1763 and the Transformation of North America. Oxford University Press, 2006.

Campbell, Charles, ed., *The Bland Papers: Being a Selection from the Manuscripts of Colonel Theodorick Bland Jr. of Prince George County, Virginia,* Vol. 1. Petersburg: Edmund & Julian Ruffin, 1840.

Campbell, Charles, ed. *The Orderly Book of that Portion of the American Army Stationed at or near Williamsburg* 6th *Regiment...from March 18, 1776 to August 28, 1776.* Richmond, 1860.

Carp, Benjamin L. Defiance of the Patriots: *The Boston Tea Party & the Making of America.* New Haven and London: Yale University Press.

Cecere, Michael. *Great Things Are Expected from the Virginians: Virginia in the American Revolution.* Westminster, MD: Heritage Books, 2008.

Cecere, Michael. *Wedded to My Sword: The Revolutionary War Service of Light Horse Harry Lee.* Westminster, MD: Heritage Books, 2012.

Chase, Ellen. *The Beginnings of the American Revolution : Based on Contemporary Letters, Diaries, and other Documents,* Vol. 1. Port Washington, NY: Kennikat Press, 1970.

Chase, Philander D. ed., *The Papers of George Washington, Revolutionary War Series,* Vol. 1. Charlottesville, VA: University Press of Virginia, 1985.

Clark, William, ed., *Naval Documents of the American Revolution,* Vol. 1-5. Washington, D.C., 1964.

Commager, Henry Steele. *Documents of American History.* New York: Appleton-Century-Crofts, 1963.

Cresswell, Nicholas, *The Journal of Nicholas Cresswell* . The Dial Press: NY, 1974.

Cushing, Harry A., ed., *The Writings of Samuel Adams,* Vol. 1. NY:G.P. Putnam's Sons, 1904.

Danske Dandridge, Danske. *Historic Shepherdstown.* Charlottesville, VA: Michie Co., 1910.

Davies, K. G., ed., *Documents of the American Revolution,* Vol. 9. Irish University Press. 1975.

Dorman, John. ed., *Virginia Revolutionary Pension Applications,* Vol. 12. Washington, D.C.: 1965.

Fischer, David Hackett. *Paul Revere's Ride.* New York: Oxford University Press, 1994.

Force, Peter, ed., *American Archives*, Fourth Series, Vol. 4. Washington D.C.: U.S. Congress, 1848-1853.

Greene, Jack P., ed., *The Diary of Landon Carter of Sabine Hall, 1752-1778,* Vol. 2. Charlottesville: University Press of Virginia, 1965.

Hamilton, Stanislaus M., ed. *Letters to Washington & Accompanying Papers*, Vol. 5. Boston & New York: Houghton Mifflin, Co., 1902.

Henings, William W., *The Statutes at Large Being a Collection of all the Laws of Virginia,* Vols. 5-9. Richmond: J. & G. Cochran, 1821

Hunt, Gaillard, ed., *The Writings of James Madison*, Vol. 1. New York: J.P. Putnam's Sons, 1900.

Journal of Continental Congress, 20 October, 1774, (Accessed via the Library of Congress website at www.loc.gov)

Journal of the House of Delegates, 1835-36, Doc. No. 43, Richmond, 1835, Virginia State Library.

Kennedy, John Pendleton, ed., *Journal of the House of Burgesses*: 1773-1776, Richmond: VA, 1905.

Marshall, John, *The Life of George Washington,* Vol. 2. Fredericksburg, VA: The Citizens Guild of Washington's Boyhood Home, 1926.

Mays, David John, ed., *The Letters and Papers of Edmund Pendleton,* Vol. 1. Charlottesville: University Press of Virginia, 1967.

Morgan, Edmund S. *Prologue to Revolution: Sources and Documents on the Stamp Act Crisis, 1764-1766*. Chapel Hill, NC: University of North Carolina Press, 1959.

Morgan, Edmund, and Helen Morgan, *The Stamp Act Crisis: Prologue to Revolution*. Chapel Hill, NC: University of North Carolina Press, 1953.

Namier, Lewis and John Brooks, *The History of Parliament : The House of Commons, 1754-1790.* Oxford University Press, 1964.

Reese, George ed., *The Official Papers of Francis Fauquier.* Vol. 2. Charlottesville: The University Press of Virginia, 1981.

Runge, Beverly H., ed., *The Papers of George Washington: Colonial Series,* Vol. 10. Charlottesville, VA: University Press of Virginia, 1995.

Rutland, Robert, ed., *The Papers of George Mason.* Vol. 1. University of North Carolina Press, 1970.

Scribner, Robert L., and Brent Tarter ed., (comps). *Revolutionary Virginia: The Road to Independence,* Vol. 1-7. Charlottesville: University Press of Virginia, 1973-1978.

Selby, John. *The Revolution in Virginia: 1775-1783.* Colonial Williamsburg Foundation, 1988.

Smith, Paul H., ed., *Letters of Delegates to Congress: 1774-1789,* Vol. 1-4. Washington, D.C.: Library of Congress, 1976.

Wirt, William. *Sketches in the Life and Character of Patrick Henry,* Philadelphia, 1817.

Zobel, Hiller B. *The Boston Massacre,* New York: W.W. Norton, 1970.

Newspapers

Dixon and Hunter, *Virginia Gazette, Supplement*, 8 December, 1774

Dixon & Hunter, *Virginia Gazette,* 14 January, 1775

Dixon & Hunter, *Virginia Gazette*, 4 February, 1775

Dixon and Hunter, *Virginia Gazette*, 11 February, 1775

Dixon and Hunter, *Virginia Gazette*, 8 April, 1775

Dixon and Hunter, *Virginia Gazette,* 10 June, 1775

Dixon and Hunter, *Virginia Gazette,* 24 June, 1775

Dixon and Hunter, *Virginia Gazette,* 24 June, 1775

Dixon and Hunter, *Virginia Gazette*, 24 June, 1775

Dixon and Hunter, *Virginia Gazette,* 28 October, 1775

Pinkney, *Virginia Gazette*, 27 October, 1774

Pinkney *Virginia Gazette,* "A Watchman," 16 February, 1775.

Pinkney, *Virginia Gazette*, 9 March, 1775

Pinkney, *Virginia Gazette,* 16 March, 1775

Pinkney, *Virginia Gazette,* 23 March, 1775

Pinkney, *Virginia Gazette, Supplement*, 28 April, 1775

Pinkney, *Virginia Gazette,* 1 June, 1775

Pinkney, *Virginia Gazette,* 8 June, 1775

Pinkney, *Virginia Gazette,* 2 November, 1775

Pinkney, *Virginia Gazette,* 2 November, 1775

Pinkney, *Virginia Gazette,* 11 November, 1775

Pinkney, *Virginia Gazette,* 16 November, 1775

Pinkney, *Virginia Gazette,* 3 February, 1776

Purdie and Dixon, *Virginia Gazette,* 21 March and 4 April 1766

Purdie & Dixon, *Virginia Gazette,* 23 May, 1766

Purdie & Dixon, *Virginia Gazette,* 23 May, 1766

Purdie & Dixon, *Virginia Gazette,* 20 January, 1774

Purdie & Dixon, *Virginia Gazette,* 19 May, 1774

Purdie & Dixon, *Virginia Gazette,* 21 July, 1774

Purdie & Dixon, *Virginia Gazette,* 28 July, 1774

Purdie and Dixon, *Virginia Gazette,* 8 September, 1774

Purdie and Dixon, *Virginia Gazette,* 15 September, 1774

Purdie, *Virginia Gazette,* 7 April, 1775

Purdie, *Virginia Gazette*, 14 April, 1775

Purdie *Virginia Gazette, Supplement*, 21 April, 1775

Purdie, *Virginia Gazette, Supplement*, 28 April, 1775

Purdie, *Virginia Gazette, Supplement*, 5 May, 1775

Purdie, *Virginia Gazette, Supplement*, 12 May, 1775

Purdie, *Virginia Gazette, Supplement*, 9 June, 1775

Purdie, *Virginia Gazette, Supplement*, 23 June, 1775

Purdie, *Virginia Gazette*, 14 July, 1775

Purdie, *Virginia Gazette*, 4 August, 1775

Purdie, *Virginia Gazette*, 8 September, 1775

Purdie, *Virginia Gazette*, 10 November, 1775

Purdie, *Virginia Gazette*, 17 November, 1775

Purdie, *Virginia Gazette*, 19 January, 1776

Purdie, *Virginia Gazette*, 16 February, 1776

Purdie, *Virginia Gazette*, 23 February, 1776

Purdie, *Virginia Gazette*, 15 March, 1776

Purdie *Virginia Gazette,* Supplement, 15 March, 1776

Purdie, *Virginia Gazette*, 8 March, 1776

Purdie, *Virginia Gazette*, 1 March, 1776

Purdie, *Virginia Gazette*, 8 March, 1776

Purdie, *Virginia Gazette*, 29 March, 1776

Purdie, *Virginia Gazette*, 15 March, 1776

Purdie, *Virginia Gazette*, 12 April, 1776

Purdie, *Virginia Gazette*, 19 April, 1776

Purdie, *Virginia Gazette*, 17 May, 1776

Purdie, *Virginia Gazette*, July 26, 1776

Rind, *Virginia Gazette*, 26 May, 1774

The Massachusetts Gazette & Boston News-Letter,
31 May, 1764

Unpublished Sources

Adams, John Diary 11, entry for 18 December 1765,
Adams Family Papers, Massachusetts Historical Society

Boston Merchants Broadside, 31 October, 1767,
Massachusetts Historical Society

"Charles Dabney to William Wirt, Dec. 21, 1805," *Papers of
Patrick Henry* Rockefeller Library CWF, Microfilm

Circular Letter from the Freeholders of Boston, 20 November, 1772, Massachusetts Historical Society.

"Lee, Henry II to William Lee, 1 October, 1774," *Lee-Ludwell Papers*, Virginia Historical Society.

"Nathaniel Pope to William Wirt, June 23, 1806," *Papers of Patrick Henry* Rockefeller Library CWF, Microfilm

Index

Michael Cecere Sr. teaches American history at Robert E. Lee High School in Fairfax County, Virginia, and was named the 2005 Outstanding Teacher of the Year by the Virginia Society of the Sons of the American Revolution. Mr. Cecere also teaches American history at Northern Virginia Community College. An avid Revolutionary War re-enactor, he currently is the commander of the 7th Virginia Regiment and participates in numerous living history events throughout the country. This is his ninth book.

Other books by Michael Cecere:

They Behaved Like Soldiers: Captain John Chilton and the Third Virginia Regiment, 1775–1778 (2004)

An Officer of Very Extraordinary Merit: Charles Porterfield and the American War for Independence, 1775–1780 (2004)

Captain Thomas Posey and the 7th Virginia Regiment (2005)

They Are Indeed a Very Useful Corps: American Riflemen in the Revolutionary War (2006)

In This Time of Extreme Danger: Northern Virginia in the American Revolution (2006)

Great Things Are Expected from the Virginians: Virginia in the American Revolution (2008)

To Hazard Our Own Security: Maine's Role in the American Revolution (2010)

Wedded to My Sword: The Revolutionary War Service of Light Horse Harry Lee (2012)

Made in the USA
Middletown, DE
22 August 2023

37172668R10197